Feminist Lives
in Victorian England

*Private Roles
and Public Commitment*

For Curt

Feminist Lives
in Victorian England

Private Roles
and Public Commitment

Philippa Levine

Basil Blackwell

First published 1990

Basil Blackwell Ltd
108 Cowley Road, Oxford, OX4 1JF, UK

Basil Blackwell, Inc.
3 Cambridge Center
Cambridge, Massachusetts 02142, USA

British Library Cataloguing in Publication Data

A CIP catalogue record for this book is available from the British Library.

Library of Congress Cataloging in Publication Data

Levine, Philippa.
Feminist Lives in Victorian England. Private Roles and Public
Commitment/Philippa Levine.
p. cm.
Includes bibliographical references.
ISBN 0-631-14802-7
1. Feminism—England—History—19th century. 2. Women in
politics—England—History—19th century. I. Title.
HQ1599.E5L48 1990
305.42'09'034—dc20   89-18577
                                       CIP

Typeset in 10 on 12pt Sabon
by TecSet Ltd, Wallington, Surrey
Printed in Great Britain by
T. J. Press Ltd, Padstow, Cornwall

Contents

Preface

When I began work in this area I was uncomfortably aware of the commonly accepted conclusion that so-called 'first wave feminism' was a limited, bourgeois and safe movement, bounded by its attachment to liberalism and more generally seen as the slightly charred phoenix rising from the still-burning ashes of individualism. I was uneasy with the categorization which thus rendered the feminist movement the satellite of a trend asserting the rights of *man*, as if that could somehow successfully and effectively encompass the demands of women and the serious political acceptance of gender. As I began to amass more and more evidence on women who chose involvement in woman-centred politics – within campaigns around legal and political injustice, around marital and sexual abuse, around economic issues – that interpretation looked less and less tenable. Feminists of this generation were sometimes cautious in their approach, favouring conservatism in dress as a means of deflecting the cruder criticisms of a bewildered public. They were limited by the unavoidable class boundaries which divided Britain so thoroughly. And yet, if we examine the lives and life cycles of women prominent in campaigns, it is clear that none of the standard generalizations apply.

I had begun by collecting data on women active in women-centred campaigns – for the election of women to local government office, for the extension of the suffrage, for the expansion of educational and employment opportunities – and had stumbled across a mass of evidence which suggested feminist networks were well in place long before our contemporary re-discovery of their power. The evidence I was finding also strongly undermined the claim that feminism arose through the assertion of *individual* rights in this period. The mistake of attempting to filter feminist activity through male experience was palpable; I needed alternative tools of construction, reconstruction and deconstruction to understand the strategies of this movement.

So what are those tools? A central part of my research was the formulation of a collective biography, a prosopography of feminism in the period c.1850–c.1900. Its function is twofold: first, to pinpoint the details of who the feminists are and whether their lifecycles reflect the choices they made in that political arena, and secondly, to draw attention to the collective features of organization so crucial to the feminism of this period and evidenced by the extensive overlap of personal and political networks. This prosopographical element has allowed me to look at the backgrounds of these women, their social location and religious activities, their marital status, their other interests and activities. In turn, the information was used to establish whether or not the active proponents of a feminist voice were in fact being drawn from a narrow segment of English society, insensitive to or unaware of the needs and lives of those differently situated.

This approach didn't so much solve my problems – more particularly that of defining a movement capable of and enthusiastic about such immense diversity – but rather reoriented the questions I asked and the ways in which I asked them. Through this means I came to lay emphasis on the autonomous activities generated by feminism rather than on seeking where the movement might be slotted into the existing and inadequate spectrum of mainstream Victorian politics. In short, my approach was fast becoming disruptive of canonic interpretations of nineteenth-century history. There is no ahistoricism in such an approach – that is rather reserved for those contemporary commentators dismissive of the movement, or anxious to sanitize it or to gloss over elements of it anathematic to latter-day sensibilities.

Part I of this study examines in detail the experiences and choices made by women at this time, their relationships with one another, with men, with society. It attempts both to see the context framing their lives and to pursue the mechanisms by which women questioned that context.

In Part II, the central organizing feature is the specific application of the politics and philosophy traced in Part I to activism, connecting relationally women's private decisions with their public practice and demonstrating their resulting distance from an orthodox politics. Part II offers a less chronologically apparent analysis than might initially seem appropriate. The decision to begin this section with the moral and sexual campaigns of the 1870s onward, rather than with, say, married women's property agitation or suffrage – both of which pre-date the sexual questions in feminist activism – derived not from an essentialist collapsing of gender into sexuality but from a sense that here, in this forcing of the private into the public eye, lay the uniqueness and identity of the overall movement. Though the sexual issues are not 'more' important than other campaigning areas, their explicit intrusion into a world dominated by formalized bureaucracy and institutionalized speech opened up the feminist arena substantially. Feminist politics succeeded in rendering public and speakable a strong undercurrent of Victorian sensibility, empowered against women by its very silence in their presence. In this respect do the sexual campaigns of this era take precedence in my account. This work is intended neither as an event-based chronological rendering of heroic moments in feminism nor as a celebration of the essential power of women but as a historically grounded attempt to see the means by which our feminist predecessors addressed the fact and sought an articulation of their subjugation in a highly ordered, singularly repressed and wildly contradictory period.

Philippa Levine
November 1989

Acknowledgements

Many people and institutions have had a hand in the making of this book and whilst they are not responsible for the conclusions, the help, advice and support they variously gave has been immeasurable.

Institutionally, my thanks must go first to the Flinders University of South Australia where much of this book took shape. In the midst of moving continents – and not for the first time – the solid head start offered by my years there made it easier to pick up the threads again, once settled in America.

Many libraries in Britain provided invaluable and fascinating material. For permission to reproduce materials from their archival collections, my thanks go to the following: the Mistress and Fellows of Girton College, Cambridge for access to the papers of Emily Davies and Bessie Rayner Parkes and to the library of Helen Blackburn; to the Fawcett Library, City of London Polytechnic for access to their Autograph Letter Collection, their Millicent Garrett Fawcett papers and their Lydia Becker letters; to the British Library, London for access to the papers of Charles Dilke and Elizabeth Wolstenholme Elmy; to the Manchester Leisure Services Committee for access to both their suffrage and Fawcett collections; to the Bodleian Library, Oxford for access to the Pattison, Pearson and Simcox manuscripts and to Royal Holloway and Bedford New College (University of London) for their permission to reproduce material from their archives relating to the former Bedford College. Barbara S. McCrimmon of Tallahassee, Florida was gracious enough to allow me generous access to her Barbara Bodichon papers.

Friends and colleagues have done much, as always, to lighten the load. David Doughan at the Fawcett Library brought his usual and delightful mix of erudition and enthusiasm to bear on my often naive questions. Patricia Hollis and June Hannam shared valuable biographical information with me, whilst Gillian Sutherland, Gail Savage, Helen Jones, Janet Howarth and Mark Curthoys allowed me to read unpublished work of theirs. Liz Stanley and David Rubinstein showed interest and confidence in the project even when I did not; both were patient letter-writers and inspired critics. Michael Brock undertook the gargantuan task of devising a computer program suited to my needs. Curt Aldstadt not only got me through the final grim stages of manuscript preparation but offered encouragement, sanity, affection and a dazzling grasp of theoretical issues.

1

Configuring Feminism Historically

Feminism is a term that trips glibly enough, though never uncontentiously, off the modern tongue, but its application to the activism of nineteenth-century women requires some discussion. The term was not in general use until the very end of the period. What justification can there be, then, for adopting it anachronistically?

Feminism has come to signify a perspective far more concrete and thoughtful (if still contested and admirably plural) than an attachment to any vague notion of 'rights' or 'equality' might suggest. Its commitment to a thorough and holistic understanding of the pervasiveness and connectedness of a host of gendered subordinations lends it consistency and vision. This book will argue that those nineteenth-century women discussed here formed just such a conscious grouping, their activities, philosophies and lifestyles demonstrating a powerful and thorough assessment of the gendered wrongs determining their society.

Beginning in the late 1850s with the establishment of the London-based Langham Place Circle, the Kensington Society and the early committees contesting the legal void which was the married woman, the latter half of the nineteenth century witnessed a series of connected, skilfully managed and high profile campaigns around a wide variety of issues closely concerning women. Despite the substantial amount of recent literature documenting this growing activity, there is still a tendency in historical circles to identify the militant minority in early twentieth-century feminism as both the prototype and the moment of the 'true' emergence of the women's movement.

Some notion of female consciousness, framed inevitably around the specific institutional disabilities and denials that derived simply from femaleness, is discernible at almost every point in English society. In the mid and late nineteenth century, galvanized by what Mary Poovey has called the 'battles for social authority' engendered by the massive changes consonant upon the rise of industrial capitalism, that consciousness took organized, articulate and increasingly populous shape.[1]

The existence of this women's movement campaigning around franchise, employment and a host of other issues is not queried by historians; the use of the descriptive term 'feminist' in this context is. Nancy Cott has argued that it is anachronistic and misleading to adopt such a neologism where it was not itself in use, or indeed in existence.[2] Cott, discussing early twentieth-century feminism in the United States, chooses to distinguish the nineteenth-century 'woman suffrage' movement, with its more narrowly delineated aim, from a more broadly conceived twentieth-century feminist consciousness.[3] Certainly there is considerable value to be derived from distinguishing conceptually both between single issue concerns and a more embracing philosophy, and between differing positions at various points in a movement's history which are consonant with its specific circumstances and context. There are pitfalls, too, in such an approach, however. Specifically, it might service a hierarchical and teleological reading of the 'stages' of the movement in its 'advance' to 'full' or 'true' consciousness.

It would be a more useful exercise, perhaps, to locate specific outcrops of activism, organization or consciousness as the historical products of social relations, rather than judge them by contemporary standards. That still leaves, however, the question of whether a term coined after the fact can be legitimately, or even usefully applied, or whether it constitutes a further lapse into ahistorical anachronism.

This book uses the term 'feminism' in describing the lifestyles and activities of women activists pursuing various changes in law, custom and practice in nineteenth-century England.[4] It does so conscious of the charge of anachronism and with a strong sense of purpose. Linda Gordon's definition of feminism as 'a critique of male supremacy, formed and offered in the light of a will to change it'[5] is one which suggests both the historical continuum in which such a struggle has necessarily operated and the breadth of vision which can successfully think about a movement with sites in more than one arena.

The principal intention of this book is to offer a reading of the later nineteenth century in which all those campaigns clustered around the aspiration of asserting women's self-determination derived from a sustained critique of the gendered order of society. In tandem with that critique, and the organized attempts to contest those social relations, women actively involved commonly adopted lifestyles consonant more with their ideas about gender than with the dominant social milieu from which they came. It is this capacity of committed women to see the necessity and the impact of gender on issues of traditional private or individual concern in addition to, and intimately connected with those traditional political concerns that legitimates the use of the term 'feminism' in this context.

In drawing parallels between their personal lives – marriage, companionship, social relations et al. – and the governmental politics constraining them, women not only offered a rejection of the separate and gendered spheres of public and private but refused, too, to conceive of a politics confined to the public sphere that excluded them. In short, they were involved in a conscious and active process of redrawing the definitional boundaries of politics. Doubtless, we would now dub this an exercise in the creation and definition of a sexual politics; the language of the nineteenth century did not countenance the term. Nor was the word 'feminism' in use.

However, the refusal to adopt the word for women engaged in so far-reaching and comprehensive a project as the contestation of existing gender relations has its dangers. Reverting to the exclusive use of terms such as the 'woman suffrage movement' posits the separation of connected women's issues, a hierarchy of concerns with the traditional political uppermost and a consequent fragmentation of a movement increasingly unified by its collapsing of public and private. For the modern women's movement, one of the most powerful early slogans – still extant though coined some two decades since – has been 'the personal is the political'. It was no less so for our predecessors in the Victorian period and it is this, above all, that is both the chief concern of this work and the justification for the use of the term 'feminism' in discussing the lives and activities of these women.

Previous writers have offered a variety of definitions and interpretations of the feminism of this period. Alice Rossi, whilst pointing out the diversity of opinion amongst women activists, none the less stresses that campaigners in women's issues were often as, if not more, active in other political and reform issues.[6] Kathleen McCrone has similarly argued that feminists were not separate from but rather an index of the rise of the bourgeoisie.[7] Ray Strachey concentrated her assessment of 'the cause' on the public face of feminism.[8] More recently, and more convincingly, Judith Walkowitz has identified female autonomy as the principal feature of nineteenth-century feminism, and Jane Rendall the championing of women's rights to social self-definition.[9]

All of these varying interpretations and definitions are rooted in a reading of the writings and activities of nineteenth-century women activists, a telling comment on the shifting interpretative vista that is history. Where Walkowitz and Rendall see some explicitly feminist concerns in their more holistic readings, these other writers remain implicitly trapped within the definitional fences erected by separate sphere ideology in their reading of feminism as a subset or a derivative of existing political positions which *do* separate public from private. A concentration on the individual single issue campaigns which severally make up feminism at this time, a tendency to over-emphasize the public face of feminism and ignore its growing impact on the tissue of women's lives, all contribute to these partial readings of the women's movement, failing to connect its various strands.

It is the connection between these strands which gives us not only the sense of a more 'global' feminist perspective embracing issues of private as of public concern, but also a means of deciding who might fall under a rubric so devised. The whole issue of definition involves not only building a picture of the movement and its concerns but further identifying its protagonists. A feminist reading necessitates some critical rethinking of the relationship between individuals and the organizational, emotional and other attachments they make in their lives to avoid both that path which leads to a hagiographical invocation of famous feminist heroines and also that which denies substance to women's private existence. In so doing, the task of historically defining the feminist (as distinct from that of defining feminism) becomes immensely complex. At the same time, such concerns raise also the vexed issue of the precise nature of the historian's authority. What is the historian's relationship with and to the entities she studies? Creating the boundaries that contain any study necessarily involves acknowledging limits and constraints without which completion would be unattainable. Texts themselves (in the broadest sense of the word) also impose a partial knowing; we can neither fully divine intention nor move outside or beyond our own discourse. We can raise questions and seek answers. This book seeks to examine the question of feminist agency.

Could a woman be a feminist without knowing it? Did she have to declare herself one? Do male sympathizers count as feminists? Could a Conservative be a feminist? These were all central questions in the task of locating those around whom to centre this study. On the question of men helpful or sympathetic to the aims and strategies of women activists, the decision was fairly simple. Women involved in the movement in the nineteenth century were very careful as to the precise boundaries of male involvement, as the following chapters will demonstrate. Wary of their own voices being submerged, women permitted men only partial admittance as helpers. Following their lead, this sample thus excluded men entirely.[10]

More controversial, of course, was which women to include. If we accept that the whole basis of historical reconstruction necessarily tends to the subjective and the arbitrary at base, we can focus the importance of this decision more on integrity and accuracy – albeit incomplete – and worry less about obscuring ideas of objectivity or worrisome notions of authority. The whole definitional issue of whom to include in a 'representative' sample of nineteenth-century English feminists raises methodological, empirical and conceptual questions. How was the sample obtained? Working on women poses, of course, greater problems in the collection of data and identification of sources than when researching in more traditional areas. Ironically, it is even easier to fail to see past the big names, simply because women in general begin from a position of greater obscurity. Interestingly, the movement itself seemed often to shy away from the creation of giants, emphasizing a more communal and collective approach to its affairs in preference to revering an individual's catalytic charisma. Inevitably, however, the combination of historical neglect and a more communal approach makes information-gathering a trying business. For that reason, as well as a determination to avoid the hierarchies posterity can bring in its wake, I sought as wide a definition of inclusion (as opposed to exclusion) as possible. Women whose writings, declarations or actions invoked a sense of gender as a concrete political category, and about whom adequate information was to be found, make up this total sample of 194 women. A further 150 or so would have been included if greater biographic detail could have been found.

Certain exclusions were maintained for practical purposes, the most obvious being an inadequacy of verifiable data. Another important exclusion was framed around the decision to concentrate rather on patterns of English than on British feminism. Scotland and Ireland, certainly in urban centres, sported active feminist organization; the English-born McLaren women helped make Edinburgh an important centre of agitation, as did those women seeking medical certification at its university. Dublin native Isabella Tod was well known in local feminist circles and kept up a lively contact with activists in Scotland and England as well.[11] Scotland, however, had its own judicial and legal system in which changes germane to women occurred at different times from those in England, whilst Ireland, separated from the island where its political fate was so often decided, suffered from that isolation politically but also maintained a strong separate culture. The concentration on England in this book reflects rather the hierarchy of my own training – with its heavy concentration on England – than any notion that English feminism was a more developed or more intrinsically interesting phenomenon.

Any sample which purports to be representative is open to question, both in terms of assessing or quantifying its representativeness and, perhaps even more importantly, in determining the legitimacy of what it represents. How can we know that it is distorting, or even accurate, when that which it represents is inevitably constructed through the sample?

Thus do we, almost invariably, and whether as historians or other interpreters of the past, fit our subjects into a pre-cast mould. The case of feminisim is of particular significance in this context, because so much of the core of feminist scholarship is concerned with recasting these moulds. And yet, feminists writing on their nineteenth-century predecessors constantly exercise themselves erroneously over their sisters' failures to conform.

Many of the writers who have identified the undeniably bourgeois (and in the US almost exclusively white) and wealthy constituency from which activists were drawn in this period have felt uneasy about the implications of those findings. One of the most intractable of such instances is contained in the common practice of separating 'bourgeois' from 'socialist' feminists and in discussing the reasons for the sparse attachment of feminists to the newly emerging socialist creeds then gaining ground. In the English example, one might in any case argue with justification that socialist politics were attracting at best a minimal hearing amongst either sex but far more importantly, we need to dismantle the assumption built into this analysis.

In the first place, the polarization of feminist practice into two camps – bourgeois and socialist – presupposes not only a coupling of feminist with other issues but also some agreement that socialism offered a 'natural' home to feminist aspiration. Neither theoretical consideration nor empirical evidence can support that relationship, and nineteenth-century feminists were themselves acutely aware of the consequences of privileging class over gender. Its effects were concrete; the family wage, the ascendancy of adult male over female suffrage, a secondary position for women's issues.

The ideological heritage of socialism was drawn from no less a patriarchal perspective than that of capitalism, and the very notion of class identification or class consciousness was itself premised on brother-hood. Women in and of themselves could claim no class position; their class derived wholly from the men on whom they were deemed dependent. It is not insignificant in this context that downward social mobility, in the case of women, was pretty well restricted to sexual libertarianism, viz., a set of circumstances in which women appeared, albeit erroneously, to be no longer under direct male control. Women with no male support system, but of a family originally deemed respectable via husband or father, retained the trappings of gentility even in the midst of penury. Only a life of prostitution could really jeopardize that security. Equally, a restricted upward social mobility was achievable; women could rise via their men. These were inequalities which did not go unnoticed by feminist women who thus preferred rather to invoke an identification through gender than class.[12] In a speech on women's suffrage she delivered in Birmingham in 1872, one of the feminist Sturge sisters made the point cogently.

I meet plenty of gentlemen carrying ladies' umbrellas, the ladies as a rule are perfectly well able to carry them themselves – therefore this is only a symbol. I wish I could think these same gentlemen were equally ready to help the little child in the streets with her heavy burden or the weary woman with her barrow of coals.[13]

Women thus consistently rejected – as this book will attempt to show – efforts to render their politics and their perspective a lesser part of existing, or even emergent, political claims. It was a stance which not only challenged attempts to minimize their importance and silence their voices, but one which also questioned the difficult dividing line between individual and collective. In seeking to find points of consonance between private life and public commitment, women captured for themselves a coherent claim of autonomy and of agency. Interpretations that seek to subsume feminism under competing (and largely male dominated) political positions deny that agency and silence their subjects.

Equally problematized in this respect are some of the readings derived from Derridean post-structuralism which also implicitly deny existence to agency in their privileged deprivileging of the text and flight into discourse. When women become mere symbols of some greater structure than their individual voices, the brute fact of their oppression and the concrete joys of their victories are lost. Mary Poovey's work has discussed that problem with great sensitivity. She talks of finding herself 'torn between focusing on individuals as if they were the agents of change' and conversely seeing individuals as '*merely* [my italics] points at which competing cultural forces intersect'.[14] Are we thus to construe that the denial of the franchise to women, or their vulnerability to and physical experience of legitimized acts of spousal violence, constitute *merely* an intersection of texts? Doubtless women and men derive their ideology, their discourse, their existence from their past and present cultural sites but not, surely, at the expense of some lingering agency of action which offers the concrete possibility of grass-roots change and at the same time does not seek to diminish or dismiss the real pain – physical and mental – which derives from the 'texts' which severally constitute power. Ironically such a position is not that far removed from the precise symbols attached to the feminine which nineteenth-century women activists sought to decentre; in such a reading, individual women are no more than the material on which symbolic unities are foisted.

French critical theorists have, of course, denied both the validity of historical scholarship and the very notion of a feminism unsullied by contact with the male realm. The explicit dismissal of feminism as practice and as philosophy by writers such as Hélène Cixous and Julia Kristeva has resulted in a position, as Janet Todd has argued, which puts 'the idea of woman before the experience of women'.[15] This study, conversely, sees no contradiction in jointly acknowledging and examining both; indeed, it is in the interstices of their divergence that understanding lies. The gap between idea and reality locates for us the pressure points which feminists could exploit to demonstrate the exploitative bankruptcy of both, and permits us to see the dangers of rewriting binary opposition in new guises.

At the same time, a reading which concentrates attention on agency and, indeed, on women's growing collective response to subjugation, does not deny or ignore diversity or, indeed, conflict. False resolution of internal tensions would do no more than obscure in its optimism.[16] Arguing that class was a poor basis on which to rest an assertion of female autonomy does not mean denying the substantial impact of class differentiation on the conduct and concerns of the movement.[17] It was, throughout the period dealt with in this volume, a movement peopled predominantly by articulate and materially comfortable women, though a substantial minority were bourgeois more in name than in circumstance. Critical, though, to the construction of a feminist position at this time was the cry for self-definition. The very existence of women, genteel by birth but not by any action of their own, yet living nevertheless on a pittance, made palpable the point: that the material factors affecting women resulted from the choices, actions and whims of men and not from the women themselves.

Social and material differences were vivid at this juncture; England's class structure was intricate and rigid in its demarcation and if its workings were sometimes subtle, the discrepancies in circumstance it produced were anything but. It was difficult for comfortably situated women to imagine the lives of poorer women, though the opposite holds less true given the high rate of employment of female domestic service at this time. The realities of the class structure thus served to separate women from one another, a factor recognized by feminists who saw the solution to that in an assertion of gender as an alternative reading and solution to that of class.

The invocation of the importance of gender in feminist circles was certainly strengthened by the tight network and genealogy of feminism emerging at this time. A glance at active feminism reveals some concentration, both geographically and socially, in specific areas. Certain cities, in particular, became strongholds of women's activity, notably London,

Bristol and Birmingham. Similarly, certain areas of the country were strong in their support; Lancashire and various parts of Yorkshire spring immediately to mind. Often, such sites saw a proliferation of feminist activists over time as generation succeeded generation, each under the tutelage of the previous one.

In the period covered here, one can identify four active feminist generations before the close of the century. There were those born at the end of the eighteenth century such as Mary Howitt (1799–1888) and Anna Jameson (1794–1860) who occupied an important position as role models for the Langham Place and *English Women's Review* circles of the 1850s and 1860s. Succeeding them chronologically were the members of those groups, and of the earliest suffrage and married women's property committees: Emily Davies (1830–1921), the Crow sisters (Jane, born 1830 and Annie), Elizabeth Garrett (1836–1917), Barbara Leigh Smith (1827–91), Emelie Gurney (1823–96), Lydia Becker (1829–90), Emily Faithfull (1835–95), Josephine Butler (1828–1906) and the slightly older Clementia Taylor (1810–1908) amongst others. Born around the 1840s, and active in the heyday of Victorian campaigning, were women such as Elizabeth Garrett's younger sister Millicent (1847–1929) who learned of feminism from her older sisters and their friends. Of the same generation were trade union activist Emma Paterson (1848–86); the first woman member of the Birmingham School Board, Quaker Eliza Sturge (1842/3–1905); her West Country cousins, daughters of William Sturge and Charlotte Allen, the eldest, Emily (1847–1892), and third of the eleven children Elizabeth (dates unknown), both active in suffrage and other campaigns. Jane Strachey (1840–1928), Caroline Ashurst Biggs (1840–1889), Helen Blackburn (1842–1903) and Clementina Black (1854–1922) were all of that generation and immensely active in a bewildering array of campaigns. Finally, there was the generation just old enough to be active in the nineteenth century and spilling over well into the twentieth – Margaret Llewellyn Davies, niece of Emily (1861–1944), Gertrude Tuckwell (1861–1951), May Tennant (1869–1946), Julia Varley (1871–1952) – more centrally involved, for the most part, in working-class issues and benefiting very clearly from the hard-won successes of earlier feminist work.

Though it is clear that family influence – through feminist sisters, mothers, aunts – could be a positive factor in some women's lives, the importance of lifestyle decisions *beyond* family influence – whether pursuing a tertiary education or rewriting the marriage contract – cannot be underestimated. The institution of the family was central to women's subjugation and it was the specific oppressions it imposed on which much feminist campaigning devolved.

The family in Victorian England was the site of confined domestication whose grip on women was firm and frequently total. It constituted one element of the polarized ordering of the social fabric which critically defined role and standing for both women and men. The binary opposition of home and work, of private and public translated into and percolated through to a bewildering range of thought, action and material circumstance. Feminists seized upon the cruelties, the injustices and the dangers that attached to that polarization, appropriating and subverting it to their design. They constructed from it an empowering and activating rather than a domestic sisterhood, one built on connections and associations of gender more than on family or class relations.

This strong network of activity and support, which promoted deep and sustained friendships among women, represents in itself one of the most singular challenges to the polarized mythologies of sex-specific behaviour and tendencies. One of the most enduring of such myths, now as then, concerns the flightiness of women's friendships contrasted with the loyalty of male bonding. In nineteenth-century England, where what Dorothy Hammond and Alta Jablow have called the myth of male friendship[18] was strong, bolstered by the institutional monopoly men enjoyed socially, educationally and judicially, feminist women were flying in the face of both myth and custom. The accusation of instability in women's friendships – an assumption replicated in anxieties over sexual fidelity and hence paternity too – deserves some closer investigation. If women did switch loyalties more readily than men, then we might point to the context of dependency framing it, and the expectations arising out of it. Women were required to move from the shadow of paternal to that of spousal authority, their obedience thus shifting horizontally from one male to another, a clear case of enforced loyalty and deference. Characteristic of feminist women was the strength of their female friendship and their refusal to diminish ties with women friends on behalf of men and even after marriage.[19] They were both celebrating the strength of their female connectedness and simultaneously defying the ascription of 'feminine' qualities required by separate sphere ideology.

In this way they were also, if less explicitly, challenging another fundamental rigidity of this system of binary opposition, in a way which sadly guaranteed their long neglect by generations of historians. In translating their feminist analysis and theory most directly into lifestyle and action, and frequently side-stepping the more usual route of political philosophies – viz., writing – they were not separating out thought and action. For the most part, feminist theory in this period was not constrained within the covers of books as was that of the better-known male theorists of the day. In consequence, and as Mary Maynard puts it,

'Victorian feminists appear as *doing* [author's emphasis] rather than as developing ideas.'[20] 'Doing' was indeed a statement of purpose; feminists thus constantly reassessed and refined their thinking and their practice. Neither the theoretical positions nor the feminist lifestyle which were so fundamental a part of it can be tamed or pruned to fit existing political theory. Though many modern commentators have attempted to root feminism in the soil of evangelicalism or liberalism (and often in both), its concerns began and remained inimical to much that was central to the tenets of such movements. Women certainly learned much about tactics and practice from their association with and exposure to these and other worlds, but the woman-centredness which formed the crux of their beliefs could find no home there. What Carole Pateman and Teresa Brennan have identified as the 'liberal accommodation to patriarchy'[21] was rapidly recognized at this time: women expectant of succour from the liberal ascendancy of the Gladstonian period swiftly had their hopes dashed. The prominence of their feminist over their party politics reflects not only their incapacity to exercise parliamentary choice but increasingly their disillusionment with government as a source of change. The amicable relations between women of radically opposed political persuasion detailed later in the book can thus be seen less as a measure of poor comprehension or indifferent loyalty than as a clear statement of the primacy of an alternative political vision coloured fundamentally by gender. The limitations of liberalism as a palliative were as obvious and as expansive as any to the feminists of this period with their coherent and cogent position.

When as devoted a feminist and careful a theological thinker as Frances Power Cobbe (as prominent for her studies on theism as for her feminism) could criticize the Revised version of the Bible for its abusive stand on women and its reliance on an all-male team of translators,[22] there can be little doubt that such women's feminism was a thoroughgoing and highly considered 'female project of cultural reconstruction'.[23]

To cast nineteenth-century feminism as no more than a struggle for equality,[24] or a movement severely restricted by a seeming attachment to formal liberalism and bourgeois theory, is not only to miss the richness that accompanied these women's determination to mesh their own private and public lives, but also to allow our own contemporary position to be hoodwinked back into the definitional straitjacket that has for too long been the source of the neglect and dismissal of this powerful, active and fascinating chapter in modern English history.

Part I

Private Roles

Part I

What is R&D

2

Family, Faith and Politics

In the mid-1950s, Noel Annan traced a series of close links that bound together that segment of modern English society he dubbed its 'intellectual aristocracy'. Of largely middle class provenance (albeit the wealthier end of that middle class), he identified a group of influential families linked by common political and intellectual values and maintaining a genealogy – through marriage and friendship – that spanned the generations from the mid-nineteenth century to the post-war years of the twentieth century.[1]

Many of those same families spawned feminist women – the Stracheys, the Sidgwicks, the Butlers, the Stanleys, to name but a few. Their common interest in the reforming movements of the period, in philanthropy and franchise reform, in university extension and women's education, would certainly have served as an obvious introduction to politics for women discovering feminism, and indeed to many of the bedrock issues that movement chose to embrace.

The question of external influence in determining the characteristics of individual choice has long been a topic of heated debate within historical circles. Historians have argued both that it is an acutely important clue to people's actions and behaviour and, conversely, that influence studies are an example of an overly deterministic historical licence. Inevitably, we are unable to rescue the full quota of these multiple historical strands which create and mould human action, and it seems absurd thus to neglect any of the potentially influential factors that structure human lives. The importance that societies have consistently attached – and in which they have been faithfully followed by historians – to such phenomena as family formation and to religious and political beliefs suggests that we should, indeed, address these features of social organization seriously. In the case of Victorian feminism, the prosopographical approach has yielded some interesting patterns in these areas of family, faith and politics which both help explain the distance that feminist thinking and action maintained from the mainstream and at the same time serve to locate it within its historical framework.

One of the most striking features of this holistic hold of feminism is the kinship networks which feminists, rather like Annan's 'intellectual aristocracy', exhibit. We can trace that interlocking series of networks in a number of ways, and perhaps most forcefully through family connections. The feminist family, rather like the reforming family, was not unknown in this period, and we can trace a complex web of feminist dynasties by looking at literal sisterhoods, at mother–daughter and aunt–niece relations as well as at more general family patterns.

Many women active in the feminist movement had grown up in families noted at the time for their unusual and unorthodox methods of child-rearing, practices not uncommonly adopted by those espousing a radical politics. Amongst the families of Victorian feminists, they represent a substantial minority. Bessie Rayner Parkes, whose father Joseph was secretary to the parliamentary commission on municipal reform which had recommended the restructuring of local government in 1833, recollected those political events early in her childhood which she felt shaped her later thinking.

I can just remember the processions at the passing of the Reform Bill . . . Truly little I knew of the inward workings of that stormy time but it has since seemed a sort of Omen to me that I began my conscious life at the time of the *People's Triumph*.[2]

Similarly, Lancashire feminist Isabel Petrie, also from an activist family, recalled that 'red letter day' in 1834 when the West Indian slaves were emancipated.[3]

Whilst radical histories such as these were not uncommon amongst feminist women, they were by no means the dominant determining characteristic. Moreover, it was not uncommon for there to be a distinct cut-off point in the libertarianism espoused by 'progressive' parents. The Leigh Smith children were indubitably granted an unusual amount of freedom regardless of gender, each of them receiving a generous annual income at the age of twenty-one. Barbara Leigh Smith none the less still experienced the heavy hand of paternal authority when she proposed as a young single woman to set up house with her lover, John Chapman. Moreover, as Jacqui Matthews points out, the illegitimacy of the Leigh Smith children, though they were otherwise impeccably middle class, gave their radical father total authority over them.[4] In a sense, it is the tension and confusion created by these conflicting messages that perhaps fuelled the distinctive practices of a feminist politics at this time, rather more than a simple equation of like-minded familial radicalism and emergent gender awareness.

Parental influence was, of course, significant. The central role of the family as an agent of socialization is a commonplace amongst historians and social scientists.[5] And in Victorian England the lengthy childhood accorded the young of the wealthier classes, with its rigorous social code, its restrictions on movement and its carefully monitored progress to adulthood, had spelt increasing parental control, especially for women whose economic dependency on parents was almost always total. Even women growing to adulthood in a radical environment experienced a profound economic dependency which differed markedly not only, of course, from the experiences of their brothers for whom independence and self-containment were the hallmarks of successful adult masculinity, but from the experiences of poorer women whose dependency – at least before marriage – was often manifested more obviously in spheres other than the economic.

Many of the women who were to become active in feminist politics had had a thorough grounding in radical political practice in childhood and had been exposed to anti-slavery agitation, Anti-Corn Law League campaigns and similar activities. Along the way, many had grown up at close quarters with the radical and reforming intelligentsia of the time as constant guests in their homes, and as members of such families.

Bessie Rayner Parkes's radical pedigree was certainly outstanding but she was by no means unique. As well as her father being a leading reforming politician early in the nineteenth century, her maternal grandfather was one of the most prominent Dissenting Radicals of his generation – Joseph Priestley. Other families boasted similar connections; the sundry branches of the Sturge family in Birmingham and in Bristol offered their daughters ample opportunity for involvement in social politics.

The Bright family was a distinct connecting thread in the provincial networks of radical non-conformist England, networks which figured prominently in the reform movements of earlier nineteenth-century politics. In the circles of Leeds Quakerism, socialist feminist Isabella Ford and her sisters had grown up with the radical liberal Bright family. During their childhood, the parents of the Ford girls had established a school offering evening classes to women mill workers.[6] The Rochdale Petries were also closely allied with the Brights as well as with the equally radical Cobden family. They all belonged, of course, to a distinct and recognizable network of radical political belief, the 'genealogy of reform' which Brian Harrison sees cemented by the impact of family traditions and connections,[7] and which has some consonance with the 'intellectual genealogy' which forms the subject of Annan's writing.

Bertha Mason, writing a history of women's suffrage in 1912, celebrated the centrality of the Brights. She quotes the recollections of Lancashire feminist Isabel Petrie Mills.

It was . . . twenty years before the first Women's Suffrage Society was founded, that, in a little parlour at Greenbank, Rochdale (the home of the Brights), I learnt my lesson, receiving a baptism, the grace of which I trust has never failed me. In the little informal meetings of a few friends seeds were sown which have borne fruit a hundredfold. There was Priscilla (afterwards Mrs Duncan McClaren) . . . Esther . . . Martha Mellor . . . and myself, the youngest, learning and thinking. There was Jacob Bright, to whom the cause owes so much, always on our side. Slavery, temperance and the need of the vote for women were the subjects most often studied and discussed.[8]

The roots of this family-influenced feminism were not confined merely to the major dissenting families of England. The Shirreff sisters, from a naval and Anglican background had also been exposed as youngsters to a wide range of opinions and ideas: 'By family ties and personal conviction they were drawn to Whig political principles.'[9] Many of England's most influential intellectuals, philosophers and scientists – men and women – were regular visitors to the Shirreff household, amongst them astronomer Mary Somerville, geologist Charles Lyell, philosopher T. H. Huxley, theologian F. D. Maurice, authors Harriet and George Grote and that quintessential nineteenth-century man of letters, Benjamin Jowett.[10]

Emilia Dilke's father, a retired Indian Army officer turned provincial bank manager, similarly numbered many of Oxford's most renowned minds amongst his social circle. His daughter was not only a pupil of John Ruskin but on close terms, too, with liberals such as Goldwin Smith, Oxford's Regius Professor of Modern History in the 1860s.

Olive Banks has argued, in the most recent of her books on 'first wave' feminism, that 'family background may be more significant for its ideological . . . than for its psychological influences.'[11] One can certainly point to the distinctive radical histories of many prominent women and to their early schooling in and exposure to organized and impassioned campaigns. Six per cent of the women in the sample used for this research were brought up in anti-slavery families; the wide range of birth dates covered by the sample distorts the figure considerably in that only the earliest born of these feminists were alive at the time of that campaign. Protests against slavery were confined largely to the period before 1840. Women born after about 1825 were thus unlikely to encounter organized anti-slavery except as a family history or reference point; 21 per cent of the overall sample were born before 1825, of whom rather less than half are identifiable as anti-slavery activists. The same is true for women born into Anti-Corn Law League families. Five per cent of the total sample were daughters of League women and men. With the repeal of the Corn Laws in 1846, the League's specific aims were accomplished; for women born after about 1835 (64 per cent of the sample), the issue was past.

In both cases, we know that there was at least some connection between the specific beliefs espoused in these single issue campaigns and a more generally libertarian outlook. The connections made by American women between slavery and their own gendered subjugation have been well-documented.[12] In England, too, many radicals understood that continuity; prominent Anti-Corn Law League campaigner Thomas Thomasson was also 'a major figure in financing the crucially important Manchester feminists of the 1870s'.[13]

None the less, we should not be too quick to assume this easy relationship, nor to accept that ideology more than psychology was the family's contribution to the development of feminism. Whilst it may be true that proportionately the number of women emerging from unusual and radical backgrounds is high, there were still many for whom feminism was a route out of the traditional patterns of belief and behaviour that pertained within the family.

A radical politics could emerge in other ways than via an unusual and politically active background – as with a Bodichon or a Parkes – or through an understanding of class mechanisms. Many women who became active and committed to women's causes came from backgrounds which arouse no particular interest or comment, and who had been reared in traditional ways. For them, family ideology was quite obviously not a formative factor in positive terms.

Women such as Emelie Gurney whose father taught at the prestigious Harrow Boys' School, Sophia Jex-Blake whose father was a lawyer of considerable standing, or Emily Faithfull, daughter of a country parson, were as prominent and energetic in the movement as their counterparts from less orthodox backgrounds. Jessie Boucherett and Frances Power Cobbe came from landed backgrounds – the former in Lincolnshire, the latter in Ireland – which yielded them some measure of financial security but did not detract from their feminist beliefs.

In the case of Emily Davies, whose father was a Gateshead cleric, some have suggested that her feminist energies were only fully released after his death, and yet even before then, and before she and her widowed mother moved to London in the 1860s, Emily was already organizing a branch of the Society for Promoting the Employment of Women in the Newcastle area and finding her significant friendships amongst feminists such as the Crow sisters and Elizabeth Garrett.

Lady Frances Balfour, active in the later years of the century and more particularly in the suffrage campaign, was the tenth of the twelve children of the Duke and Duchess of Argyll and brought up in the unremarkable manner typical for the children of the aristocracy. Balfour was almost thirty, and eight years into her unsuccessful marriage to Eustace Balfour, when she joined the suffrage movement. In her autobiography she remarks that at no point was she 'not a passive believer in the rights of women'.[14] She explained 'how far from knowing much about the Cause, the circles to which I belonged then were'.[15] Women such as Balfour or Boucherett, then, were shielded in many ways as children from exposure to radical or feminist ideas by their family backgrounds. For a Boucherett or a Cobbe that screening would have been particularly marked, brought up as they were on rural landed estates.

Their rural roots also make them stand out amongst the predominantly urban feminism of this period. The movement was largely city-based in character, and an urban radical background clearly facilitated for many women an early appreciation of an attention to these matters. It was to be late in the century before any form of organized rural politics were at all effective. Few women activists remained living in rural areas but moved rather to more populous cities and towns, at least for a portion of their campaigning years. None the less, Boucherett always retained an affection for her rural origins and frequently returned to her Lincolnshire home in her active adult years.

For the most part, these were women whose backgrounds were secured in material comfort and social assurance. A few – and they were unusual given the level of constraint imposed by the class system at this juncture – did emerge from working-class families. For the most part, this latter group formed the later chronological element of the sample, women born towards the end of the century, recipients of the new, if limited, state educational provision and of the gradual growth of participant politics.

Margaret Bondfield came from a working-class family and spent many years immersed in trade unionism and labour politics before rising to parliamentary prominence. Hers was a large but reasonably well-off family. Margaret, the second youngest child, spent some time in a private school before completing her education at the local Board School. Her father was a textile foreman. Her mother bore eleven children between 1852 and 1877 and not surprisingly worked exclusively within the family home. She was, nevertheless, an active political canvasser.[16] From the age of thirteen, Margaret was a wage-earner. She worked first as a school monitor earning three shillings a week. At fourteen, she was employed in a retailing job, and remained in similar employment until assuming full-time trade union activities. Bondfield joined the union movement in 1894 when she was twenty-one, in the aftermath of the flurry of new unionism in the early 1890s and of the depression which helped subdue it. In her autobiography, Bondfield never suggests that it was family beliefs *per se* which catalysed her entry into the political arena. From her observations, it is clear that she saw the family as an institution moulded by politics, but it was more her shopfloor experiences and bouts with unemployment that shaped her political reference points.

Bondfield was unusual not in yoking her class analysis to her politics which, for working-class women, was a common route into feminism in the ensuing years, but in making that connection at so early a date. Throughout the nineteenth century the number of women joining the feminist ranks from manual or industrial backgrounds remained predictably small. There were a number of women from relatively poor backgrounds but theirs was a poverty of a different order, poverty born of a non-manual background and exposing them to a very different set of childhood influences than women of identifiably proletarian stock.

Anna Jameson was one of five sisters whose father was an impoverished artist. She was forced on to the job market at the age of sixteen, but, though she worked sporadically as a governess for some fifteen years thereafter and never really knew financial ease, her first job was of a very different order than that of Bondfield or the other trickle of working-class women joining the movement in this period. She was governess to the children of the Marquis of Winchester and though it was doubtless neither a handsomely paid nor an unduly comfortable position, its cachet was considerably greater than that awarded the manually-employed woman.

Frances Buss, too, came from a background of impoverished gentility. Her early introduction to the teaching profession – which was to have such important consequences for girls' education when she founded the North London Collegiate School – came through family necessity. She and her mother ran a small London school as their principal source of livelihood. Both in determining status and in exposing women to the depradations imposed by the double standard, class could thus clearly act as an important factor in determining beliefs, more starkly perhaps at a time when class-consciousness at every level was so acute a topic of social concern.

Many women, however, fought bitter parental battles as part of their route into feminist awareness. Even the Garrett sisters, whose extraordinary contribution to the acceding of women's rights in this period covers so many important areas, experienced parental suspicion and doubt. Once she had convinced her father of her right to study and practise medicine, Newsom Garrett became Elizabeth's most vocal proponent but his initial opinions on the course his daughter wished to pursue had been less favourable. Her mother, Louise, remained throughout this turmoil involved in a more orthodox female and religious lifestyle than her many daughters.

In the case of Annie Rogers, who spearheaded the campaign for educational provision for women at the University of Oxford, family background was more influential in encouraging academic talents than any political aspirations. The same was true of Margaret Wynne Nevinson whose father gave her illicit lessons in Greek contrary to the express wishes of his wife.[17] For Rogers and Nevinson alike, it was academic attainment more than radicalism which catapulted them into women's activities, and both women acknowledged a greater degree of paternal over maternal influence in their formative years.

Nevinson, like Sophia Jex-Blake and Helena Swanwick, endured a measure of family hostility to her unusual educational aspirations. In the case of Nevinson and Swanwick that hostility was predominantly expressed in maternal fears over their marital chances. Mothers did affect the choices made by their daughters, despite the conviction of many authors that the maternal contribution was often a more negative one than the paternal. And yet how does one assess meaningfully the impact of mothers (or fathers) on their daughters' lives? Olive Banks sees mothers as more 'discouraging' of their daughters' ambitions than fathers,[18] M. Jeanne Peterson argues that 'emotionally . . . mothers were sometimes less significant than fathers',[19] but Pat Jalland conversely sees female bonding between mother and daughter as influential in girls' development.[20] These differing interpretations of the determination of maternal role point us critically to the difficulties inherent in feminist and women's history, as well as in reading biography too literally. Far less importance has been routinely attached, by biographers and others, to the lives of women, especially of married women. Biographers commonly dispense with the lives of wives and mothers in a nugatory manner, effectively dismissing them as mere adjuncts to their main and largely male concerns. The higher public profile enjoyed by men makes it far easier for us to chart their possible or potential influence on their daughters. And for the most part, especially earlier in the period, the mothers of feminists were necessarily women for whom the choices created and pursued by their daughters were seldom available.

With the steady growth of feminism through the century, women born at the latter end of the period were far likelier to have mothers or other female relatives of feminist persuasion and sympathy than had earlier generations. The specifics of mother–daughter relationships were not the only family connections of significance. In seeking to establish the overall influence of the family in determining adult choices, both mothers and fathers were significant, as were a host of other family connections.

Mothers, in particular, clearly played an important part in influencing the choices of their daughters throughout this period, as did aunts, though perhaps less frequently. As Barbara Caine notes, the 'central socializing agent' in the lives of women was their home life and it would be surprising if, as Banks and Peterson have suggested, mothers played no more than a negative role in the choices feminist women made.[21] Contrary to Banks' view, Hilda Martindale acknowledged the debt that she and her sister owed her mother, Louisa, and in doing so gave us a fascinating account of one woman's route into feminist understanding. Widowed only three years into her marriage, Louisa Martindale was faced with raising two small daughters entirely alone. That their subsequent careers were so successful – Louisa, the elder, as a doctor and Hilda as a Home Office factory inspector – owes much to their mother's growing feminist awareness. She moved towns in order to ensure places for her daughters at one of the new academic girls' schools, encouraged their tertiary studies at the new women's institutions and took them as youngsters to hear speeches by such controversial women as Josephine Butler and Annie Besant.[22]

It was not uncommon to find daughters succeeding or even partnering their mothers in various administrative capacities within the organized women's movement. The daughters of two Bristol activists, Mrs Beddoe and Margaret Tanner both held posts, as had their mothers, within local feminist organizations in the south-west. Alongside the more obvious mother-daughter pairings of Matilda and Caroline Ashurst Biggs, Harriet and Helen Taylor, Lady Stanley of Alderley and Lady Kate Amberley, and the Howitts, there were also mother and step-daughter combinations. Charlotte Manning, prominent in early London feminist circles, and Priscilla McLaren both influenced their step-daughters to active participation in the women's movement.

Lady Strachey, prominent in the suffrage movement of the mid-nineteenth century and a poet of some contemporary standing, bore four sons and five daughters. Unusually, her daughters were as successful as her sons in public life. Amongst her offspring were Joan Pernel Strachey, Principal of Newnham College, Cambridge from 1923 to 1941 and Philippa Strachey, suffragette secretary of the London Society for Women's Suffrage. Their brothers include biographer Lytton Strachey and Oliver Strachey whose wife, Ray (née Costelloe), wrote the first major text on the women's movement, *The Cause*, in the 1920s. She was, for the record, also educated at Newnham College and was the parliamentary secretary of the National Union of Women's Suffrage Societies.

Two of Elizabeth Whitehead Malleson's three daughters studied at Cambridge, whilst Philippa Fawcett, only child of Millicent Garrett Fawcett, captured high honours in the mathematics tripos at Cambridge in 1890. Her mother was showered with congratulations and compliments to which her simple response is an interesting indication of feminist mother–daughter relationships. Writing to the historian Charles Pearson in Australia, she maintained, 'I need not tell you how greatly delighted I was that women's education should be helped in this way by my own child.'[23] And to the compliments of a Mrs Thursfield, she movingly responded, 'You will know that I care for it mainly for the sake of women; but of course I also feel myself especially blessed in the fact that the thing I care most of all for has been helped on in this way by my own child.'[24]

In some instances, a mother's support for her daughter's unconventionality lay concealed within the family. Both Margaret Llewellyn Davies of the Women's Co-operative Guild and Leeds socialist-feminist Isabella Ford had mothers who, though they upheld a feminist position as far as we know and encouraged the activities of their daughters, chose to limit their own public involvement. None the less, they sanctioned their daughters' choices.

Even where there is no specific evidence of such encouragement, women frequently recognized some common bond with their mothers. Frances Power Cobbe called the death of her mother 'the great sorrow' of her life. 'She was the one being in the world whom I truly loved through all the passionate years of youth and early womanhood; the only one who really loved me . . . No relationship in all the world, I think, can ever be so perfect as that of mother and daughter.'[25]

The Garrett sisters kept up a regular correspondence with their mother, though they shared little in common with her politically or socially in their adult lives. The strength of such female bonding in a society which encouraged sexual segregation so vigorously is unsurprising. Pat Jalland has shown that mothers frequently experienced strong jealousy and resentment towards their daughters' husbands, even though they knew that marriage represented the pinnacle of a woman's social success.[26] Less positive, perhaps, in its outcome, the strength of such feelings demonstrates the possible power of the mother–daughter bond.

There were, of course, also women whose relations with their mothers were more ambivalent. In 1870, Kate Amberley defended her motives in informing neither her mother nor her mother-in-law of a speech on women's rights she had delivered to the Stroud Mechanics' Institute in that year. 'The reason I did not tell you about my lecture was, that before I gave it, I did not wish to be discouraged in any way, by the ridicule or opposition that either you or Lichfield House [where her mother, Lady Stanley, lived] or many others in London would have thrown on it.'[27]

It is difficult to assess how far Kate Amberley was guilty of an injustice to her own mother in this instance. Lady Stanley was, after all, one of the earliest benefactresses of Girton College, Cambridge. She had opposed the erection of a chapel, arguing that no money should be diverted from the more pressing and central aim of education.[28] Her mother-in-law, Lady Russell, also sent Kate her congratulations on the speech![29]

In the case of Helena Swanwick, the ambiguity was more her mother's than her own. Though Helena's mother thought higher education for women desirable, that broad-mindedness did not extend to her own daughter. 'If I had had to struggle to go to High School, I was to have a much harder struggle to go to College.'[30] Whether offering support – direct or indirect – or active, if often ambivalent or bewildered discouragement, the relationship between daughters and mothers was clearly an influential one.

Carroll Smith-Rosenberg noted a similar, and often determinant, attachment between mothers and daughters in the domestic female friendships she charted in nineteenth-century America. The 'mutual emotional dependency' which marked their relations was such that daughters grew *into* their mothers' worlds.[31] A similar pattern of incentive within a specifically feminist, rather than female, context derived its strength from these earlier sources but rewrote the content accordingly.

Aunts often played a direct role in encouraging their nieces into an active feminism. Margaret Lewellyn Davies had her aunt Emily Davies as a role model and Emilia Dilke maintained a close and affectionate relationship with her niece Gertrude Tuckwell. During Gertrude's adolescence, lengthy letters between aunt and niece explored the options open to an enquiring and energetic young woman. Emilia's belief that 'the woman is an individual having claims and rights of her own and duties to *herself*' clearly influenced Gertrude who, from an early age, pursued an independent career.[32]

The close working and personal relationship of aunt and niece Katherine Bradley and Edith Cooper was an unusual one but can be seen as another outcrop of the feminist movement. As 'Michael Field', the two women composed and published a considerable body of poetry and drama in the late nineteenth and early twentieth centuries as well as conducting a lifelong intimacy of passionate intensity.

In some instances, the involvement of whole families in a cause clearly acted as an encouragement for women. Influence and encouragement worked across both horizontal lines of kinship – between sisters and cousins – and vertically between generations too. When the Bristol Women's Suffrage Society first met in 1868, it had considerable male and paternal backing. The invitation to attend the meeting at 3, The Mall, Clifton read:

Mr Commissioner Hill permits his daughter to invite so many as his drawing-room will hold to meet there on 24th January, 1868, at 3 p.m., for a friendly consultation on this public question, although from the narrowness of the space the Meeting cannot be public.[33]

When Barbara Leigh Smith consulted these same friends, the Davenport Hill sisters, about the first draft of her polemic on the laws of married women's property, Florence and Rosamund in turn went to their supportive and legally trained father for advice. Florence wrote to Barbara in August 1854 to report that she had discussed the text with her father Matthew, but that on the issue of marriage to a deceased wife's sister, Florence's intention was to 'enquire of my brother Alfred who my father considers more conversant with the laws of property, marriage &c., than he is.'[34] Alfred went on to draft the Matrimonial Causes Act of 1878 which had been pioneered by his sister's friend, Frances Power Cobbe. (See chapter 6.)

Successive generations of the Davenport Hill[35] family made a considerable impact on Victorian society, both at home in England and abroad during the course of the century. Feminist Frances Power Cobbe remembered the children of reforming lawyer Matthew Davenport Hill as forming 'a centre of usefulness in the neighbourhood of Bristol'.[36] Like Cobbe, Matthew's daughters found themselves attracted to the slum work of Mary Carpenter in that city. Both Florence and Rosamund (who were good friends of Cobbe as well as of Barbara Leigh Smith) were for many years prominent in a host of feminist activities in England; their cousin Emily – the daughter of Matthew's sister Caroline, who had emigrated in 1850 to South Australia – vigorously took up similar charitable works in the colonial context. Amongst Caroline's other brothers were Rowland – Penny Post – Hill and one of Britain's first prison inspectors, Frederic Hill.[37]

This impressive display of a family's personal values was not unusual. It was a common phenomenon in reforming circles at this time and has been noted by a number of commentators. Diana Worzala and Brian Harrison both see its influence as a cradle of mid-Victorian feminism, in encouraging political awareness and activity amongst daughters and sons alike.[38] It is a view which suggests the strong continuity between an earlier emphasis on reform and a subsequent feminist conviction. Though seductive in its logical simplicity, it is an argument that needs to be applied with some care. Reform was, after all, not infrequently the province of aristocrats such as Lord Shaftesbury who approached these social issues from a very different viewpoint and took a markedly different political stand on their implementation. His views on what was to become known as the 'woman question' at no point corresponded, however, with that of the radical reformers.[39]

Though feminist commitment was generally limited to the women of a family, both inter- and intra-generationally, they did encourage the support of their menfolk, particularly where there were parliamentary connections to exploit. They never relinquished the reins of control to male sympathizers as so often happened in other areas of concern, for as Olive Banks points out, it was unlikely that men would devote their 'whole life to the women's movement in the way that was by no means uncommon' amongst women.[40]

Radical fathers such as the London solicitor William Ashurst certainly took a serious interest in women's issues. Ashurst encouraged his four daughters in their independent and unusual lifestyles, but it was they and not he who played the active and vocal role in the feminist politics of the period in their different ways. All four daughters were feminists, involved additionally in a variety of other radical campaigns, most notably Italian republicanism; Emilie, the youngest daughter, was Mazzini's literary executor.

The four Ashurst daughters – whose family often self-consciously referred to themselves as 'the clan' – are a good example of the sister-hoods with which nineteenth-century feminism is littered. They shared a common overall feminist commitment and many of the same friends, but given the differences in their age and personal proclivities, became engrossed in different activities. Eliza, the eldest, died young in childbirth but during the 1840s, when in her early and mid-twenties, had espoused a whole range of radical causes and was regarded askance, according to Eugene L. Rasor, as an 'avant-garde' feminist.[41]

Caroline, born in 1822, married politician James Stansfeld and with him became involved in the agitation over the Contagious Diseases Acts, as did her youngest sister Emilie who acted, between 1870 and 1876, as the salaried editor of the campaign's journal, *The Shield*. Both Caroline and Emilie were also active in the causes of women's suffrage and Italian republicanism. Matilda, the third of the four sisters, though rather less prominent in feminist campaigns, bore a daughter who was to be a mainstay of the suffrage movement in the 1870s and 1880s, Caroline Ashurst Biggs. Caroline, growing up in the company of women as active, dedicated and articulate as her mother and two aunts (Eliza had died too young to have been significantly influential), was an obvious candidate for the growing women's movement.

Sisterhoods like the Ashurst network abound in the history of nineteenth-century English feminism.[42] Maria and Emily Shirreff's close partnership was not abandoned when Maria married Thomas Grey in 1841. The sisters continued to write novels and feminist tracts together as well as establishing the Women's Education Union and its highly successful offshoot, the Girls' Public Day School Company.

Rachel and Harriet Cook, Henrietta Müller and her sister Eva (later McLaren), Sarah, Hannah and Anne (later Cowen) Guilford from Nottingham, though their feminist practice sometimes differed, are all examples of these extraordinarily powerful and unified sisterhoods. In the case of Anne and Fanny Metcalfe they, like the Shirreff sisters, worked in close union, founding together the Highfield School for Girls in the North London suburb of Hendon.

The Müller daughters – Henrietta and Eva – active slightly later in the period, are a fine example of the complex web which embraced feminist activists at this time. Henrietta, who remained single, was active in feminist journalism and in local government circles as was her sister Eva. Eva married into the Bright-McLaren network but before moving to Bradford upon marriage had worked closely with Octavia Hill and Josephine Butler.

The London Langham Place Circle of the 1850s and 1860s boasted a significant number of such sisterhoods – the Crows, the Lewins, the Drewrys, the Leigh Smiths. The situation was no different beyond London; alongside the Davenport Hills, Bristol was also the home of the Quaker Priestman and Sturge sisters. The Winkworth sisters – Catherine, Susannah and Emily – were well integrated in feminist and intellectual circles during their youth in Manchester. When they moved to Bristol in 1862 they found a similarly compatible network there where they fell in with Mary Carpenter, Florence and Rosamund Davenport Hill and Frances Power Cobbe.

The best-known feminist sisterhood of this period must undoubtedly be that of the Garretts. Writing to her friend Harriet Cook, Elizabeth Garrett signalled her sense of family destiny and uniqueness. 'My strength lies in the extra amount of daring wh[ich] I have as a family endowment. All Garretts have it.'[43] Not only did this family of six sisters and four brothers produce both Britain's first United Kingdom-trained woman doctor and the leader of the constitutional suffrage movement, but the eldest sister, Louisa Smith, was also active in the early London National Society for Women's Suffrage. Another sister, Alice Cowell, was Dr Elizabeth Garrett's successor on the London School Board in 1874 and Agnes Garrett, also a feminist activist, established – in partnership with her cousin Rhoda – the first all-female house-decorating partnership in the country.

Rhoda Garrett, Derbyshire cousin of the more famous Suffolk Garretts and another vocal women's activist, brings us to what David Rubinstein dubbed, in the case of the Garretts, a 'cousinhood'.[44] We can extend such cousin-based networks well beyond the Garretts, however. Florence Nightingale numbered both Anne Clough, first Principal of Newnham College, Cambridge, and Barbara Leigh Smith Bodichon amongst her cousins whilst Clementia Taylor, a radical active across the range of feminist campaigns, was a cousin of Barbara Bodichon's friend and educational associate, Elizabeth Whitehead (later Malleson).

Dorothea Beale of Cheltenham Ladies' College was a cousin of the feminist writer Caroline F. Cornwallis who died in 1858. The articles she published in the *Westminister Review* shortly before her death have widely been considered to be amongst the first shots fired in this revivified round of the feminist struggle. Elizabeth Sturge, writing her autobiography in 1928, remembered that her introduction to the suffrage issue came when 'as a girl I was present at an obscure meeting in Bristol [at which] my cousin, the late Eliza Sturge of Birmingham, was chief speaker.'[45]

For women especially, in this period, the family was the primary site through which their lives were ordered and contained. Frequently that meant also that the choices they made were heavily reliant upon family obligation and opinion. Barbara Caine's study of the large family of Potter sisters skilfully highlights the simultaneous arms of emotional support and of control which were the collective sisterhood's means of dealing with its errant or distressed members.[46]

In the Garrett family, a surprisingly traditional family who produced none the less an astounding succession of publicly prominent feminists, a similar policing function was apparent. When Henry Fawcett proposed marriage to the young Millicent Garrett, her older sisters assumed a dominant advisory role in the proceedings. Elizabeth – who had some time earlier rejected a similar proposal from her sister's suitor (we do not know whether Millicent knew of it at this stage though others of the sisters certainly did) – leapt into action. Their parents had insisted upon a waiting period before granting the lovers permission to marry, and during that time Elizabeth was anxious to elicit for her sister Millicent the advice and opinions of the London feminist circle. Millicent was not

altogether impressed by this plan and confided her dilemma to their
eldest and married sister, Louisa.

Lizzie [Elizabeth] . . . offered to get for me Mme Bodichon's, Miss Crowe's and
others' opinions of Mr Fawcett. I don't know Mme Bodichon – if I did, of course,
I cannot say what weight her opinions might have with me; but at present,
judging from Dr Bodichon's appearance, I should say that it was improbable that
we should agree in the choice of husbands . . . I have not written to Lizzie, for I
am afraid of vexing her, which I should be dreadfully sorry to do, for I know that
it is out of pure love for me and anxiety for my happiness that she wrote as she
did.[47]

It was this same sister, to whom Millicent had confessed her anxieties,
who was also responsible for her introduction to organized feminist
politics. Louie, as she was known amongst the sisters, took Millicent to
an election meeting in support of John Stuart Mill in 1865 and then on to
a party at the London home of radical suffrage organizer, Clementia
Taylor.[48]

These are some of the ways, then, in which family background served
to influence women's route into feminist understanding, at both the
psychological and the ideological level, though the distinction between
the two cannot always be determined with clarity. For some women,
familial and parental encouragement and engagement led to their own
involvement. For others, it was a reactive mechanism against the values
of one or both parents that energized them. In a sense, the common
denominator for them all was reaction, for even in enlightened family
settings, daughters seldom received the same upbringing as sons. Even
where they did, external values inevitably made themselves felt. Psychology and ideology are not always factors of separable quantitative
discovery; it is their enmeshing that is perhaps of more significance.

We should thus be wary of over-determining the importance of family
influence not merely because as many women came to their feminist
understanding out of traditional families as out of unconventional ones,
but also because it would be an easy step from there to seeing them as
politically passive pawns moulded wholly by their history. A host of
other determinants, ideological and psychological, stemming from support and from the dynamics of reaction, served as catalysts and partial
explanations for the marked growth of feminist activity at this juncture.

One area of considerable importance and interest is religion. These
were women who came to adulthood in a society saturated and governed
by religious precepts. Though Anglicanism remained the dominant form
of Christian worship at this time, its position was being significantly
eroded on both flanks; by the growth of alternative Christian denomina-

tions critical of its practices and doctrines on the one hand, and by the gradual but palpable process of secularization on the other. At no point in the nineteenth century was a profession of unbelief socially acceptable; few were willing to commit themselves even to a qualified agnosticism. Religion continued, despite declining attendances at formal worship, to function as a central force in England throughout our period. We should not, therefore, be surprised by the frequent invocation of the divine, and the seemingly devout stand which so many feminists of this period took. More interesting and more significant than their religiosity are the specific denominational choices they made and their constant questioning of the fundamental precepts of religious belief. Religion remained, after all, in the words of Seymour Drescher, 'a primary form of cosmopolitan social organization' reaching well beyond the confines of personal conscience.[49]

For women especially, religion acted as an agency central in determining the specific pattern of their lives. The relationship between the increasing 'feminization' of religion and its relegation to the world of privacy and contemplation (and thence to the domestic private sphere) had informed a growing acceptance of women's central role in preserving and disseminating belief through piety and often through its philanthropic concomitant. The success of early nineteenth-century evangelicalism has been seen as a strong factor in the new emphasis laid on highlighting the public-private divide.[50] The weight thrown by this cross-denominational evangelicalism on the family as the focus of personal salvation imposed on women a major role in moulding the spiritual direction of the family. Its message, though, could be a confusing one. Although it offered women a role and a worth in life as well as an opportunity to harness their energies around a religious framework, at the same time it tied them definitionally to the idea of separately constructed roles dependent on sex.[51]

Women entering the feminist movement rarely chose to reject religion wholesale. Indeed, many of the campaigns in which feminists involved themselves relied at least in part on an expression of devout belief as the motor for organization. Though there were a handful of women who were at best indifferent to the authority of the Church, most feminists remained at the very least nominal believers, and many took the issue seriously enough to consider conversion to beliefs with which they felt a stronger accord.

Most of the women in the sample were born to Anglican parents. Of the many non-Anglican beliefs represented in the feminist community, the most significant religious minorities remained the Unitarians and the Quakers, as other historians have also found.[52] Religion at birth was retrievable in just under half the total sample. The relative proportion of

Quaker and Unitarian to Anglican women is striking; 21 per cent of the total were *known* Anglicans and 20 per cent either Quaker or Unitarian, the former comprising 9 per cent and the latter 11 per cent of that total. The true Anglican figure is undoubtedly higher and one might feasibly include in that same category women born into other state churches such as the Church of Scotland, as was one woman in this sample.[53] Women of dissenting beliefs were far likelier to make those beliefs a public and political issue than were those from establishment backgrounds. One might safely assume (though the quantitative element in this survey does *not*) that in the larger proportion of cases of unknown religion, the women were at least born into Anglican households.

Many of the best-known feminists of this period were the daughters of the small but active communities of Quakerism and Unitarianism, denominations known for their relative radicalism and interest in social conditions and welfare. Both sects were significant, not only in producing or encouraging feminism, but also for their considerable contributions to the business community and the political world. Many of England's best known industrial firms were owned by Quakers, and both these religions produced distinguished and frequently radical politicians throughout the century. Both had small but active populations whose high profile in the community often made them seem more numerous than they actually were. In neither religion, however, despite their relative advantages, were women allotted a role even approaching that of the men. Whilst they were considerably freer in scope and activity than in many other forms of Christianity, they still occupied a palpably subordinate position. Elizabeth Isichei has argued that it was precisely this paradox which 'sensitize[d] their minds to the relative position of the sexes'.[54]

In comparative terms, though, they fared well. In the women's movement, as in radical and philanthropic circles, Unitarians and Quakers alike were highly regarded. The Winkworth sisters – Susannah, Catherine and Emily – were the daughters of a well-to-do silk manufacturer and lived in Manchester in early adulthood. In those years, they became involved in both literary and feminist circles, principally through the agency of feminist and novelist Elizabeth Gaskell. The Winkworths had been born into the Church of England and came, in fact, from clerical stock, having a reverend grandfather in Berkshire. They were, nevertheless, clearly impressed by the Unitarians with whom they mixed in Manchester.

It may seem strange that among the names of those to whom we thus looked up for intellectual nourishment or guidance, none should occur of members of the

Church of England . . . Our Church friends were, many of them, excellent people, and perhaps on the average superior to the *average* of our orthodox dissenting friends in education and refinement; but there was not one person of commanding intellect among them . . . The Unitarians in Manchester were, as a body, far away superior to any other in intellect, culture and refinement of manners and certainly did not come behind any other in active philanthropy and earnest efforts for the social improvement of those around them.[55]

Indeed, one sister – Susannah – eventually converted to Unitarianism.

Others, too, were attracted by these faiths. Frances Power Cobbe made a point of attending and trying out a Unitarian service though she found it decidedly not to her taste.[56] That it was Unitarianism with which she experimented, though, is important. Both Unitarianism and Quakerism were known as spawning-grounds for feminism. The Unitarians numbered Bessie Parkes and Barbara Leigh Smith, Clementia Taylor and Elizabeth Whitehead, Elizabeth Jesser Reid, Anna Swanwick and Florence Nightingale among their number whilst the Sturges, the Brights, the Priestmans, the Howitts and Isabella Ford were all from Quaker backgrounds.

Though women of Quaker and Unitarian disposition formed so significant a minority in the English feminist community of this time they were not the sole representatives of non-conformity within the movement. A handful of women from other varieties of Dissent were as active; there were a sprinkling of Congregationalists including Margaret Bondfield, Laura Chant and Yorkshire feminist Florence Balgarnie, and a small number of women from the various Methodist sects. Rochdale feminist Isabel Petrie Mills came originally from a Free Methodist family, marrying in 1848 into the Methodist New Connexion. She and her husband, John Mills, together shifted into Congregationalism.

As a young woman living in the family home in 1840, Isabel had witnessed the startling material consequences of doctrinal dissent. 'One memorable day two men entered our house and carried off the dining-table and a copper coal-box . . . The articles were to be sold for non-payment of Church Rates!'[57]

Experiences such as this served often to invoke a sense of social injustice in their recipients, 'a group consciousness rooted in religious persecution'.[58] Jane Marcus noted the unsurprising concurrence within activist ranks of those fighting against slavery and denominational restrictions simultaneously and in favour of such causes as an extended franchise, temperance, trade unionism and international peace.[59]

Once again we should be wary of assuming too simple and unproblematic a consonance between religious belief and feminist practice. In the first instance, though their numbers were certainly substantial proportionally, non-conformist women were still a minority among feminists. More importantly, perhaps, religion continued in effect to offer women at best a confused and mixed message and remained a critical source of sex role segregation.[60] Despite its sometimes liberating face, religious propensity could also connote an unchallenged political passivity.

This conflict between religion's limited assignment of activity to women on the one hand, and on the other its adamant belief in both their lesser authority and their essential sinfulness was nowhere more apparent than in the evangelical movement which spanned both low-church Anglicanism and Dissent. The influential work of Leonore Davidoff and Catherine Hall has demonstrated amply the considerable part played by evangelical religion in formulating and promoting the ideology of the separate spheres appropriate to men and women.[61] As they point out, however, this construction was not without its internal contradictions. 'Although the man had full recognition and power as head of the household, Evangelicalism offered women a life work, which, while subordinate, carried dignity and moral weight.'[62]

Evangelicalism, though primarily associated with the low-church Anglicanism of the earliest years of the century, did, as already noted, cross denominational lines. Brian Harrison sees the various arms of the moral reform movement of the period as culling their supporters and their activists from a 'hard core of "middling" non-conformists and evangelicals'.[63]

Despite their obvious doctrinal differences, these groupings were fully aware of their meeting points. Emily Davies tells an amusing tale of her clerical father which highlights aptly the mutal understanding which brought such people together, as much within feminism as in other social movements informed by these beliefs.

The editor [of the *Gateshead Observer*: Emily's family had moved north to Gateshead from Chichester in 1839 on John Davies acquiring an ecclesiastical living there] was a Unitarian, but he and my father were on friendly terms. On one occasion in later years, they met in the street, and after a little talk my father exclaimed, 'Ah, Mr Clapham, if only you could be brought to a knowledge of the truth, you might be the most useful man in the parish.' Mr Clapham replied, 'I was just thinking the same of you, Sir'.[64]

Feminists, unlike their male counterparts, seemed able to work with considerable unity within those doctrinal differences.

One highly significant factor in the specific incidence of Dissent, and to a lesser extent of evangelicalism, amongst such women is the political and religious geography of feminism it allows us to trace. It is not coincidental that women such as the Anglican Winkworth sisters or the

Methodist Isabel Petrie Mills were reared in the industrial county of Lancashire where non-conformist traditions were strong. The areas where there was a marked incidence of feminist activity were often also areas in which non-Anglican Christianity had secured a foothold; Manchester and Birmingham in the northern industrial zones and Bristol where Quakerism was an influential force.[65]

In addition to suggesting some of the regional patterns to the emergence of feminism, nurtured and supported by concentrations of sympathetic religious radicals, this geography points, too, to the diverse regional make-up of the movement. Feminist circles in northern industrial centres where non-conformity was strong show a higher proportion of dissenting activists than in the Anglican and more rural south. The Manchester Unitarians, the Birmingham, Leeds and Bristol Quakers, all produced strong feminist contingents from within their number.

The point takes us back, too, to the connections between family and politics. In these contexts most acutely, though within Anglicanism as well, the cross-regional patterns of kinship and religion show marked feminist significance. Thus Quaker families like the Brights, Sturges, Peases and Gurneys, and Unitarian families such as that of the related Leigh Smiths and Nightingales, or even such Anglican families as the Garretts – all of whom had family branches spread across the country – produced active women from all areas. In his study of Unitarian abolitionist activities, Douglas Stange notes 'the familial unity of Bristol Unitarians'.[66] None the less, family influence was not always paramount. The Garrett daughters are not noted for having shared the strict evangelicalism by which their mother ordered her life.

These kinship links are explicit in the recollections of Methodist-born Isabel Petrie Mills. The Quaker Brights were close family friends of her Celtic father and Yorkshire mother, themselves a typical family of regional non-conformity. Bright's eldest sister, Sophia, bore two feminist activist daughters – Lilias Ashworth and Mrs Ashworth Hallett – both in the Quaker strongholds of south-west England where Sophia had settled on marriage. At the first Anti-Corn Law League meeting called in 1843 at Toad Lane, Rochdale (home of the Rochdale Pioneers' Co-operative), Isabel remembers seeing not just John and Sophia Bright but also the other sisters Priscilla (later McLaren) and Margaret (later Lucas), both of whom were prominent feminists. She talks also of her acquaintance with such Quaker and feminist families as the Peases, Gurneys and Priestmans as well as with Anglican feminist Octavia Hill.[67] These extensive connections of family and friendship point clearly to the close relations between politics, region and religion which so sustained the alternative politics, feminism included, of nineteenth-century bourgeois England.

A number of women who chose to identify themselves as feminists at this time underwent important religious conversions or traumas during the course of their adult lives. Around 8 per cent of the sample chose to switch faiths, a handful joining the Catholic church (including Bessie Rayner Parkes under the influence of Irish feminist Sarah Atkinson, and poetess Adelaide Proctor) and one – May Tennant – switching from Catholicism to Anglicanism. Again, the incidence is proportionately high, suggesting that these were women who took such beliefs seriously and gave considerable thought to their actions and their conscience in such matters.[68] Gail Malmgreen considers, too, that 'the 'new woman' was often a new religionist'.[69]

Not all of those for whom a crisis of conscience catalysed such actions chose to immerse themselves in the comfort of traditional faiths. For Frances Power Cobbe, her religious doubts and subsequent acceptance of a theistic position had resulted in a painful rift with her orthodox family, with Frances banished from the family home for a year. Doctrinal and theological issues remained a constant question for her until the revelation of theism came to her in her late twenties. From then on, she actively pursued a link with theists across the world, developing her theological standpoint and publishing copiously in this area.

Anglican-born Emelie Gurney was attracted by the more mystical elements of religion. 'I have an intense pleasure in being converted', she confessed to her friend Caroline Stephen.[70] Mystical religion attracted a number of activist women in this period. Theosophy, with its non-Western mystique, drew many to its path including the radical Annie Besant and outspoken London School Board member, Henrietta Müller. The young Emelia Strong (later Pattison, and afterwards Dilke) was also captivated by this mysticism. As a teenager, her habitual method of atoning for her sins was to lie 'for hours on the bare floor or on the stones, with her arms in the attitude of a cross'.[71]

Religion was often the wellspring of feminist understanding and activity, whether women had undergone psychological or spiritual crises of this sort or had remained within a more conventional and orthodox context. Constance Maynard, first Principal of the denominational Westfield College, Louisa Hubbard and Octavia Hill all found their Anglican beliefs a direct source of intellectual and emotional sustenance as was Unitarianism for Florence Nightingale. Despite the contradictions it also implied, religious belief offered a model of love and friendship, of devotion to a cause, of the triumph of once untenable beliefs.

Even within the dominant context of mid-nineteenth-century piety, there was still room for some measure of religious cynicism. Sheila Herstein sees the children of Unitarian Benjamin Leigh Smith and Anne Longden – among them, Barbara Leigh Smith – 'drifting through intermarriage and broadening social connections into nominal acceptance of the Church of England'.[72] And Millicent Garrett Fawcett, whilst remaining within the Church of England and having been raised by a devoutly evangelical mother, clearly saw more sense in hard political footwork than in seeking divine intervention in mortal matters. When Josephine Butler organized a prayer meeting to coincide with a parliamentary condemnation of the Contagious Diseases Acts in the early 1880s, Fawcett applauded the rather more practical attitude of the American participants. 'Tears are good, prayers are better, but we should get on better if behind every tear there was a vote at the ballot box.'[73]

Barbara Leigh Smith established her experimental Portman Hall School in the 1850s, more than fifteen years before even the relatively uncontentious proposals for 'unsectarian' rather than 'secular' universal education reached the statute book for the first time. She and her fellow workers took a decidedly pragmatic approach to the problems they knew faced them over the question of religious practice. Elizabeth Whitehead recognized that her lack of manifest spiritual zeal might tell against her suitability to educate the minds of the young. 'We are known to be ungodly people attending no church in the parish, but I hope this will not stand in my way – if it does with the school-master I shall attack the stronghold of the vicarage . . . I feel very courageous this morning.'[74]

In a similar vein, the unusual marriages Elizabeth Wolstenholme and Florence Fenwick Miller made attest to the growing, if small, number of women for whom traditional religion was no longer an organizing principle. Wolstenholme was visibly pregnant when she married, whilst Miller chose a civil ceremony for her marriage in 1877 and did not adopt any part of her husband's name whatsoever.

The religious choices which feminists made link closely, as well, to the specific political stances to which they adhered. A few literally yoked their politics to their religion through membership of religious organizations whose political affiliation was explicit; Sarah Dickenson, active in the women's trade union movement and in suffrage activities in the north of England, was a member of the Labour Church and Gertrude Tuckwell and Margaret Llewellyn Davies were both brought up in Christian Socialist households. Llewellyn Davies's father was a radical cleric, brother of Emily Davies, and her mother, Mary Crompton, was a Unitarian feminist. Hers was, indeed, an ecumenical household. Brian Harrison has remarked that for Margaret Bondfield, religion and politics were inseparable.[75]

The palpable connections between politics and religion in this period are familiar historical territory. In the case of feminist political practice, the high incidence of dissent and the seeming preference for a liberal politics is not entirely coincidental. Many women had, as we have seen, been politicized in their youth by their family's ostracism from the mainstream or by their involvement in the pressure-group politics clustered around dissent and evangelicalism. And though they often deliberately distanced their feminism from the remainder of their politics, claiming for it the status of a separately conceived and separately constructed entity, there are none the less some observable though by no means rigidly observed corollaries.

Many, as we have seen, learned their earliest political lessons through parental example and encouragement and often retained at least some attachment to these infant loyalties. Such experience was not limited to the radical fringe in which women such as the bohemian Ashurst daughters, Isabel Petrie Mills or Bessie Rayner Parkes grew to adulthood. The Shirreff sisters were reared within – and in the case of the younger sister, married into – the higher echelons of Whig-Anglican establish-ment politics, as noted earlier. The significance in the feminist context is the capacity of all these women, not only to recognize their enduring similarities above those differences, but also to separate out their feminist practice. They recognized the yawning gap between their feminism and the practice of governing politics which was largely unsympathetic to their cause, and yet as active and involved women they still chose to retain some adherence to that politics.

The political creeds outside feminism and pursued by feminist women spanned the broad spectrum of British politics. Of those with known political affiliation, the Liberals and Radicals far outnumber their competitors. Twenty-seven per cent of the sample are identifiable as Liberals/Radicals and a further 5 per cent as Conservatives, though in practical terms the distinction was often far less discernible. On occasion, it led to confusion. Commenting on her sister Emelie's politics to Eliza Ashurst early in 1845, her friend Mazzini's tone was semi-teasing and semi-serious. 'Emilie fancies she is one of the Benthamite utilitarian tribe; not a bit; there is poetry enough in her to drive away to the realm of Hades a whole legion of Benthams; one of these days she will awake and find that she has been labouring under a dream: an ugly one.'[76]

This apparent lack of political clarity has confused historians seeking to interpret the politics of feminism within a mainstream context. Writers as diverse as Elie Halevy and Carol Dyhouse have pointed to a political conservatism amongst active women, or to a seeming socialist-conservative dichotomy which left no room for the political middle ground.[77] Certainly there were women who allied themselves either to the socialist or the conservative camp, but for the most part non-party definitions of political outlook serve a more valuable function in the feminist context.

The attractions of socialism grew somewhat with the greater number of working-class women involving themselves in the movement and, of course, with the actual strengthening of its position within British politics, which the Labour movement signifies.[78] None the less, for women, the relationship between feminism and socialism was rarely a simple and frequently an unhappy one; the debate over the primacy of class or of gender remained an unresolved question in the labour movement, though not in the feminist movement, throughout this period and beyond.[79]

Within mainstream governing politics in this period, Conservatism in one sense could offer politicized women a less contradictory identity. For Liberal adherents, there was a demonstrable assumption that the whole tenor of liberal political belief favoured the formal emancipation of women. Conservatism, with its accent on traditional and hereditary rights, presented a less optimistic face, but with the increase in organized constituency work that followed the passing of the various measures of parliamentary reform after 1872, it offered women an active though distinctly subordinate political role. Thus could the energetic Lady Knightley divide herself severally between the philanthropic activities expected from a woman of her class, the Conservative Primrose League and, at the same time, the National Union of Women's Suffrage Societies.[80] It was of no especial consequence in the ambience of female Conservatism that her counterpart, Lady Jersey – also an active Tory wife – was prominent in the Women's Anti-Suffrage League. Conservatism offered women not a feminist perspective but a seemingly gender-neutral activism. The growth of Liberal Unionism in the last years of the century absorbed a number of active women who, whilst retaining a liberal creed in most respects, found the Irish issue problematic. Millicent Garrett Fawcett, Lady Stanley, Frances Balfour and Kate Courtney were among those who shifted to Liberal Unionism, though not thence to Conservatism as did the organization.

Party politics was, in significant ways, something *apart* from that all-encompassing feminism with which activist women ordered their lives and choices.[81] Their feminist principles relate more cogently to a libertarian or reforming outlook, though even that parallel needs to be approached with caution. Brian Harrison, in particular, has argued this connection with some force and plausibility, pointing to the contiguous membership of feminist and reform organizations, to their parallel techniques of persuasion and campaigning.[82] Olive Banks has gone so far as to argue that feminism was 'one aspect of a wider movement for social and political reform'.[83] This is a tempting and functionally convincing analysis but it falls short in denying the consciously holistic philosophy informing nineteenth-century feminism. Whilst a large number of feminists professed libertarian views on a wide range of issues and understood their consonance with a feminist politics, the practical politics of the reform movement in fact consisted of fragmentary single issue pressure groups where cross-connecting ideologies, whilst obvious in retrospect, were not always explicitly drawn out. In the case of feminism, the relationship between separate campaigns and an overall ideal was manifest, if not always wholly consensual. In this sense, the movement differed significantly from these other modes of libertarian campaigning. Feminism offered a consistent creed that functioned as a theoretically understood cross-over from campaigning politics to philosophical stance.

The resultant and unique creed which emerged from this understanding was one able to cross not only party lines but a host of unorthodox as well as mainstream topics in addition. Vegetarianism, anti-vivisection, anti-vaccination and 'rational dress' were all amongst the less traditional stances embraced additionally by women identifying themselves with feminism, alongside its more traditional and long-standing associations with anti-slavery, opposition to the corn laws and, more enduringly, temperance.[84]

Such alliances were frequently couched within a specifically woman-centred perspective; support for temperance had strong economic and indeed physical justification, whilst the argument against the practice of vivisection often relied on an explicitly gendered, if sometimes essentialist, interpretation. Anti-vivisectionists were clear that the practice they so abhorred resulted from the overt masculinity created when 'Man suffers the Woman in him to fall'.[85]

Though the range of political opinions amongst activist women thus differed markedly, their stance was. so fundamentally grounded in a feminist ethic that could support difference that these political diversities rarely spelled insurmountable problems or hostilities for women within the movement. Emily Davies's views point to some of the ways in which what elsewhere might render contradiction a hindrance, was subsumed within a wider acknowledgement of shared values. Davies hailed, as we have seen, from an Evangelical and highly respectable background; her father's views had shifted from a youthful Liberalism to an espousal of Burkean Conservatism. Though her brother Llewellyn, it may be remembered, had strong links with the Christian Socialist movement, Emily chose more cautious boundaries, both politically and spiritually. Millicent Garrett, who as a child had found Davies's manner forbidding, called her 'the least revolutionary of revolutionaries',[86] a similar judgement to that of her biographer, Barbara Stephen. 'In all that concerned women, she was a revolutionary; in all else, a conservative.'[87] Emily's correspondence refers frequently to her distaste for radicalism – 'the more I see of Radical women, the less I desire to increase their number'[88] – and yet at no point in her full and varied life did she actively desist from their company, whether socially or within the campaign sphere.

Whilst, in the Edwardian era, both tactical and even ideological differences became divisive factors within feminist ranks, in this earlier period women retained a strong sense of mutuality which overrode difference.[89] Frances Power Cobbe related with some relish the exchange about her politics between those quintessential liberals Harriet Taylor, and her partner John Stuart Mill.

Mrs Taylor said: 'Ah, Miss Cobbe is a bitter Conservative!' 'Not a *bitter* one,' said Mr Mill. 'Miss Cobbe is a Conservative. I am sorry for it, but Miss Cobbe is never bitter.'[90]

And in some senses, such a politics clearly *was* borne of a contradiction, albeit a fruitful one. Whilst, in one sense, women opted to separate their feminism from the rest of their politics, and in particular from party politics, they none the less directed both energy and attention to attaining a voice and indeed a presence in that central institution of party politics, Parliament. As party lines grew more distinct in the second half of the century and an observable demarcation between Conservative and Liberal thinking became practically and ideologically more apparent, both the pragmatism and the cynicism of women for this male politics increased.

If we are to wait for Women's Suffrage until the Liberal Party is educated up to the point of bestowing it, I fear it will not come either in my lifetime, or yours . . . I think it a mistake on the part of any woman to be a party woman first and a Suffragist only in the second place.[91]

Elizabeth Elmy was, of course, correct in reserving her faith in the Liberal party on the matter of the franchise, but she knew, too, that tactically it was a question that needed to be forced to the forefront of Parliamentary attention whenever possible. This reliance on the whims of male politicians and need to dance to the rhythm of the parliamentary timetable was accepted and understood by feminists as a token of their prolonged exclusion from civic participation; without it their cause could not advance but they remained sceptical as to its effective capacity to alter the *status quo*. In consequence, though they thus acknowledged and organized around the tactics of public politics, their definition of their own aspirations was never limited merely to such achievements or ends. Parliament, male political behaviour, the campaign trail, were means and not ends within the feminist philosophy.

3

Reappropriating Adulthood

For Victorian women, there was no simple divorce between childhood and adulthood; the continuity of their dependence and their exclusion from full citizenship blurred the distinctions between the two. None the less, feminist women in particular frequently challenged the restrictions imposed upon their sex at a practical level as much as in their campaigns. The lifestyles they adopted as adults form a central feature in our understanding of the determination of feminist practice.

For women far more than for men, adult life was shaped and constrained centrally by marriage. This rite of passage which so symbolized a recognition of adulthood, in fact, served merely to deepen women's dependent status and highlight the continued denial of their adult status. Notwithstanding, it remained the orthodox pinnacle of feminine achievement throughout – and well beyond – the late nineteenth century. At the same time that it conferred status on women, it ensured, too, their effective disappearance from public scrutiny. 'Victorian and Edwardian political biographies seldom mention the wives, except for brief comments on their selfless devotion and loving dedication to their husband's public duty.'[1]

Amongst feminists, it was to be the very last years of the century before any thorough-going hostility to the institution of marriage seeped into feminist thinking. One of the most remarkable features of Victorian feminism was its concerted attempt to remould rather than reject marital practice whilst at the same time not annul the worth of the single woman.

Forty-five per cent of the total sample used in this study did marry, though many at a relatively late stage in their adult life, reflecting perhaps what Olive Banks sees as their 'anxiety over subordination in marriage'.[2] Pat Jalland's figures show that 'at any time, about one-third of all women over thirty were likely to be unmarried',[3] with that figure declining as the age cohort rises. Many feminists only married late in their thirties, and of those whose marriages were known to be unhappy most had married very young; 58 per cent married after the age of twenty-three, and of the ten documented unhappy marriages in the sample, seven were in cases where the marriage had occurred before the bride was twenty-two.

Increasingly, and as the feminist voice gained in confidence, women who did marry were careful to do so in a supportive and unrepressive environment. The marriages which feminists made throughout this period represent an area in which the coterminous nature of their beliefs and of their living arrangements can be viewed in high relief. Marriage seldom led such women to abandon either their feminist beliefs or friendships; they sought rather, and in a variety of ways, to find marital arrangements that were compatible with their views despite the legal disadvantages under which they continued to labour for the greater part of the century. Their preference was far more for integration than for wholesale rejection.

The decision to marry or to remain single could be an anguishing process, hedged not only with personal emotional considerations but with the enormous and often unsubtle pressures ordering Victorian bourgeois circles. Anne Jemima Clough was fairly certain, even at the age of twenty, that marriage was not high on her list of priorities but she knew the impact of those norms. 'I do think of it sometimes and there is a vast deal of nonsense in my heart too.'[4] Writing her memoirs in 1926, Margaret Wynne Nevinson recalled just how strong those pressures could be: ' . . . in the Suffrage days, speaking at meetings up and down the country, shy young women, longing as I longed for economic independence, would come and whisper the same story to me, they are being urged to get married.'[5] It was clearly a dilemma of some magnitude. The movement in its earlier years had had no wish to condemn what it saw as the potential gains of marriages based on mutual affection and respect, and unencumbered by legislative enactments of the double standard. At the same time, feminists were anxious to dispel the image of inutility which clung so obstinately to the single woman. The marriage question thus cut directly across the lines of other central campaigning issues – employment, married women's property, sexuality and even education. Though it was to be late in the 1880s, and in the wake of the social purity campaigns, before attitudes towards marriage hardened into a specific 'campaign' issue, one of the most characteristic features of earlier generations of feminists was indubitably their individual and private attempts to live their feminist practices within marriage, or to reject the institution on independent grounds.

Brian Harrison has argued that in the circles in which feminism found so many champions, 'a political partnership between spouses inevitably grew out of their domestic partnership'.[6] The evidence suggests rather that it was a woman's politics that determined her choice of partner.

Women from radical religions, from which a good proportion of feminists came, were also likelier to make active marital selections based on similar criteria. Nancy Hewitt's work on the feminist Quaker women of early nineteenth-century America has shown how their courtship and marriage patterns were built upon 'combining mutual respect and affection with hard work'.[7]

Back in England, revealing anecdotes abound. Alice Scatcherd refused to wear a wedding ring, scandalizing the upright proprietors of hotels where she and her husband stayed. Florence Fenwick Miller retained her own name after marriage. Elizabeth Wolstenholme married only because she was visibly pregnant and distressing her co-feminists. Elizabeth Garrett Anderson maintained her medical practice through marriage, childbirth and severe family illness. All these women's lives represent attempts to maintain a feminist profile not just on the campaign trail but also in their 'private' lives. It was here, crucially, that they challenged the separation of public and private by refusing to separate out the politics of feminism from their lives as women in a patriarchal order. As M. F. Cusack argued in 1874, 'while marriage is honourable in all, it is not the one end of female existence'.[8]

Cusack's belief was apparent in a number of ways, not only in women's determination to render the decision to marry a genuine area of active choice in their lives, but also in a changing perspective on their interpretation of the nature of love. Emilia Dilke's miserably incompatible first marriage to Mark Pattison foundered, according to her account, because of his desire for a wife who was merely a 'contented machine'.[9] Emilia's experiences with Pattison, which she described as 'the incessant peck, peck, peck of the cruel beak,'[10] did not, however, quench her beliefs that where two people 'shared the same moral and intellectual ideal – then marriage is the greatest bliss that life can offer'.[11] It was not long after Pattison's death that she made her second and far happier marriage to the beleaguered Liberal politician Charles Dilke, unshaken in her decision by the legal strife he faced in a highly-charged and intensely public divorce proceedings.

When George Eliot married the young John Cross after the death of her long-term lover, G. H. Lewes, it was her feminist friends who upheld her decision in the face of the pressures of propriety. A letter of support from her friend Barbara Bodichon reveals the capacity of feminist women for reshaping and reconsidering the emotional and social precepts on which they had been nurtured. 'Tell Johnny Cross I should have done exactly what he has done if you would let me and if I had been a man. You see I know all love is so different that I do not see it unnatural to love in new ways – not to be unfaithful to any memory.'[12] This forging of new marital and emotional relations was not restricted to rewriting the marriage contract. Activists – married and unmarried alike – were sensitive to the needs and the standing of single women. Whilst they caustically attacked a value-system which condemned women to economic dependence yet could not fulfil that 'ideal', feminists sought also to reconstitute a positive image of singleness as an issue of personal choice rather than an uninvited catastrophe.

It was her childlessness that often coloured the negative perceptions which attached to the woman who remained unmarried.[13] In a society which attempted to divide the domestic and the public so sharply, family life was paramount in the maintenance of the social fabric. The spinster in this context was effectively denying her maternity and was thus outside the family norm. The unease over the spinster's failure of maternal fulfilment raises, however, one of the many arenas in which ambivalence about gendered behaviours emerged at this time. Whilst the unmarried woman herself became the focus of disdain or pity, she also invoked both fear and disapproval for her perceived unwillingness to conform. She was both the passive recipient of misfortune and simultaneously wilfully defiant of orthodoxy.

The figures for child-bearing among feminist women are sadly distorted by the paucity of available and reliable data. None the less, the general demographic pattern of reduced family size in the middle class discernible from the 1870s, suggests that reality and ideology were, in any case, moving farther and farther apart even in more conformist strata of society. Amongst married feminists, many either remained childless or bore small numbers of children. Women such as Lady Strachey with ten children, Lady Stanley with ten children and twelve confinements, or even Amie Hicks who emigrated briefly to New Zealand with her relatively small brood of six, were rare in the feminist community. One or two children – as with Millicent Fawcett and her sister Elizabeth, Hertha Ayrton, Elizabeth Elmy, Bessie Parkes, Ursula Bright, Florence Fenwick Miller or Harriet Taylor – was a more common pattern in this group. Many also remained childless: Emilia Dilke, Emma Paterson, Barbara Bodichon, Sophie Bryant, Anna Jameson, Clementia Taylor and Emilie Venturi are good examples of childless women, some at least of whom had made conscious decisions to remain so.

In her study of the Potter sisters, Barbara Caine suggests a palpable dynamic between childlessness, activism and type of marriage; it was Beatrice Webb and Kate Courtney who, of the sisters, remained childless.[14] It is with some irony that Caine points out that only Beatrice, the eugenicist, ever practised contraception![15]

The number of women *known* to have borne children in this sample is 16 per cent, which constitutes 36 per cent of those who married. Even allowing for the distortion induced by lack of available data, the figure is low and suggests that other priorities than the traditional pursuit of motherhood informed the lifestyles of these women. Though European marital fertility appears to have been low throughout the 1860s and 1870s, childless marriages in the 1870s in the population overall account for only 8.3 per cent of total marriages.[16] Even if this computation is inaccurately low, as demographers contend, it has some meaning in relation to statistics of confinement. In 1750, the average number of confinements per marriage was five to six,[17] and though the figure falls throughout our period, it still suggests that feminist women, amongst whom both pregnancy and confinement remained low, were choosing to control their fertility perhaps more than other groups of women, though they remained very quiet about it.[18]

The fact of marriage often made childlessness a less material factor in the lives of wedded feminists than in those of their single co-workers. Millicent Garrett Fawcett's unflattering childhood memory of Emily Davies fits the stereotypical picture of the cold, unloving and unloved spinster, alas. 'Her manner towards us was not winning. She always seemed to be letting us know of how little consequence we were.'[19]

A more flatteringly human portrait of a spinster – that of Lydia Becker – was offered posthumously by a Manchester acquaintance of hers, and its tone suggests that feminists were increasingly anxious to portray the unwed woman not as a parody of masculinity but in as human and, indeed, 'womanly' a light as possible. Denying 'the idea that the platform ever superseded the home in . . . [Becker's] mind', Mrs Alexander Ireland wrote of her first encounter with Lydia in glowing terms.[20] Becker had been Jacob Bright's dinner companion when Ireland met her in the autumn of 1867. Confronted with a new-born child, Lydia Becker 'took the little one in her arms with a womanly tenderness I can never forget, and holding one of the dimpled feet in her hand, said, with a decided impressiveness: "Now I do hope that, before this child comes of age, the women's suffrage will be fully established."'[21] The story is a significant one, for it represents a moment of resurrection, the restoring of both humanity and womanhood to women stripped of their identity by their *absence* of marital status.

It was, of course, a double-edged weapon, for it brought spinsters back into the fold by defining femininity along traditional lines. Nevertheless, its restorative function was an important one in combating the denial in which the lives of single women were cast. Amongst feminist women, moreover, it is clear that spinsterhood was frequently an active choice made, perhaps for the pursuit of a career (as with factory inspector Adelaide Anderson, headmistresses Dorothea Beale and Frances Buss, politican Margaret Bondfield or economist Clara Collett) or perhaps because they found male company less to their taste, as did Constance Maynard, Sophia Jex-Blake or Frances Power Cobbe.

Towards the close of the century spinsterhood began to take shape as a concrete political position deemed preferable to marriage amongst a portion of the feminist community. From the late 1880s, as the critique of male sexuality became both more public and more developed, many feminists began to see singleness as both epitomizing a new morality and finding an independence unachievable within the confines of male-female relations. Olive Banks has argued that there is a discernible relationship between marital status and ideology amongst activists in this period, which routinely privileged singleness over marriage.[22] It was only towards the close of this period when the very institution of marriage – as distinct from the restrictions operating within it – became a target of political action, that that was so. Marriage was certainly always an ideological battleground for the movement, but it is interesting to see how the shape of that conflict changed. For many of the earlier feminists, achieving an acceptably mutual marriage was a political point; later the point was made rather by disavowing the whole exercise of marriage. Amongst the earlier women, there was seldom a sense of capitulation accompanying their marriage. Centrally, they saw their marriages as a site wherein feminist practices could be mapped out and established within the domain of normative heterosexual relations, a stance which set nineteenth-century feminists, with their characteristic pluralism, apart from their Edwardian counterparts.

With the establishment of the anti-marriage lobby, late in the nineteeth and most particularly early in the twentieth century, came another interesting shift in philosophy and tactics, the 'rejection of the significance of the personal' within the movement.[23] Political interpretation in these two periods of highly visible feminism thus differed substantially; for the younger women, born at the close of the period, the challenge was to confront the public sphere head-on, whilst for the earlier generations, it was the attempt to collapse the two spheres that fuelled their actions.

Marriage was also an important source of those inter-generational contacts which so sustained the alternative politics of this period. Elizabeth Garrett Anderson's husband, James Skelton Anderson, was a relative of factory inspector Adelaide Anderson; Josephine Butler was a member of the Whig Grey family into which Maria Shirreff married; suffrage activist Lady Frances Balfour was related by marriage to Eleanor Sidgwick, active in the women's educational movement at Cambridge. In Quaker families, the connections multiply. The four families of Gurney, Nichol, Pease and Sturge, all of whom were associated both with a variety of radical causes and with feminism, were inter-related in a complex genealogy. All these different kinds and varieties of connection, through marriage and family or through political association, served to reinforce the idea of a relatively narrow elite sharing a set of values and a certain social homogeneity much as did Annan's 'intellectual aristocracy'.

A study of the occupational backgrounds on which feminism drew at this juncture also exhibits this characteristic social and economic clustering. Not only the occupations in which we find women activists themselves employed, but those of their fathers and husbands as well, point us towards a certain social homogeneity in determining the potential constituency of feminism. In many ways, the occupational status of the men in feminist families can offer a more accurate index to background and standing than the occupations of the women, given the attitudes and problems relating to women's work in this period. Where patterns of female employment illustrate the attempts to challenge the status quo of labour and education, that of their menfolk highlights rather the class basis of activism – including income and social status – with all its varied implications. (See chapter 8 for a fuller discussion of this issue.)

Both family and marital background in this perspective suggest an overwhelmingly bourgeois composition to the movement. The church and the law follow slightly behind business as the three major sources of paternal wealth and employment, though a substantial minority came from land-owning families as well. Fourteen per cent had fathers who were in some form of business, either as manufacturers, bankers, or similar. Eight per cent each had clerical or lawyer fathers (included here is one Justice of the Peace), whilst academic and political fathers both numbered around 5 per cent. A further 4 per cent were daughters of naval or military personnel, their fathers generally of some standing, and 3 per cent were fathered by medical men. Many women involved in feminism thus enjoyed some substantial degree of material comfort in their lifetime.

The bulk of the sample were from families in recognizable professions or areas of influence, largely deriving from Class II of W. D. Rubinstein's seven-scale system of socio-occupational status.[24] There were also some who hovered uncomfortably on the fringes of respectability. Teachers, artists and poets as well as engineers trod the tightropes of acceptability and respectability delicately, and thereafter we begin the descent of the social ladder with such artisan occupations as clockmaker (Hertha Ayrton's father, Levi Marks), pianomaker (Emma Cons' father), and boot and shoemaker (Mary Smith's father) as well as Julia Varley's father alongside whom she toiled in the Bradford textile mills.

Few women had 'working' mothers employed in paid work outside the family home, again a salient factor in determining the overall class basis of the movement. Those whose mothers did work for wages tended to be among the poorer women in the sample; Frances Buss ran a school with her mother which provided a larger portion of the family income than the meagre earnings of her artist father and Mary Smith's mother worked independently of her husband as a grocer. These were unusual instances, however. In the cases cited here, moreover, it is 'respectable' and genteel poverty that we are generally finding, and not the less 'refined' variety where manual work was the sole, and inadequate, solution to financial hardship.

Inevitably, given the narrow channels of social mobility afforded in the Victorian period, marital social standing for the most part reflected women's family histories. Poor women remained poor; the daughters of professionals married men in stations similar to those of their fathers and male siblings.

An occupational breakdown of the husbands of feminists produces few surprises in this context. The most significant group of husbands are politicians – 9 per cent of the women in the sample married men whose principal career was politics, largely Parliamentary. A further 5 per cent wedded academics, moreso in the later years of the century when restrictions governing fellowships at Oxford and Cambridge colleges were eased in this respect. Lawyers and businessmen are close rivals for feminist partners, the former with 4 per cent and the latter with 5 per cent of the total.

Some interesting changes in career patterns, both paternal and spousal, can be discerned. None of the feminists in this sample, even those from military families, married military men. Similarly, far fewer married into trade and business than hailed from that background. In some respects, this reflects changes occurring in the structure of business. Business men began moving over into politics towards the later years of the century, maintaining their businesses at a profitable distance. Where women hailed from, and remained within the business community by marriage, the pattern is an interesting one. The men they married belonged, in large part, to a more 'enlightened' if still paternalistic class of employers; we find no Gradgrinds among their number. Matilda Ashurst's husband, Joseph Biggs, was, for instance, 'a manufacturer noted for his excellent treatment of his workpeople'.[25] Isabella Ford's father, a Leeds silk manufacturer, was similarly inclined in his business dealings and was involved, besides, in various educational and charitable ventures in the region. Given the largely humanitarian attention paid by radical women in this period to issues such as labour conditions, workhouse structures and the like, it is of some significance that the values they espoused should have been shared by their partners.

As for the absence of liaisons with men in the military, it would be beyond the bounds of interpretative licence to look for any nascent pacifism here, more especially given the stand many feminists took in 1914. However, the lifestyle demanded by high military rank would have been inimical to many women of independent mind, with its constant potential for upheaval and mobility.

Striking, too, is the absence of civil servants amongst both husbands and fathers in this sample, at a time when we see a rise in the number of women civil servants. The men associated with feminist women seem to have chosen an active participatory role in politics over that of servant of the state.

For poorer women, a rise in social status was rare. Women from manual and artisan backgrounds tended to remain there. Phoebe Marks, later Hertha Ayrton, is one exception. She hailed from an immigrant working-class Polish-Jewish family living in Portsea. Through the offices of those well-connected feminists who befriended her she became a student at Girton College, Cambridge before marrying mathematician William Ayrton in 1885 at the age of thirty-one. More common were the experiences of women like Emma Paterson (née Smith) whose father was a teacher and husband a cabinet-maker, or Isa Craig (née Knox) who married an iron merchant and hailed from a family of hosiers. Sarah Dickenson's marital relationship was perhaps the most symmetrical; she had both a father and a husband who were enamellers by trade.

None of the details or statistics concerning the employment history of males closely associated with feminist women are startling. We might perhaps have anticipated the bias towards some form of political involvement these relationships exhibited; women from political families gained early access to, and familiarity with, both the process and the personnel from whom they demanded changes.

The occupational breakdown of feminists themselves is also illuminating. Forty-six per cent of the sample can claim a history of paid employment for at least some portion of their lives, and for many, a career was a singular and militant manifestation of their feminist beliefs. In a number of cases, where women became medical practitioners, printers or publishers or government factory inspectors, they owed their novel livelihood in large part to the explicit actions and support of the feminist community.

Two catalysts to women's labour emerge distinctly in this period, in practice as much as in theory; on the one hand, there were those women who assumed waged labour more as a principle, a practical identification of their feminism fuelled by belief more than by necessity, and on the other hand there were the women for whom stark necessity and not choice was the motive. At the theoretical level, more markedly with the growing perception of a demographic imbalance, feminists recognized and campaigned around the need to expand the employment opportunities generally available to women. (See chapters 7 and 8.) At the same time, there was a growing recognition amongst them, too, that more than mere economics dictated that need for expansion. Women were claiming employment as a right as well as a financial necessity, in which all women should have a choice, and as a reminder of the ideological bankruptcy of the separate sphere order. Thus we find feminists whose occupations rested primarily on a crusading principle side by side with women who, though in more traditional occupations, sought to bring a feminist understanding to bear on the conditions therein.

A handful of women were employed, of course, in one capacity or another within the women's movement. Isa Craig, Emma Paterson and Emilie Venturi née Ashurst all received pay from feminist organizations for their services as secretaries or editors whilst others such as Gertrude Tuckwell and May Tennant worked for individual feminists, these two acting successively as secretaries to Lady Dilke in her trade union work. Clerical work was an increasingly common occupation among women at this time, and many feminist women chose to offer their clerical and administrative skills in the movement rather than in the commercial world. Countless others, of course, put in long hours as unpaid workers for the cause.

The largest group of women in paid employment throughout the period covered by this study were women active in education as headmistresses, teachers, governesses and the like. Many taught in, and had great influence on, the new feminist girls' academies proliferating from the 1860s on; 13 per cent of the sample fall into this category. For the most part, they were women who found employment in fee-paying and feminist schools. Many women from upper working-class backgrounds were also moving into teaching in the years following the establishment of state schooling, but the divide between the pupil-teacher schemes adopted by the Board Schools and the heavily academic accent within the bourgeois institutions, continued to divide the teaching profession along lines of class as well as gender.[26]

Literary women form another major grouping in the sample. Taken together, women working as poets, novelists and writers, editors, journalists and translators amount to 17 per cent of the total sample. The nineteenth century has often been called the age *par excellence* of the woman writer, as indeed of the woman reader. Jihang Park's analysis of women's inclusion in biographical compendia of the period shows that in the 1862 edition of *Men of the Time* (and despite its misleading title) writers – excluding journalists – along with actresses and musicians, constituted 78 per cent of the female entries.[27] For many women, a literary occupation was attractive in that it demanded neither designated hours nor attendance at a place of work. Journalism similarly 'was also compatible with maintaining a home and family'.[28]

This compatibility with other duties and expectations obviously lent writing some attraction for active women. At the same time, its freedom from the specific kinds of drudgery – time-keeping, institutional discipline – associated with many occupations was an interesting comment on women's distaste for that type of regimentation. Though writing and publishing remained problem areas in a host of ways, professional attachment to them was still an effective pursuit of and for activist women.

Some middle-class women pursued more unusual paths. Agnes and Rhoda Garrett's house-decorating business in London (see chapter 7), like Mary Somerville's reputation as an astronomer, made these women stand out even in feminist circles. Others channelled their talents in specifically feminist ways. Emily Faithfull established the Victoria Printing Press in London's Great Coram Street in 1860 as a conduit for training and employing women as compositors. She had begun her experiment with an all-women's printing society in Edinburgh in 1857 and moved thence to London. Whilst women's organizations in traditional areas such as millinery and embroidery were not, at this time, unusual, non-traditional areas such as this were still novelties. Amongst Helena Downing's (née Shearer) many woman-centred activities was the foundation in 1875 of the North London Photographic and Fine Art Repository which boasted an all-female staff of operators.

For women whose employment was most obviously an outcrop of the feminist movement, this conscious praxis was never uncomplicated. Sensitive to the critical attention of a largely hostile media and public, they found themselves often pushed to greater and greater achievement and, indeed, sacrifice, Margaret Wynne Nevinson recalled that as a young teacher at the South Hampstead High School for Girls, her headmistress had asked her to arrange her impending marriage so that it would not interfere with the preparations for the Cambridge Local Examinations![29]

There were, too, a handful of artisan women: bookbinders and textile workers, upholstresses and watch engravers, and also a small number of theatrical women whose position must have been a precarious one in an age when the theatre was still, for many, the incarnation of disreputable living. Women artists fared rather better, perhaps because painting was amongst the dilettante skills encouraged in young ladies where stage-acting and performing certainly were not. Barbara Leigh Smith Bodichon enjoyed two successful exhibitions of her watercolours in London, in 1859 and 1861, and derived a reasonable income from her painting.[30] Emilia Dilke earned some considerable reputation as an art historian, publishing substantially in the field.

Female employment in the later nineteenth and early twentieth centuries was rising slowly,[31] a phenomenon which reflected both the changes in occupational structure brought about by the capitalist economy, and the feminist encouragement to such activity. For many feminists, paid work was often as much a statement of principle as an economic function. 'I was determined to fight for my own living and be a burden to no one', declared schoolmistress Mary Smith of Carlisle.[32] Smith hailed from a poor family and had little choice but to rely on her own skills for her livelihood. Even so, she remained fiercely committed to an ideal of material independence.

None the less, we should be wary of over-determining a *feminist* component in these changes. Women's fights to gain recognition in and access to medicine were occurring at the same time as male doctors were seeking to exercise increased control over women's bodies through the creation of a specific and highly specialized obstetrics and gynaecology. Lower down the medical hierarchy, the parallel and simultaneous creation of nursing as an appropriately feminine occupation left gendered role definition untouched and unchallenged, with its designation of nursing as an auxiliary service occupation enhancing the status of the medical experts.

The mere fact of an increase in female employment, or in the creation or institutionalization of women's occupations, does not of itself constitute proof of the diffusion of feminist values. Much of the occupational expansion to which women had access served merely to entrench the problems faced by working women, though the reality was often complex. Staying with medicine as a case study, whilst nursing in many ways fed the essentialist views of woman's natural sphere, the rigorous codes which governed and strengthened it at this time still declared a serious intent to allow women independent waged pursuit. At the same time, women fighting for access to higher level medical training concurred with that declaration of intent but also challenged both the male monopoly of authority and knowledge and broad notions of sex-related suitability.

For traditionalists, the question of women's employment was cast singularly and unproblematically in the mould of an alternative rather than an addition to marriage as a primary career. We know that for countless poorer women the reality was rarely so simple; in feminist circles, too, though generally for different motives, there was not always an assumed path *from* waged labour *to* marriage and family duties.

Many feminist women maintained an employment history after marriage, paid or unpaid (see chapter 7). Elizabeth Garrett Anderson continued to practise medicine; Alice Acland did a three-year stint as editor of the Women's Corner in Samuel Bamford's *Co-operative News* as well as assuming the secretaryship of the newly-formed Women's Co-operative Guild in 1883, Amie Hicks went from rope-making to midwifery and trade union activism. Some women – Maria Grey, Emilia Dilke, Millicent Garrett Fawcett among them – pursued their writing careers regardless. There were others who, though abandoning paid employment, continued with volunteer work, often of a feminist or radical kind. After May Tennant (née Abraham) gave up her factory inspectorship upon marrying in 1896, she continued to raise money on behalf of factory women and to involve herself in a variety of feminist activities.[33] Margaret Wynne Nevinson, though she never worked again as a schoolmistress after her marriage, did research for Toynbee Hall and worked, geographically close by, as a rent collector for the East London Dwellings Company, both in a volunteer capacity. It was only after the birth of her second and last child that she remained *physically* at home.

It was, of course, always a challenge for women to juggle a life that crossed boundaries so defiantly as to maintain work alongside marriage. Despite the institutionalization of that barrier through the establishment of marriage bars, formal and informal, there were none the less a handful who, in the face of scorn, hostility and sheer incomprehension, found the courage and capacity to do so.

Increasingly in this period, access to more middle-class employments depended upon greater and more advanced educational qualifications, an area opening up only slowly to women. The correlation between educational study and subsequent career for women is far less significant than for university men, not merely because so many fewer openings were available to women graduates but further because, even for educated women, family and social pressures were still far likelier to emphasize marriage and motherhood over material achievement in the working world.[34]

Not surprisingly, only 30 per cent of the total sample received any measure of formal education, and nor was that always of an efficient or academic sort. (See chapter 7.) In the later years, a sprinkling of women were the favoured recipients of the fruits of earlier struggles but for the most part, it was self-education and determined struggle that characterized women's access to education in this period, and a strong practical recognition of how crucial education was to be for feminist advancement, personally and collectively.

In formal terms, only a few women were the recipients of an organized and adequate education. Surprisingly few of the sample attended the new feminist academies; the dates of this study militate substantially against that, as so many of the women discussed here were of the founding rather than of the subsequent generations. Olive Banks has shown that 'the attractions of feminism to the girl who had been to college as well as college to the girl who was already a feminist' are quantifiable factors.[35] None the less, in this sample, the numbers exposed to the new schooling remain low. Five per cent attended Queen's College, Harley Street and 2 per cent Bedford College, the new secondary institutions of the late 1840s, whilst 4 per cent and 1 per cent respectively entered the new women's colleges at Cambridge, Girton and Newnham. Janet Howarth and Mark Curthoys found, in their study of women university students, that the 'clientele' for the Oxbridge colleges and for London's Royal Holloway College 'was drawn overwhelmingly from the professional, commercial and industrial classes',[36] the same constituency from which feminism derived the majority of its recruits. It seems, at first sight, surprising that the overlap should be as small as this, but it was, of course, later generations of women who were able to use the new facilities to greater effect.

Informal means of education, it would appear, were more numerous and significant, and even within the new institutions, many limitations still served to constrain women considerably. Janet Courtney recalled the educational apartheid endured by the early Oxford women. 'We pursued courses devised for us and specially adapted, so kind and perhaps slightly condescending 'members of the University' thought, to our feminine limitations.'[37]

It was a segregation which, combined with other and related factors, militated not only against the acquisition of a good education but also against the opportunity to follow it up profitably in career terms. Acquiring an education formalized by institutional recognition was only one of the battles women faced; the pursuit of an education as a means of enhancing their opportunities for employment further complicated their lives. Howarth and Curthoys have pointed out 'the way in which academic specialization was constrained by career prospects, family and schooling'.[38]

M. Jeanne Peterson has argued, using the well-placed Paget family as evidence, that Victorian women of the 'urban gentry' could, in fact, obtain 'a fine education, whether formally or informally'.[39] It is certainly the case that many women exhibit, in their choice of reading, in their grasp of contemporary issues, in their letter-writing, an ease with the literate culture of their day. Of her sample of aristocratic and *haut bourgeois* Victorian women, Pat Jalland remarks that though most had been 'denied a formal education, many were widely read, articulate, and knowledgeable about politics. Lady Balfour recalled that "politics absorbed my generation"'.[40] Millicent Garrett Fawcett, though her formal access to education had been minimal, was – notwithstanding – a well-regarded political economist and the first woman admitted to the Political Economy Club at the bidding of Charles Dilke.

Educated Victorian women were a self-selecting, highly-motivated group, whose dissatisfaction with inadequate schooling and sense of injustice watching brothers depart for school and university frequently sharpened their feminist awareness. Countless memoirs tell of ambitious young women monitoring with frustration the educational progress of their brothers and frequently hanging on their coat-tails for enlightenment and information. (See chapter 7.) As both Peterson and Olive Banks have pointed out, 'active feminists were . . . even for their class and period, unusually well-educated.'[41] They were still, however, ill-served in this respect and acutely aware of the comparative deficiencies under which they laboured.

For W. D. Rubinstein, that accent on the liberating role of education was a sure sign of bourgeois rather than aristocratic values. For an established elite, education was less a necessity than a luxury, whilst meritocracy was a fundamental founding principle of middle-class values.[42] We can appropriate that notion within feminist terms by seeing that women, as the aspiring 'class', chose those same meritocratic means as one method of 'upward mobility'.

Inevitably it is in the wealthier and professional ranks that we find the most enduring evidence of a class of educated women. In the light of Rubinstein's cogent criticisms of assuming too direct a relationship between educational background and elite status,[43] we should exercise caution in seeing these women as an 'intellectual aristocracy', more so in the light of the enormous disabilities they faced in achieving even the trappings of parity with their brothers' educations.

This examination of the occupation, education and lifestyle of discernible feminism has pointed to its overwhelmingly bourgeois constituency throughout this period. Placed in the context of the remarkable cultural ascendancy and expansion of the English middle classes in the nineteenth century, it is not surprising. This does not, however, mean that we should dismiss or despatch this variety of feminism because of the inevitable 'limitations' imposed by its class base.

Feminist women at the time were fully cognizant of, if not always lured by, the dynamics of class relations. Just as they expressed deep dissatisfaction with the constraints imposed on their educational and political aspirations, and indeed their physical freedom, many feminists were equally eager to explore beyond the restraining class boundaries that mapped out their physical and intellectual terrain. And for some, it was palpably an uncomfortable process.

As a young woman in England's north-east, the respectable and well-brought-up Emily Davies was anxious to broaden her horizons. Though not one of her more successful experiments, she made 'some attempts at getting to know lower middle class people' in the early 1860s.[44] Later in her life, moving in the more illustriously cosmopolitan circles to which her educational and feminist work exposed her, she still continued to feel a sense of class unease and never really fully accustomed herself to the elite company which now surrounded her. Invitations from aristocratic feminists, though personally flattering and offering her stimulating company, continued to discomfit her. She confessed that discomfiture in a letter to her friend and Girton colleague, Elizabeth Adelaide Manning. 'It is rather nice seeing the people, but I don't feel as if I had exactly a raison d'être among them. Miss Garrett's case is different . . . because successful physicians always consort with the aristocracy.'[45]

Emily's acute readings of the class divisions which so ordered her world endorse the point that class mobility – as we have seen in the context of marriage – remained a restricted phenomenon serving to contain feminism, at least in the earlier period, within largely bourgeois networks.

Lady Balfour, writing to her friend Millicent Garrett Fawcett, casually mentions that she has dined recently with Lord Salisbury,[46] a privilege restricted to but few women. It may have been a milieu in which Emily Davies never felt fully comfortable, but it was wholly outside the experience of women from labouring backgrounds, and we should not be surprised to find that even when visiting his well-heeled feminist companions, Arthur Munby never attempted to bring his bourgeois social life within the remit of his lover, country-born domestic servant Hannah Cullwick. Even within the relative freedom offered by an alternative politics such as feminism, class boundaries in the social context remained largely intact.

Measuring and assessing class position is always a precarious exercise and we must beware of an overly schematic perspective which might mask, or conversely, emphasize unduly the distinctive social categories at work within Victorian feminism. As already noted, one of the factors useful in assessing class is occupation; female occupation, given the relative novelty value it still had in the white-collar sector, is a less accurate guide perhaps than male occupation, that of father, husband or brother. Olive Banks has argued that a clearer picture of class identity for the feminist woman emerges rather from the occupational status of her father than herself, noting that her own sample was 'more middle class in terms of its own occupation than in terms of its social origin'.[47]

For women generally, class status did rest far more on familial and thus paternal identification than on their own identification, but even here the distinctions could often be fine. The fathers of both Helen Blackburn and Isabel Petrie Mills were engineers but of a very different order. Blackburn's father was a civil engineer, and though it was not quite a 'top-drawer' profession, it was markedly more substantial than the engineering position held in proletarian industrial Rochdale by John Petrie. Occupational status thus went hand in hand with both a regional and a religious index. Whilst Petrie was a Lancashire non-conformist, Blackburn's Irish father moved his family to London in 1859 when Helen was seventeen. He enjoyed a substantial practice there, and it was there, too, that his daughter became involved with the activities of the Society for Promoting the Employment of Women and in the London suffrage movement.

These instances demonstrate the palpable if dense relations between class, religion and region which complicate any simple equation of occupation and class for this period. The case of Unitarian feminist Anne Cowen offers another example. She herself was clearly a prominent political and feminist figure in late nineteenth-century Nottingham as was her town councillor husband. Declared liberals and non-conformists, it is interesting to note the secure nature of their social standing given that their wealth derived from the iron trade. Anne's husband was an ironmaster, a business which, whilst lucrative, was unlikely to guarantee social prestige outside the circles of radical provincial non-conformity.

Despite the largely bourgeois constituency from which feminism derived its protagonists, there are also a surprising number of women whose position is less clear and who existed in a kind of class limbo of semi-gentility. Anna Jameson and Frances Buss were women for whom, as we have noted, garnering a living was more necessity than feminist principle and for whom, equally, the idea of undertaking manual work to earn that living was quite simply inappropriate. Mary Smith, who lived proudly, though far from lavishly, off the proceeds of her one-woman Carlisle school, came from lowly stock but, as a schoolmistress, entered an acutely class-contradictory world. Women, far more than men, found that many of the occupations into which they moved in the nineteenth century were, in the process of their 'feminization', stripped of any specific class connotation.

For feminist women, the adoption of principles derived from a feminist perspective both clarified and clouded their lives. Whilst it clarified the gendered configuration which controlled even the definition of femaleness, it served to make their social interactions in a non-feminist environment less comfortable. Their re-appropriation of adulthood through choice and independence set them at odds with prevailing custom and law but allowed them to establish freedoms long denied on the basis of sex.

4

Understanding the Empty Places: Love, Friendship and Women's Networks

In nineteenth-century feminism, as much as in that of today, women understood that their feminism affected their lives. At the simplest level, attachment to the cause was unlikely to incur substantial approbation. More importantly, though, involvement brought women to reflect in immediate and personal ways upon their relations with one another and with men, upon their overall political understanding and upon their decisions about the course of their own lives.

The results were often distinctive, and allow us in retrospect to identify some of the characteristics of a feminist-derived culture. It was not, as American writers have noted for this period in their own country, a women's culture framed primarily around domesticity, but rather it was weighted more towards a collective understanding of oppression and the need to challenge it in diverse and often previously unexplored ways. The acquisition and nurturing of a feminist position, more particularly in this period when it inevitably marked some abdication of social status, could not but shape distinctively the lives of women passionately committed to their cause.

Women embraced a feminist perspective in every area of their lives, a massive step in an era when the full and stifling weight of bourgeois ideology was at its peak, and when failure to conform to its directives constituted not merely rebellion but moral degradation. To be identified as a feminist in mid- or late nineteenth-century England was to court contempt, ridicule and hostility. At the same time, though, feminism undoubtedly offered encouragement and sympathy to women striving to repudiate the role to which their sex traditionally assigned them.

Women seldom chose to channel their entire energies into one specific area of protest, and most can be found offering at least financial support or institutional strength to a whole range of distinct but connected campaigns. The same women appear again and again as members of and subscribers to the various organizational causes pursued by feminists in this period; the connections between the fight for educational extension and the expansion of occupational opportunities, or between the right to vote and the legal minority of the married woman (or indeed, all four!) were transparent enough. These multiple organizational commitments suggest both the sheer quantity of time, money and energy which women were willing to invest in the movement and, of course, qualitatively, a feminist philosophy which made links between seemingly disparate issues.

Heavy political obligations do not necessarily dictate or constitute a lifestyle consistent with belief, however. The most significant character-istic which marked out the separate existence at this juncture of a feminist movement was the translation of those political ties into a close web of social connections. Women found kinship with one another in their moments of relaxation as much as on the campaign trail, and those familiar names which swell the membership lists of women's political pressure groups are also prominent within a distinctive feminist social calendar. Political co-operation and good friendship were closely allied, and a body such as the Kensington Society offers a good illustration of this tendency.

An all-women debating society established in 1865, the Kensington Society combined these political and social functions with intellectual pursuits not readily available elsewhere to women.

The agitation for the opening of the Local Examinations had brought into communication with each other a good many people having more or less common interests and aims, and it seemed desirable that the cessation, for the moment, of the special occasion for co-operation should not result in our losing touch of each other. With a view to supplying some sort of link between us, a small Society was started, for the discussion of questions of common interest.[1]

The Society met four times a year at the Kensington home of its President, Charlotte Manning. The members initiated topics for discus-sion, ranging from predictable issues such as women's suffrage and education to questions of practical concern – philanthropy or the 'ser-vant question', which speak volumes for the class basis of the member-ship – and currently fashionable philosophical topics such as 'sentimen-tality'.

The Society comprised a representative assortment of mid-Victorian feminists, and though the meetings were always held in London, members from all over the country sent in contributions. As well as London-based feminists such as pioneer medical women Elizabeth Garrett and Sophia Jex-Blake, married women's property laws activist

Emilie Gurney, Helen Taylor, Emily Davies and Frances Power Cobbe, there were many non-Londoners. Some were itinerants like Barbara Leigh Smith Bodichon who divided her time between her native England and Algeria where her husband had lived for many years, or Jessie Boucherett, living largely in London but using her rural Lincolnshire estate address. Others were corresponding members – Dorothea Beale, headmistress of Cheltenham Ladies' College, Elizabeth Wolstenholme in Manchester or the Heatons, mother and daughter, in Leeds. The list is interesting, for we might equally be looking at the membership list of any one of a number of feminist organizations, or indeed at the guest list of a feminist hostess. It is the integration of these elements offered by the Kensington Society which suggests so strongly the dovetailing of the social, the political and the intellectual within the feminist community.

This active process of fusion within directly identifiable feminist activities, and in the personal lives of active women, illustrates the strength and the breadth of feminism in this period. It was a movement far broader than its organizational manifestations, its petitions or its demonstrations, reaching directly into the choices with which these women sought to structure their lives.

They belonged largely both to an urbane and sophisticated elite in Victorian society and also, separately, to a distinct women's culture to which they were prepared to devote both time and money.

The specific networks of kinship discussed in chapter 2 where families, and more importantly, women within families, succoured a nascent feminism amongst one another, inevitably spilled over significantly into, and were amplified by, interlocking networks based not on family connection but rather on friendship and social bonds.

It was through the Crow sisters – Jane, Annie, Elizabeth and Sophie – that Emily Davies met their school-mate Elizabeth Garrett who was to remain for her a close, dear and lifelong friend. In her turn, Emily introduced Elizabeth to the Leigh Smith sisters – Barbara, Bella and Annie – who lived in the house opposite her brother's rectory in London's Marylebone. Emily's brother was, of course, the father of Margaret Llewellyn Davies who was so prominent in the foundation of the Women's Co-Operative Guild in the early 1880s! Emily Davies had been delighted when the Crow sisters came to live in Gateshead in 1848: 'We had much in common with them and saw a great deal of them.'[2]

In effect, what they were creating for themselves was a social milieu of active women, prepared to take steps for the benefit of their own sex, whose friendship offered support and sustenance in the fight. One of the most striking features of feminist friendship in this period is the absence of vituperative enmity. There were inevitable political disagreements over tactics as well as occasional flashes of personal dislike, but the overall impression gained by exploring the close social bonds of women in this period is one of considerable amity. They shared not only a common understanding of their own position but a genuine interest in one another in more personal ways. It is this melding of the political and the personal which lends nineteenth-century feminism so distinctive a cast in the politics of the period.

The social aspects of Victorian feminism reveal a conscious and active interest in pursuing and maintaining such networks. Women involved in feminist activities made a point of approaching one another and entering into communication with one another. Bessie Rayner Parkes (later Belloc) conducted a fearsomely large correspondence with a considerable portion of the Victorian intelligentsia. Whilst her male correspondents were often radicals – Richard Cobden, F. D. Maurice, Austen Holyoake – her women correspondents were largely women we can identify as feminists: Lady Stanley, Dr Elizabeth Blackwell, Isa Craig, Sarah Atkinson (who, it may be remembered, was instrumental in converting Bessie to Catholicism in 1864), Barbara Leigh Smith Bodichon, novelist and archaeologist Amelia Edwards, Margaret Llewellyn Davies, educationalist Constance Maynard and a host of other women spanning the generations. The list is a long one and this breadth of acquaintance – either personally or in correspondence – was a common feature amongst Parkes's feminist companions.[3] Women in Victorian England were frequently keen and busy correspondents; Pat Jalland has noted that, particularly after marriage, regular and detailed letter-writing was often a lifeline for women in maintaining their contact with their families.[4] Feminist women reached well beyond family networks in their correspondence.

Frances Power Cobbe, who campaigned in almost every major feminist cause, noted that with the somewhat surprising exceptions of writers George Eliot and Harriet Martineau, 'I think I may boast of having come into contact with nearly all the gifted Englishwomen of the Victorian era.'[5] Cobbe's statement suggests that this was a community small enough for such a wide acquaintance to be possible. Even so, there was still an active desire at work; after all, the sample used for this study comprises some 200 women spread over the length and breadth of the country.

Mary Bruce described feminist scholar Anna Swanwick as 'always anxious to make acquaintance with those who were working for the cause of women's advancement'.[6] Edwin Pratt maintained that Louisa M. Hubbard, founder and editor of the feminist periodicals *Woman's Gazette* and *Work and Leisure*, 'was in communication with perhaps every woman of any mark who was working in the same direction as herself'.[7]

The social lives of these women frequently overlapped as they chose to spend time in each other's company. Certain women played a central role in providing a social focus amongst feminists. Emily Davies remembered, in particular, the parties given by Emily Faithfull, founder of the all-female Victoria Printing Press, as well as those of Barbara Bodichon and Clementia Taylor, at whose houses she met the entire range of London feminists. Lady Amberley's diaries recall the women with whom she shared teas and dinners, and the list reads like the roll-call of any of the major feminist organizations of her time; she talks of entertaining Frances Power Cobbe, Lady Byron and Dorothea Beale to tea, as well as meeting Lady Goldsmid, George Eliot, Octavia Hill and Ursula Bright at parties given by women such as Emelie Gurney of the Married Women's Property Committee. Suffrage activist Helen Taylor became godmother to Amberley's first-born son – better known as Bertrand Russell – in 1872.

Close social contact of this sort was by no means confined to the metropolis. Centres such as Manchester, Bristol and Oxford saw similar social concentrations emerging through the common feminist strand. All the Manchester feminists knew one another – Ursula Bright, Lydia Becker, Elizabeth Wolstenholme, the Winkworths, along with Mrs Gaskell and the Brontës, and in later years Emmeline Pankhurst. The Winkworth sisters recalled the Gaskell household as a central point of contact. It was there that they first met Langham Place activists such as Adelaide Proctor and Anna Jameson.[8]

It was these same women – women with sufficient income and leisure, and indeed, domestic aid – who would often provide venues for political meetings: many a women's suffrage committee meeting was held at Aubrey House, the London home of Clementia Taylor. These occasions, as much as the more informal setting of a party or dinner, provided invaluable social links for women. Louise Creighton, musing on the value of women's conferences, felt that 'the chief advantage almost seems to be the coming together of so many different people, and the opportunities one has for getting to know women of all kinds.'[9]

Josephine Butler's sentiments were akin to those of Creighton, but she made more direct the connection between social gatherings and the fight for women's rights. Writing at the end of the century, some years after the vindication of her activism by the full repeal of the Contagious Diseases Acts, she remarked on the importance of that link.

As I look back through our long warfare there rise before my mind not only our united band in untiring conflict with injustice, but many pleasant adventures, social gatherings, and sweet friendships, taking their rise in a common aim, cemented by fellowship in trial and in hope, and ripening, year by year, for the higher communion of the life to come.[10]

In a society as stratified and rigid as Victorian England could be, single-sex socializing was not unusual. Much of the conventional social round common to the wealthy involved the segregation of the sexes, and American historians have argued cogently, as we have seen, for the development of a specific women's culture based around the domesticity imposed by that segregation.[11]

The social pattern common amongst feminists, however, was of a different quality. The contact these women were seeking was one which frequently combined social elements with their other interests, intellectual and political. Margaret Bondfield remembers Elizabeth Garrett Anderson arranging a series of 'unforgettable holidays' at Girton College. There, Bondfield's Bradford trade unionist friend Julia Varley 'learned of the possibilities of life that education brought'.[12]

Nor was age a dividing factor amongst women who sought a woman-oriented lifestyle. Commenting on her friendship with Lady Emelie Goldsmid, Kate Amberley described her as 'an old lady who sympathizes with me about women's rights and women doctors, etc.'[13] Clearly the two found much common ground in their shared feminism.

It was the combination of this relaxed and informal social ambience with a more serious contemplation of ends and aims which was so unusual and so palpably attractive to women more accustomed to the strait-jacket of domestic middle-class life. When Barbara Leigh Smith established her experimental Portman Hall School off the Edgware Road in London in 1852 under Elizabeth Whitehead's direction, the volunteer teaching staff was culled from amongst their feminist associates; friends Eliza Fox and Octavia Hill worked alongside Barbara's own sisters.

Though their circles of friendship were often predominantly female, most of these women kept mixed company too. The celebrated Arthur Munby, known for his fascination with working women and for his lengthy and secret involvement with servant Hannah Cullwick,[14] was a regular visitor to the Taylor household, Aubrey House, in the London suburb of Notting Hill. Among the many other guests he met there, none were more frequent visitors than the women of Clementia Taylor's feminist circles – Barbara Bodichon, Elizabeth Garrett, Lydia Becker, Frances Power Cobbe, Elizabeth Whitehead Malleson.[15]

The Taylor household was an important focus of social and political mixing in radical and feminist circles at this juncture. It was here that Munby recalled meeting the American writer and feminist Louisa May Alcott as well as the male consorts of Taylor's feminist friends. Sheldon

Amos and Frank Malleson, both married to activist women, were known to Munby through both the more convivial atmosphere of Aubrey House gatherings and as fellow workers at the Working Women's College. William Shaen, another well-known mid-century radical, had been a school-friend of Clementia's husband, Peter. Around his family, we find a similar social network comprising a strong strand of feminism as well as radicalism. The Shaen household was one of the first in which the Italian republican Mazzini found companionship in England and through whom he went on to meet and form firm friendships with the Ashursts, Harriet Martineau, the Mallesons and the Toynbees as well as with Peter and Clementia Taylor.[16]

Many of these women belonged not only to specific women's organizations but to mixed clubs of some kind or another as well. The relationship between the early feminist movement and the National Association for the Promotion of Social Science is only the most obvious of such connections, and clearly in the mid-century, an important one despite the restrictions it continued to impose upon women members.[17] Though women's presence as speakers could, on occasion, cause the association to face its own ambivalence, it nevertheless provided a meeting place where women could air their concerns in a mixed environment and where there was at least some semblance of interest and the opportunity for a hearing. 'The association was of immense use to the Women's movement in giving us a platform from which we could bring our views before the sort of people who were likely to be disposed to help in carrying them out.'[18]

It was through her association with the Ideal Club in the 1890s that trade unionist Margaret Bondfield met not only other activist women – Emilia Dilke and her niece Gertrude Tuckwell among them – but also such men as Bernard Shaw and Sydney Webb. And for Bondfield, as for other radical women, the labour movement offered them 'companionship and an outlet for emotions'.[19] Mixed clubs, though, however radical in intention, were frequently intimidating to women members. Judith Walkowitz's work on the Men and Women's Club, founded by socialist Karl Pearson in 1885 to discuss sexuality, illustrates how the dynamics of the group were constructed in a specifically gendered way. The women members found themselves constantly silenced and criticized by the male members. It is particularly significant that the club broke up after four years, in Walkowitz's words, 'mainly because men were dissatisfied with women's performance'.[20]

It is in this context that we might examine women's preference for one another's company, a milieu at once less disapproving and more reinforcing than even seemingly sympathetic male company. Often their preference for single-sex gatherings was paralleled also by the simple but forceful question of the physical constraints limiting women's freedom of movement. In some respects, bourgeois women were even more confined than their poorer sisters on whom the dead weight of respectability did not always impinge quite so crushingly. The growing incidence of women's social clubs in the last third of the century, both in London and in various provincial centres, provided middle-class women – and more particularly those who were single – with an alternative social environment to that of their homes. Where working-class women might at least find occasional relief from the domestic burden in the pub (though it remained principally a male environment), for 'respectable' women movement was confined largely to a residence-based social world. The opening of all-women clubs and reading rooms, a phenomenon which Estelle Freedman has termed 'social feminism',[21] afforded women a valuable escape route which at the same time, being exclusively female and clearly middle class, rendered them on the right side of propriety. Women seeking their contacts in such an environment were freed from the need for chaperonage; in a sense, and ironically, respectability thus served on occasion to empower women.

In particular, the new female clubs were seen to provide a congenial meeting point for the growing number of single, and mostly professional, working women whose lives outside the hours of their employment continued to suffer severe restriction and were often drab and lonely. We should, perhaps, draw some distinction between the feminist community at large and the working women for whom they saw themselves functioning; feminist women, in a sense, had a ready-made community of interest but not all working women identified themselves with the movement. Eva Anstruther, assessing the women's club movement in 1899, maintained that 'It was only when women *took to work*, asserted their independence, and set up for themselves to earn their own living, when in twos and threes, and one by one they came and settled in lodgings and residential flats, it was only then that something in the nature of a club became apparent.'[22]

Anstruther calculated that by 1899 there were twenty-four such institutions in London. The Pioneer Club, founded in 1892, was widely regarded as catering for a specifically feminist market. It numbered 300 members at the turn of the century whilst the more socially-oriented and older Alexandra Club had a membership of some 900 women. Bath, Liverpool and Manchester – all significant regional centres of feminist activity at this time – had similar clubs by the end of the century as did both the major Scottish cities and Dublin. Just as these new women's organizations offered new social opportunities for women breaking out of the mould by taking up careers of various sorts, so they also provided a new channel for the development of women's friendships.

The common sexual segregation which dominated more traditional social mores made close friendships between women an acceptable emotional outlet. Both Blanche Wiesen Cook in the American context and, for England, Martha Vicinus, have pointed out that it was often these female friendships which helped women resolve the problems of independence and rebellion which a feminist stand invariably involved.[23] The singular and distinctive characteristics of this common theme of friendship within the feminist movement of this period is, as is the case with the kinship networks, the extraordinary closeness which ensued. Even women living at opposite ends of the country made attempts to get to know one another, to sustain contact even if only through correspondence, and to maintain links with other feminist women. Alongside these wider and more casual circles of social and organizational acquaintance, we can trace numbers of close and important personal relationships.

Such friendships were often intense and passionate, involving declarations of love and promises of eternity not dissimilar to those found in the language of romantic heterosexuality.[24] Women had little fear, it would seem, of forming strong emotional attachments to other women, and the question of whether such attachments ever resolved themselves into specific sexual contact is, whilst important for other reasons, not necessarily a valuable index of the quality of relationship.[25] It would, of course, be a powerful and fascinating exercise to trace possible stages in lesbian self-recognition through physical and sexual attachment, but aside from the difficulties of historical recovery involved in such a venture, the nineteenth-century women's movement offers so many examples of deep and unashamed love between women – who often chose to spend their lives together – that the specifics of genital contact seems an irrelevant index of these friendships.[26]

A re-examination and reassessment of such friendships is valuable in focusing our attention on the depth of, and need for, companionship and away from the common interpretation of women's homosocial friendships as mere sublimation for the company of men. As Estelle Freedman points out, the 'concept of the woman-identified woman has historical roots in the female friendships, networks and institutions of the nineteenth century'.[27] Women, in choosing female friendship as the primary source of emotional sustenance in lives that were often caught in contradiction, were meshing their political understandings with their social and emotional being; it was an explicit rejection of the division between public and private with which they had been so thoroughly inculcated. In this respect, some interesting differences emerge in understanding the distinctions between male and female homosocial relations in this period. Whereas in choosing male friendship as a prerogative, men were rejecting the private sphere and embracing notions of

masculine consonance and identification, women's friendships – certainly in a feminist context – involved a specific meshing of
public and private, and thus a firm rejection of the dualism that divided
the sexes.

Friendships amongst feminist women ranged from close mutual support to shared living arrangements. Their common characteristic was the
reciprocal provision of what Constance Maynard called 'the long, long
clasp of living love'.[28] Writing from the Australian colony of New South
Wales where she had accompanied a shipload of emigrant women,
Langham Place feminist Maria Rye acknowledged the value of that
reciprocity in strengthening her against the loneliness and isolation she
was experiencing there. In a letter to Barbara Bodichon in 1865, she
confessed, 'I have been longing to hear from you and longing to
write . . . You are quite right in saying that I ought to remember that I
have staunch loving friends at home – believe me that I have and do
remember it with the most implicit faith and repose.'[29]

Carroll Smith-Rosenberg points out that friendships such as these were
not 'isolated dyads, but . . . normally part of highly integrated networks'.[30] Rye could look not only to her friendship with Bodichon but to
other women, too, in her feminist networks for this sustenance.

Friendship, then, was integral to the networking so characteristic in
nineteenth-century feminist circles. Did it, however, initiate or precede
that political development? Diana Worzala's vision of the organizations
of the earliest feminists of this era rests on a notion of social intimacy
built around family acquaintance and similarity of backgrounds, out of
which grew the various committees which we recognize as the embryo of
the movement.[31] It was certainly the case that close friendships such as
those between Barbara Leigh Smith and Bessie Rayner Parkes,[32] and
between Parkes and Mary Merryweather, offered an established footing
facilitating the movement's growth. Women with similarly radical predi-
lections and background were bound to find a common cause, though
not necessarily a catalyst to action. Moreover, so many good friendships
grew out of and in tandem with collective commitment, that it is difficult
not to see an intrinsically parallel development of campaigning feminism
and feminist friendship.

It was through her own active discovery of feminism in the 1870s and
1880s that the young widowed Louisa Martindale forged a bond with
Elizabeth Wolstenholme Elmy. The two women lived some three
hundred miles apart – Martindale in Sussex and Elmy in Cheshire – but
they conducted a correspondence founded on feminist discussion. Elmy is
particularly interesting in this context. She was, without doubt, one of
the foremost feminists of her generation, active in a dazzling array of
campaigns, frequently in arduous administrative capacities. As a result,

she was familiar with a huge number of her co-activists around the country, and yet lived the greater part of her adult life – though there was a lengthy stint when she taught in Manchester – in the Cheshire town of Congleton from where she conducted a regular and lively correspondence with other and far-flung feminists. One very moving note preserved in her letters illustrates the refusal of feminist women to categorize their friendships or communications in established ways.

How many years have we corresponded I know not – but all the time I was under the impression that you were in very good if not affluent circumstances and a little bird has just whispered in my ear that such is not the case – how will you have kept this from all your admiring and grateful friends[?] . . . You have given up so much of your time and money too as well I know – and now I wish you for my own peace of mind to accept the enclosed cheque with only one condition, that it is spent on *yourself alone*.[33]

Elmy married in 1874, but this change in her personal circumstances effected no decrease in her activism. She not only continued to sustain her mammoth correspondence, but helped establish various new women's organizations before the end of the century. For her, as for other feminists, marriage was seldom detrimental to a woman's feminist position or lifestyle.

The closely-knit networks within women's circles were invaluable in creating a new and freer social world for single women, but they never excluded married women. For single women, and particularly those taking up paid employment, female friendships provided a counterbalance to their growing distance from domestic and family networks,[34] whilst nourishing their new political perceptions.

The intensity of such friendships led women, on occasion, to question the married future which they knew was assumed for them. Constance Maynard refused an offer of marriage, at least partly because the love her suitor offered her seemed pallid beside the emotions she felt for her friend and co-teacher, Louisa Lumsden. Maynard remained unmarried; her highly charged emotional life found an outlet in a series of passionate though doomed attachments to other women.[35]

Bessie Rayner Parkes, on the other hand, though eschewing marriage in her youth, did finally marry at the age of thirty-eight. When she declined a proposal of marriage at twenty, one of her foremost reasons was her passion for Barbara Leigh Smith. Her diary is full of constant and adoring references to Barbara.

Oh how dearly I do love and reverence Barbara; how I long for her to love me dearly.

Her face seems to me a summing up of her self; how I love to look at it, to gaze long and drink in its revelations . . . [36]

This level of passionate commitment inevitably had its painful element, though again it is significant that feminists seemed skilful in resolving such problems. Trade union activist Edith Simcox's love for novelist George Eliot brought her much torment. In her manuscript autobiography, she confessed, 'I love her just as much as ever and a touch would bring me back to unconsciousness of everything but the love. But I have no hope . . . '[37] And yet, despite the hopelessness which succeeded Eliot's union with George Lewes, the two women retained social contact thereafter.

One of the most singular characteristics of these friendships is demonstrated by their retention of multiple social ties. Women close to one another happily and frequently discussed their other close companionships without seeming rivalry.[38] As close as the young Bessie Rayner Parkes was to Barbara Leigh Smith, she could still calmly respond thus to a confession of Barbara's. 'You say you are still in love with Miss Howitt; I think by her letters she dearly loves *you* so it is all right. How *heartily* she expresses her ideas and feelings. I like it very much.'[39]

Friendship was thus a central factor in determining life decisions amongst these women, and indeed, as we have seen, often *was* a life decision. Frances Power Cobbe, for instance, lived the greater part of her adult life with sculptress Mary Lloyd, and Amelia Edwards's constant companion on her travels was a female companion known only in her works as 'L'.[40] Similarly, Octavia Hill went from a deep friendship with Sophia Jex-Blake that so worried her parents that they intervened, to a brief and unfulfilled engagement to marry in 1877. Thereafter she formed a partnership with Harriet Yorke which endured for the remainder of her life.

Though marriage might on occasion be thus delayed or avoided as a result of a preference for deeply-felt female friendship, it was rarely diluted if and when it did occur. Despite the anxieties expressed by Catherine Winkworth that, after the marriage of her friend Charlotte Brontë, 'we can never reckon on seeing her much again', one of the most significant features of feminist friendship at this time was its capacity to withstand the potentially isolating mechanics of marriage.[41] And in this respect, feminists differed considerably from other women. Pat Jalland has argued that for Victorian women, marriage was a finality which involved their 'inevitable movement away from . . . former family and friends'.[42] Liz Stanley's assessment of this strong factor of friendship within feminism as the 'bedrock' of our contemporary understanding thus goes straight to the heart of the movement's dynamics.[43]

Stanley's insistence on the diversity of women's friendships in this period[44] points us to the dangers of stereotyping nineteenth-century feminists as a wholly homogeneous social grouping. June Hannam's work on Leeds feminist, Isabella Ford, highlights the resultant 'complexity of the women's movement' at this time. Ford's social contacts, like Margaret Bondfield's, stretched across both the socialist and Marxist wings of the labour movement and at the same time to those sections of the women's movement where socialist principles were regarded as a suspicious dogma.[45] This breadth of acquaintance and tolerance was a distinctive feature of the movement which saw women of significantly different temperament and make-up working to accommodate one another. Though Emily Davies frequently bemoaned the problems of working with radicals, she nevertheless frequented the parties and dinners of that arch-radical, Clementia Taylor!

Feminist women were, as Edith Somerville wrote in a letter to her lover Violet Martin, creating 'profound friendship that extends through every phase and aspect of life, intellectual, social, pecuniary'.[46] The implications of that friendship, grounded as it was in a practical and principled understanding of the need to translate political philosophy into personal existence, were thus markedly collective in character.

The feminist culture which grew on this notion of the simultaneity, and indeed symbiosis, of personal and political objectives was one which stressed shared experiences and shared aims, if not always strategies. It was a philosophy which ran counter to the ideology of individualism which informed the mainstream of Victorian ideology so influentially. Though the politics of individualism had always been tempered in some measure by interventionist policies, it remained none the less one of the most powerful ideological tools of the period. The collectivity which constituted the women's movement was a move away from that individualism, understanding directly the need for combined action, not only within campaigning politics but socially and emotionally as well. Feminist practice offered an implicit critique of Victorian individualism.

Whilst I and other happily circumstanced women, have had no immediate wrongs of our own to gall us, we should still have been very poor creatures had we not felt bitterly those of our less fortunate sisters, the robbed and trampled wives, the mothers whose children were torn from them at the bidding of a dead or living father, the daughters kept in ignorance or poverty while their brothers were educated in costly schools and fitted for honourable professions.[47]

The philanthropic and class element was not entirely quenched in Cobbe's assessment of women's wrongs, but her passionate recognition of the injustices of inequality brought with it a firm belief in the need for collective action to right it.

Collectivism of this sort led directly, within the context of a feminist understanding, to a distinct woman-centredness. The social networks we have explored lie at the conjunction of collectivism and this female and feminist orientation. The Hellenic scholar, Jane Ellen Harrison, happily opted for the institutional life offered by a fellowship at Newnham College, rather than family life.

By what miracle I escaped marriage I do not know, for all my life long I fell in love. But, on the whole, I am glad. I do not doubt that I lost much, but I am quite sure that I gained more. Marriage, for a woman at least, hampered the two things that made life to me glorious – friendship and learning. In man, it was always the friend, not the husband, that I wanted. Family life has never attracted me. At best it seems to me rather narrow and selfish; at its worst, a private hell. The role of wife and mother is no easy one; with my head full of other things I might have dismally failed. On the other hand I have a natural gift for community life. It seems to me sane and civilized and economically right.[48]

Emily Davies thought that women had, in fact, always congregated together. She labelled Bessie Parkes an idealist for interpreting the women's movement as unique, or at any rate, different in its emphasis. In a somewhat irritable letter to their mutual friend Barbara Bodichon, she noted, 'There is nothing at all new in women's working together. All over the country there are ladies' associations, ladies' committees, schools managed by ladies, magazines conducted by ladies, etc., etc., which get on well enough.'[49]

In a similar vein to Emily's argument, historians of earlier periods have stressed the importance of childbirth rituals from which men were wholly excluded and which served as a symbol in many ways of the primary source of women's power.[50]

Parkes, however, was more prescient in this instance. The coming together of women in feminist circles derived its *raison d'être* from a wholly different perception of women's place than those philanthropic and quasi-domestic ventures which Emily Davies cites as evidence of women's togetherness. Those instances fed largely into existing social mores. Feminism, on the other hand, effectively gave women the strength of purpose to challenge those same mores. Women were not working with other women because it was a permissible and respectable activity but rather because they chose to make active statements as to their vision of a feminist future. Their companionship, socially and politically, was a mutually reinforcing bond, the power of which both married and single women understood.

For Sophia Jex-Blake, it was a powerful enough force to override the usual social obligations. 'I believe I love women too much ever to love a man.'[51] Equally, however, married women continued to seek the company of other women, as we have seen. Emilia Pattison (afterwards Dilke, on her second marriage) 'declared that while good male society could be found in many places, what was also necessary to a woman was the sympathy of active-minded and intelligent women'.[52]

Kate Amberley, rather more happily married than Mrs Pattison, none the less reserved – as we have seen – a good deal of her time for her feminist associates. She employed the professional medical services of the newly qualified Elizabeth Garrett and notes that Garrett 'sent the medecines (sic) to me as she does not profess to attend men'.[53] Garrett had qualified in medicine, not only to promote the twin feminist causes of advances in women's education and women's employment, but also to service, thereafter, the specific medical needs of women and children.

Women's consciousness of this need to assert the primacy of feminist concerns even spilled over at times into a preoccupation with language. It was a common practice amongst feminists to maintain their original surnames on marriage. Few went as far as Florence Fenwick Miller who, when she married Frederick Alford Ford in 1877, simply kept the name she had been given at birth. Most women retained their names, adding them to their married names, as did sisters Millicent Garrett Fawcett and Elizabeth Garrett Anderson as well as countless other feminists.[54]

The setting up of the early women's colleges at the University of Cambridge brought the linguistic problem to the fore with the issue of titular propriety: 'Is there no euphonious feminine to be discovered of one of all these names – Rector, Warden, Provost, etc., which prevail at Oxford? . . . Dean *has* a feminine in Spanish, but alas, it is duenna.'[55]

Edith Simcox similarly found the common masculine assumptions of the language a distinct irritant in the political arena. When the Secretary of the International, of which she was a member, wrote signing himself 'yours fraternally', Simcox was less than impressed. Her reply, resigning her position on Council, made clear her dissatisfaction. 'I signed the letter. . . . "yours fraternally" by way of a parting protest against the English of the friends of woman.'[56] Women's determination to fight their battles for themselves arose out of such instances. The language of brotherhood was only one example of a common problem, largely unacknowledged outside the feminist community.

Woman-centredness was, then, a common feature of nineteenth-century feminism, though the degree of women's commitment inevitably varied from individual to individual. An interesting exchange between George Eliot and Edith Simcox illustrates the point. Simcox relates the story in her autobiography, and though there was doubtless a strong element of emotional strain running through the discussion, it neverthe-less does serve as an example of those differing levels of commitment which could be accommodated.

[Lewes] had had a letter from a young Cambridge man, who had dreamt so vividly and repeatedly that she [Eliot] was ill that he couldn't help writing to ask – enclosing a directed card for reply, 'only a dream' or something of the sort, to prove that he wasn't in quest of an autograph. She said perhaps that would make me more charitable to men-folk. I protested I wasn't otherwise, and she said that she had always owed me a grudge for not being grateful enough to the Station Officer who was kind to me when the train was snowed up beyond Loggia [Italy]. She said unlike most people, she believed I should have thought more of the adventure if a woman had been kind to me. I said I might have if I had had the opportunity of being kind to a woman. But that I had no prejudice whatever against men. He and she said as they have before, that among chance acquaintances men are more appreciative and courteous to her than women. I said that I had found women kinder than men, which she was 'glad to hear', as showing they could be kind to each other – so I didn't explain either that I had always taken their kindness as a sign that I was half a man – and they knew it; or that I thought it rather hard she should visit, as a fault, my constitutional want of charm for men.[57]

The conversation between the two women is interesting, not only for the light it throws on the position of the committed feminist but in pointing up the twilight zone into which women not subscribing to accepted notions of femininity were willy-nilly forced. Eliot was not alone in doubting the wisdom of this pro-woman feminist stand. Janet Courtney's retrospective work counselled that 'for some time we have been in danger of producing a type which finds its ideals in a world of women rather than in the world as it is'.[58]

Feminist orientation was inevitably a threatening idea to those outside, whilst signalling endurance, commitment and support to those within. It provided a common interest which bonded women from differing political stances and different backgrounds, and even on occasion across the strife-ridden barriers of class.

The rejection of separate spheres which feminist friendships thus represented offered women a coherent means of ordering personal feelings and political commitment into a lifestyle consonant with the challenge of the feminism which so frequently absorbed their energies. In doing so, it created the potential for the growth and development of a separately conceived and strong feminist culture in later nineteenth-century England.

Part II

Public Commitment

5

Disrupting the Dark Continent

Feminist attention to issues of sexuality and sexual behaviour offers an interesting case study of the way in which the women's movement attended to and ultimately challenged the neatly laid-out, though seldom realistic, separate spheres of public and of private behaviour. Modern historical studies have illustrated in abundance the dangers of too literal a reading of the historical signs; where once we thought the Victorian age a time of silence and neglect of matters sexual, we are now inclined to see the more insidious ways in which sex permeated the very fabric of Victorian propriety.[1]

It would, of course, be absurd to ignore the repressive strand of fear through which much of this fascination was filtered, and which frequently led to a rigidity in linguistic conventions which sealed the subject-matter off as a closed and discrete issue. It was in such an environment that feminists attempted to make public and give voice to the inequalities and injustices arising from this paradox. In this area of feminist attack, more than in any other, women had to confront prejudices and assumptions which struck at the very heart of male identity. The challenge was intensified by the careful control of the language of sexuality so characteristic of this period. Rachel Harrison and Frank Mort have suggested more precisely that nineteenth-century debates on sexuality reveal 'not so much the absence through repression of non-procreative sexualities as the beginnings of a proliferation of categories or subjectivities of sexual deviance within official discourse'.[2]

In reality, repression was the underside of obsession, and we need to understand the dialectic of Victorian sexuality as framed by this dynamic. Ironically, however, though sexuality was deemed the ultimate area of privacy, the private world was also the arena occupied by women. This fractured schizophrenia which thus subdivided the private sphere further along gendered lines, was the source of much contradiction in

Victorian thinking on the subject of sexuality, as on the subject of women or what constituted 'woman'.

Despite the accent on privacy with which sexual matters were hedged, they none the less remained issues of considerable public clamour and concern, in which legislative principles were enunciated very distinctly. Government took a considerable role, not only in determining the boundaries of sexual behaviour, but in ascribing specifically gendered roles to men and women in legal contestations over the dissolution of marriages and child custody.

Thus, despite attempts to constrain and confine sexuality within the private sphere, it none the less remained constantly public. Feminist strategies challenged fundamentally the contradiction of that ever-increasing polarization of the public and the private wherein public statements and actions served to proscribe private behaviour.

The feminist challenge to this subjugation has also suffered from an overly literal interpretation. Only within the last decade or so have we come to re-evaluate the widely-held and unflattering judgement that articulate women in the nineteenth century promoted prudery and repression on questions of sexual behaviour, rather than seeing that they were offering instead a challenge to what they perceived as a well-established and well-protected area of male privilege.

It was with the changing role of the state in legislating sexual activity that nineteenth-century feminists were primarily concerned. Their leadership of the opposition to the implementation of the Contagious Diseases Acts of the 1860s has sometimes served to obscure historiographically other factors in the determination of a specifically feminist position – or more accurately, positions – on sexuality. That struggle, none the less, does offer a dramatic and important springboard for understanding the central issues which both characterized and altered feminist thinking.

The provisions enacted by the Contagious Diseases Acts (see p. 83) brought into sharp relief the precepts governing women's lives and sexual existence along lines of both class and gender. Despite the highly visible existence of a prostitution governed principally by poverty, women were none the less expected to assume a role of passionless propriety. The 'moral mother', as Nancy Chodorow dubbed her – that quintessential product of nineteenth-century myth-making – 'was a historical pro-duct'.[3] Out of women's lives were constructed the moral paradigms with which the Victorians sought to pattern the social fabric, and yet which simultaneously constrained its ideologues within the boundaries of fear. Attitudes to sexuality, and more particularly to female sexuality, had undergone significant changes during the course of the previous century, with a highly moralistic tone becoming increasingly dominant.[4]

At the same time, the state's growing willingness to act as moral arbiter was consonant with its tentative but tangible steps to greater overall political control. By the mid-nineteenth century, this perceptible change in politics and ideology had brought with it, inevitably, a host of contradictions which served to mark radically not only the sexual divisions between men and women but distinctions between what was considered appropriate for women of differing social classes. As we have seen in Part I and will discuss again in chapter 8 more fully, class was a factor which, in this period, can never be underestimated in gauging our retrospective responses. Women's politics – though invariably enmeshed simultaneously in a class politics – at least recognized the destructive potential of that divide and offered a challenge to rendering class pre-eminent above gender in political analysis. Elizabeth Janeway has pointed out that 'female sexuality . . . has always been used as a sort of glue to hold structures together'.[5] In the Victorian period especially, that 'glue' fulfilled more than one role, both sexually and across class lines.

Prostitution – more particularly in the mid-century years – was the focus and the nucleus of much of the furore over sexuality, and the catalyst for important changes in feminist thinking. Its centrality to the determination of a public morality runs the gamut of the interpretative spectrum. For the champions of idealized womanhood and Victorian moral puritanism, the prostitute woman was a concrete manifestation of moral disintegration and degradation, signifying a canker on the body politic whose presence was necessarily contaminating.[6] For the feminist advocate, on the other hand, she was – in Judith Walkowitz's words – 'a paradigm for the female *condition*, a symbol of woman's powerlessness and sexual victimization'.[7]

Interestingly, these two divergent viewpoints converged in seeing the state as a fitting agency of change. In their different ways, both saw state intervention as remedial, despite the deep mistrust of state interference rooted in classical Liberalism. Their view of what steps the state should take to ameliorate the problems posed by prostitution were wildly different, based on their polarized understanding of prostitution itself. In both cases, however, the significance of their even accepting the state as an agent of change is of critical importance in signalling a loosening of liberal individualistic ties. In the parallels feminists drew between their quest for political representation and their rejection of male-defined sexual norms, they looked more and more to the state, and to the changes they wished to see in it, to intervene on the side of justice and equality.

The Contagious Diseases Acts of the 1860s, which permitted the arrest and genital examination of suspected prostitute women in designated 'high risk' areas, as a means of curbing venereal disease in the armed forces, had energized the emergence of this new feminist response to the state as a forum for controlling sexual behaviours. Throughout the 1870s, when repeal agitation was at its most forceful, the feminist activists who spearheaded the challenge to the acts increasingly articulated the parallels between sexual and political domination. Their challenge to the state's clear implementation of a double standard served to refine, extend, and indeed to radicalize their broader philosophy; women active in repeal circles were also involved simultaneously in a myriad of other women's campaigns and used any and all available platforms to demonstrate the critical connections that drew together the various demands of their movement and their understanding of the connections between sexual and political subordination: 'women used sex to talk of power'.[8] The argument that women's presence in Parliament would secure more equitable treatment across gender lines was certainly a powerful one for women seeking to make explicit both the conceptual connections and the practical links between their varied activities. In 1875, the *Women's Suffrage Journal* declared its belief that 'there is a real connection between this systematic degradation of the personal rights of women and their political disabilities'.[9]

In the years prior to the Contagious Diseases Acts, moral issues had rarely been explicitly raised by campaigning feminist activists. Even the blatant inequities enshrined in the Matrimonial Causes Act of 1857 (see chapter 6) had engendered surprisingly little organized protest. Women had focused their energies most intensely in earlier decades upon education, employment and the legal rights of married women. The need to establish women's fitness in areas as palpably public as political representation or in the labour force were seen at that juncture as having precedence over discussions of private behaviour and attitude. The gendered division of spheres forced women, at least in the movement's earlier stages, to challenge those notions not by collapsing the definitional boundaries of gender as they would do – with some qualifications – from the time of repeal agitation on, but by stepping *out* of them to assume specifically public roles. In effect, it was necessary for women to understand fully the nature of the sphere to which they were denied access before they could begin to challenge the very ideology which posited their exclusion from it. By the 1870s, however, as the first professional women doctors began to emerge, and a feminist culture to be established through schools, colleges and regional networks of a political and social nature, the women's movement gained both confidence and an ever sharper cognizance of the extent, urgency and connectedness of their labours.

The passing of the Contagious Diseases Acts catalysed that stage of understanding, not only because they were such glaring examples of profound inequity but because they dealt with an issue which, whilst sensational enough to attract widespread attention, literally and figuratively articulated and demonstrated the disingenuousness of separate sphere ideology, and acknowledged the reality of its failure. The implementation of the Acts gave feminists the perfect foil with which not only to argue the logic and justice of their case but also to expose the sheer density of the power which entrapped their sex. Alongside its pragmatic abandonment of moral strictures, the regulation legislation enacted by the state was emblematic, too, of much broader inequalities. Feminist campaigners took every opportunity to point out its class implications, the connection between poverty and prostitution induced by women's economic dependency, and the lack of choice in employment and education exacerbating the problem. The overall powerlessness of women which the Acts exploited was the message which feminist campaigners were most anxious to promote.

The various chapters of the Acts, passed in 1864, 1866 and 1869, permitted the apprehension of a suspected prostitute so that she might be – in the words of the 1866 Act – 'convey[ed] . . . with all practicable Speed to [a] Medical Officer . . . for the Purpose of ascertaining whether or not she has a Contagious Disease'. She could then be detained for twenty-four hours. If found to be suffering from a venereal disease, the woman was to be held for treatment for a period not normally exceeding three months. No magistrate's order was necessary to render detention legal. Refusal, 'wilful neglect . . . to conform', or leaving the hospital without formal discharge were summary offences for which a gaol term could be imposed.[10] By 1869, eighteen scheduled districts throughout the British Isles – largely naval and military garrisons – were covered by the Acts' provisions, and alarm was spreading rapidly amongst those who opposed their implementation. Whilst opposition was not limited to the feminist community, theirs was the most vigorous of the sources of dissent and the one most able to communicate vividly its inequities.

In many respects the legislation itself demonstrated, both in its provisions and in its language, the moral confusions engendered by the dichotomous nature of separate sphere ideology. It was women – and increasingly feminists as much as those forced to practise prostitution – who were transgressing the moral boundaries. The constant use of the term 'public woman', both in the Acts and in the Royal Commission subsequently monitoring them, is illuminating. The phrase was less a euphemism born of delicacy than a clear and critical statement of transgression; in every sense the prostitute woman defied the ideal of Victorian womanhood, as the feminist also came to do in her outspokenness. She was sexual in an age of proud passionlessness, active where passivity was the hoped-for norm, and directly involved in commercial, albeit illicit, bidding and transaction. The preference amongst parliamentarians for the term 'public' was certainly accurate, but it was also shocking in its juxtaposition with 'woman', the very antithesis of 'public'. The alarm over venereal disease was certainly justified, accounting, as it did, for 29 per cent of all army hospital admissions in 1862, but it was also a means of vocalizing more deep-seated alarms about contamination and challenge. Where the hapless prostitute became a paradigm of powerlessness for feminists, she was a paradigm of lawlessness and of moral degeneration for the patriarchal state.

The Acts highlight for the modern observer the confusion and unease which underpinned the dominant sexual ideology of Victorian England. Despite some unconvincing statements to the contrary, the major function of the legislation was not to rid the island of commercialized sex but rather to ensure that its presumed concomitant, venereal infection, was held in check. The Acts looked not to the customer but to the vendor as the prime contaminater in the sexual exchange, and focused on providing a safe source of uninfected women for men who remained free from coercive treatment or inspection. Indeed, it was when routine genital examination in the military had sparked a rank-and-file protest that the Acts were first considered. The Royal Commission appointed to assess their efficacy reported in 1871; the language employed by the Commissioners is once more revealing. Discussing the second chapter of legislation passed in 1866, they noted that it 'not only recognized prostitutes as agents in the propagation of the disease, but sought so far to control their conduct as to render the practice of prostitution, if not absolutely innocuous, at least much less dangerous'.[11]

In effect, the legislation proposed to deal primarily not with a moral issue but with the practical – if ideologically imbued – problem of contagion. Fear of infection and disease was a multi-layered and constantly-present strand haunting the Victorians; at every level it was a threat to order, whether physically and physiologically or politically conceived. The scapegoating of the prostitute woman, however, represents an interesting and significant shift illuminating the changing attitudes and the hardening of fears about female sexuality in this period. Traditionally, the military had been seen as harbingers and bringers of disease and epidemic, most particularly when they were an invading force.[12] The regulation of prostitution heralded a change in attitude which saw the threat emanating more specifically from *within*. This was a plague which was not brought back by rats aboard ships nor by sailors' and soldiers' exploits with foreign women, but a disease endemic in Britain's own 'disorderly' and female populace.

The lawlessness which was prostitution lay at the heart of this gripping fear. Prostitutes were women outside the control of the dominant ideology who were seen to be spreading disease as well as profligacy uncontrollably. That profligacy was both sexual and economic in nature, and the issue of control thus translated yet further from the private to the public sphere. The presence of 'public' women on the streets also disrupted the authority of policing agencies, another challenge to male power. In their distance from the rigorous codes of 'femininity', such women became deviants, deviance translated to illness and thence to disease and also – importantly – to the urgency of the need for incarceration, whether represented as medical or punitive. If we compare the regulation of prostitution, which specifically authorized a period of incarceration, with the changing response to mental illness and insanity in this period, the consonance of the examples is striking.[13] The fear of deviance and its contaminant properties was palpable. Prostitute women refusing to submit to treatment incurred a charge of criminality, thereby virtually guaranteeing their incarceration and labelling as criminal. The adoption of an incarcerative institutional response to insanity, a need to separate the mad from orderly society, displays similar concerns.

The personification of disease, of disorder and of degeneracy by individuals such as prostitute women was a means both of distancing and simultaneously of grasping at a mode of controlling rebellious or dissonant voices. By the time that campaigns around sexual questions came to be a common feature of its politics, feminism had already experienced considerable public derision and hostility that had labelled its supporters misfits, outcasts and deviants. The addition of sexual causes to those they already championed, whilst it perhaps increased the level of clamour somewhat, caused only a quantitative and not a qualitative difference in the responses they stirred.

It is interesting to note the subliminal way in which the various disorders perceived to plague the country and threaten its moral stature were run together even by reasonably sympathetic observers. In his diary for 1860, Arthur Munby recalls the following scene in London's West End.

In the Haymarket was a youngish woman, quite drunk; it was pleasant to see the interest which the group of prostitutes around took in her – one offering to subscribe for a cab to send her home in, which the police wouldn't allow, another picking up her shawl and running after them with it; all pitying her, yet showing a feminine disgust at her drunkenness.[14]

Despite Munby's consciously rehabilitative humanization of the participants in this incident, his attitudes, none the less, provoke some fascinating connections. Here were two disorderly but different challenges to the established role of women and to the authority of the police – a group of prostitute women and a woman intoxicated. Not only do the prostitutes show sympathy with the drunken woman but they are sufficiently bold to attempt bargaining with the police, and even after proving unsuccessful can still intervene on her behalf, taking her shawl to her as she is apprehended. In Munby's eyes, they clearly redeem themselves by being simultaneously concerned at her plight but repulsed by her behaviour. There is a certain naivety to Munby's comments; drunkenness – female or male – can hardly have been new or shocking to those frequenting the heart of London's seamier nocturnal entertainment district. The passage is interesting, though, both in bringing together the varying ways in which women could effectively, if not necessarily wilfully, deny their allotted role, and in showing the specifics of their relations with the symbols of male authority, in this case the police. The contested domain of the streets is a silent but present factor in Munby's account. Despite Munby's reading of their attitude as essentially, and indeed naturally, feminine, the relations he portrays between the various actresses in the scenario do not correspond to the properly submissive role which a 'true' femininity would demand.

The period in which prostitution came to be widely perceived as an urgent social problem was also one in which class lines were increasingly strongly drawn.[15] Fear of class unrest was a common concern in the parliamentary debates of the nineteenth century, with further resonances in the fears and insecurities upon which colonial aggression also drew. It is not without significance that the zeal with which imperial conquests were undertaken, and the language in which such colonization was couched, filtered down into the means by which government sought to control the perceived dangers of class and sex. Working-class slums and female sexuality were as much *terra incognita* as was the 'dark continent' of Africa where Britain expropriated so much land and founded so many colonies at this time. The mapping and taming of all these different categories of territory was a priority of governments of both mainstream political parties, caught up as they were in the creation of a strong and unified English identity. The language of class, the language of sex and indeed the language of imperialism at this time, all display common characteristics – a concern with domination, control and authority, a fear of contagion and infection. The triad of race, class and sex was apparent early in the development of modern English political culture.

The campaign to secure abandonment of the Contagious Diseases Acts was successful, in feminist terms, not only in achieving eventual repeal in the mid-1880s, but in finally giving women activists a voice with which they felt they could extend their analysis of gender inequity into that sexual and moral arena. Once they had articulated their anxieties over the meaning and implications of this legislation, further analyses which brought home the contiguity of sexual, political and economic inequality ensued. In the late 1870s, when repeal agitation was firmly established as a leading feminist concern to which a substantial number of England's more prominent campaigners were prepared to lend their energies, new organizations concerned with the significance of sexual politics began to emerge in feminist circles.

The most obvious of such new manifestations were, of course, the various social purity groups whose fundamental premise was a challenge to the double standard.[16] A plethora of organizations sought to encourage state legislation on moral issues; the Social Purity Alliance, the Moral Reform Union, the National Vigilance Association and the Association for the Improvement of Public Morals were amongst those groups who, in the 1870s and 1880s, began to articulate a moral rearmament which challenged the rights of unrestrained male carnality.[17]

The social purity movement – with its emphasis on a single moral standard applicable to both sexes and fashioned on the principles of a Christian ethics – was, however, only one of the ways in which the post Contagious Diseases Acts movement gave more and more credence and emphasis to this critical area of feminist challenge. In similar vein, the support of many feminists for teetotalism followed a similar logic, drawing connections between alcoholism and violence against women. Campaigns dealing with marital violence and the assault of women constantly denounced the social acceptability of drunkenness amongst men and its consequences for women.[18] Again, while the case for abstinence was generally couched in the language of the gospels, much of the impetus fuelling feminist teetotalism stemmed from a clear understanding of the gendered implications of drink and not necessarily from a puritan distaste for pleasure. The challenge was, once again, to a double standard that privileged male preference and pleasure over female health, safety and liberty.

A further outcrop of the new ability to voice concerns in moral areas led to the growth of a new variant on the idea of women's rights to unfettered choice in personal decisions. Feminist activists were acutely aware that the battle-cry of freedom was, in effect, a double-edged sword. They called, not for unrestrained freedom so much as for socially necessary constraint, but a constraint applied more equitably along ungendered lines. Just as earlier campaigns had emphasized women's rights to engage in paid labour or to choose an occupation without reference to sex, later nineteenth-century feminists desired to extend that notion of choice into decisions about personal lifestyle. The right to choose celibacy as a socially acceptable alternative to marriage and procreation became an increasingly important strand of feminism, and substituted in the nineteenth century for explicit calls for more sexually free lifestyles. Feminists remained largely silent on homosexual preference and on contraception throughout this period; nor did the provision of child care become an issue of note in the movement much before the 1930s.

Several factors govern the choices women made, both in remaining silent and in becoming vocal, in these various areas. In the first instance, the political culture in which, even as they challenged it, they were fundamentally immersed, was nowhere near an acceptance of the kind of extended welfare provision implied by child-care facilities. The struggles within both the women's movement and the labour movement had considerable distances to travel before such ideas could even be entertained; at this juncture gaining a foothold for single women in the paid labour force was still an issue. The working mother would have to wait considerably longer for attention to her needs. Moreover, the politics of the late nineteenth century were still so thoroughly steeped in a Christian tradition which upheld heterosexual and familial values that neither extra-marital nor non-heterosexual liaisons were, in most circles, acceptable. Occasional and exceptional relations of this kind were certainly made public, but were effectively contained within narrow social parameters and invariably confined their protagonists to the social margins, if not to an often tragic vilification.

It was on marriage in its more traditional sense that much of the subsequent feminist moral outrage focused, more particularly since women were uncomfortably and increasingly cognizant of the thin moral line which, in reality, separated respectable marriage from commercial sex. As Susan Kingsley Kent has so pithily put it, 'the respectable woman found herself a seller in a buyer's market'.[19] It was a theme which, in the very last years of the century, came to dominate the more radical critiques of marriage and to inform the championing of celibacy as a feasible and desirable alternative to normative heterosexual relations. In their rejection of heterosexual sex, we can see the coalescence for many feminists of their realization of the proximity of marital relations and prostitution. Sex on male terms meant effective disempowerment for women. Mary Shanley points out that in rendering adultery the principal ground on which marriages might be dissolved, the law was in effect assuming 'that sexual relationships and the legitimacy of a man's offspring were the basic considerations of the marriage contract'.[20]

In 1857, with the passing of the Matrimonial Causes Act, decisions on divorce became, at least nominally, the responsibility of the secular courts. The Act is interesting in connoting specifically sexual grounds which made divorce tenable, focusing principally, although by no means equally, on the issue of monogamy. Though both husband and wife could petition for divorce on grounds of sexual dereliction, men were accorded far greater liberties both to remain within or to end their marriages. Whilst husbands could seek divorce in any instance of adultery, a wife's petition had specifically to state compounding and aggravating factors such as brutality or 'unnatural' sexual acts of varying kinds in addition to adultery. The Commission appointed to recommend changes in the laws of marriage had, in 1853, recommended that divorce *a vinculo* should be limited to cases of proven adultery and 'shall only be granted on the suit of the husband and not (as a general rule) on the suit of the wife' except 'in cases of aggravated enormity'.[21] By maintaining the distinction between total divorce (*a vinculo*) and effective separation ('bed and board' or *a mensa et thoro*), the 1857 legislation created and extended a double standard which affected both sex and class. Gail Savage's comment on this Act that 'the operation of the law on the whole afforded protection to more men than women' is an important one.[22]

The Matrimonial Causes Act was promulgated a full seven years before the passing of the first of the Contagious Diseases Acts and its justification of a differing moral code applicable to men and women was as explicit, if not more so, than that which would govern the lives of prostitute women during the twenty-one years of regulation. It was, additionally, as punitive in some respects as was the regulation legislation. In assessing custodial rights over children, adultery on the part of a woman was in itself sufficient grounds for denying her custody of, and often any access to, her children. Moreover, the Act also discounted an adulterous woman's rights to maintenance, a severe blow in an age of such complete female economic dependence. The message of the Act was that women, given no choice in the matter, had to earn their support by observing an appropriate code of sexual and social behaviour. When the provisions for divorce were, in part, extended to poorer women by the introduction of separation orders granted to victims of marital assault, the same restrictions on female sexuality were written into the legislation.[23]

Thus, even before the Contagious Diseases Acts ushered in a new era of articulated sexual debate, Parliament was constructing the acceptable parameters of sexual behaviour along gendered lines and with remarkably little opposition. Neither the Matrimonial Causes Act of 1857, which first made explicit the differing values which government would forthwith place on male and female transgression of marital vows, nor the subsequent extensions and refinements of the period (the Matrimonial Causes Act of 1878 and the 1895 Summary Jurisdiction (Married Women) Act), generated the degree of anger or attention which devolved on, for instance, the regulation of prostitution.

Marriage not only deprived a woman of economic and legal status and rendered her obliged to fulfil conjugal demands that would almost inevitably burden her further with frequent pregnancies, but it was by no means a safe haven from the brutal realities of public life. The feminist position on marital violence – spearheaded in the late 1870s by Frances Power Cobbe – was a far more focused and public feminist perspective than many, and certainly attracted more attention than did, say, statutory rape. Prosecutions for marital violence commonly attracted only lenient sentencing from magistrates, in marked contrast to their response to crimes of property, as feminists were quick to point out. Their allusions to the idea that men regarded women as one element of their property were bolstered by the frequent invocation of the weighty legal opinion of the eighteenth-century jurist William Blackstone, that wives might receive 'moderate correction' from their husbands. In 1867, John Stuart Mill challenged his fellow parliamentarians to compare the sentences meted out to those who abused their wives with those common in property theft cases. Mill's angry declaration of the problem implicitly invoked the feminist perception that this was a problem which women endured for lengthy periods. As Mill concluded, with such a comparison on hand, 'we should then have an arithmetical estimate of the value set by a male legislature and male tribunals on the murder of a woman, often by torture continued through the years'.[24]

In the context of the dangers that women could identify as stemming directly from sexual relations – prostitution, venereal disease, marital assault – we should not be too quick to judge feminist responses as prudish and narrow. Certainly, their view of sexuality often veered to the negative, although the recent studies of Pat Jalland have demonstrated amply that many couples mutually enjoyed the physical facets of their relationship.[25] One of the most constant and powerful motifs in the feminist thought of this period is the persistence, however, of that idea of sexual danger, of sex as dangerous to women.

Sexual danger for women assumed many forms; alongside marital violence, infection, coercion into paid or unpaid sexual acts, this was the period in which the serial killer 'Jack the Ripper' stalked the streets of London's East End, butchering women. Many believed that the prostitute women who were the principal victims of his violence were merely meeting their grisly moral nemesis at his hands. The killings brought home the encompassing vulnerability of women at the hands of men, and the sexual proximity of that vulnerability.[26]

It was not only by psychopaths with deft surgical skills, however, that women were threatened. Feminists had long and repeatedly rehearsed the truism that regulation legislation intimidated women in public places; their fear of apprehension, whether by prospective clients of prostitution or by a vigilant and aggressive police force, served to render the streets an inhospitable environment for all women. And at home, the spectre of

marital assault competed with the risk of venereal infection in endanger-
ing women's health and safety. Gail Savage's work on divorce petitions
in England has shown that in cases where the wife was petitioning for
dissolution, the transmission of a sexually incurred disease was common
grounds for seeking divorce.[27] Interestingly, and as Savage has noted, the
message thus coming from the Divorce Court was distinct from that
relayed by the Contagious Diseases Acts.[28] These latter, as we have seen,
designated women the primary infective agent; divorce petitions – which
to some extent move us up the social ladder – acknowledge rather that
men might carry and transmit such diseases. When Josephine Butler's
anti-regulation journal, *The Storm Bell*, called the Contagious Diseases
Acts 'a plan for providing healthy women for profligate men', the
specifics of that danger were apparent.[29] For feminists, it was by male
sexuality and not by women's actions that the moral economy of English
society was endangered.

The negativity that emanated from this sense of menace explains not
only the choice of issues upon which feminists decided to act, but to a
large extent, those areas which remained unchallenged. It is certainly
possible to oversimplify the movement's neglect, both of birth control
and of upholding homosexual preference as a measure of its conservatism. It may, indeed, be that some tactical consideration or some
genuinely felt discomfort with these areas prompted their dismissal from
close and sustained consideration. It seems unsatisfactory, however, to
rest the argument there on so baldly pragmatic a reading of the signs.
It was not, after all, as if the movement displayed a rift in its thinking
on these issues as it did, on occasion, in other areas. The absence of
these areas of concern is conspicuous in being so remarkably uniform
throughout the movement, a seeming declaration of consensus.

An alternative and libertarian approach to both issues could, however,
be read as largely damaging to women by exposing them further to the
control implied by male-defined sexual behaviour. In the case of contraception, the argument is a well-known one. The separation of procreation and penetration could justifiably be interpreted as a means simply of
making women even more vulnerable to a male desire conveniently
removed from the threat of unwanted pregnancy and thus harder to
parry. The silence on matters of contraception might also be seen,
however, as a means of allowing women to shelter behind religious and
Biblical precepts which treated that separation as sinful. It was ironic that
women thus walked an uncomfortable tightrope between the dangers
incurred in pregnancy and those which contraception might realistically
offer. In not making specifically public their reasons for rejecting
participation in this arena of struggle, feminists were perhaps exercising a
cautious conservatism. That they chose not to make their fears a major

area of debate suggests that the consensus might have been an uneasy one and that its implications, if unvoiced, did not go wholly unrecognized. After all, a vocal element in the movement attacked marriage as a form of licensed prostitution while others warned that heterosexual relations would almost certainly invite venereal disease. By the 1880s, feminists in general were far less coy about their public declarations and their language; sexuality had become a central and immovable pivot in their overall perspective, colouring many other campaigns and constantly occupying the political limelight. The choice not to enter into specific areas of obvious female concern and inevitable contestation suggests something more deliberate and important than just queasy sensibilities or 'feminine' manners.[30]

On the question of homosexuality, the pointers are less distinct. The late nineteenth century with its quickened, if visceral, interest in deviance had developed harsh homophobic tendencies.[31] A steady legislative intent to deal punitively with male homosexuality can be tracked right through the century, from the re-introduction in 1826 of the death penalty for acts of sodomy (repealed again in England and Wales in 1861 though not in Scotland until 1889), through the wide-ranging anti-homosexual provisions contained in the 1885 Criminal Law Amendment Act, to the crackdown on soliciting represented by the Vagrancy Act of 1898.[32] Feminists did not oppose any of these measures, nor indeed the sentiments fuelling them; their distaste for and mistrust of any and all manifestations of male sexual desire effectively trapped them.[33] Homosexuality was, for feminists, one further index of male carnality; there were no pressing reasons for feminists thus to come to the defence of men's sexual practices. The libertarianism of a pro-homosexual position runs counter to the largely negative interpretation of all and any male sexuality which the women's movement had adopted by the closing decades of the nineteenth century.

It was a tendency of late Victorian ideology, more than the specific preferences of feminists, to equate morality so explicitly with sex.[34] The control of sexuality came to connote the control of broader social arenas. Prostitution thus came to be an issue not just of sex but also of gender roles, of public health and of public order, with the appropriate authorities assuming control. Amongst feminists, however, the equation was never fully endorsed. They continued to draw attention to other moral and ethical areas in which sexuality had no explicit point of reference.

The temperance cause – not limited, of course, to feminist sympathizers – was one such area of moral regulation where a morally, though not a sexually gendered interpretation prevailed. Feminists represented alcoholic consumption as a catalyst for male violence and irresponsibility, the direct consequences of which were visited as much on the drinker's family as on the drinker himself: men drank away household monies; men drank and then beat their wives; men drank to stimulate their baser passions. The issue of alcohol – or as Frances Power Cobbe called it 'brain poison'[35] – was coterminous with the issue of control. When men drank they were beyond the reach of reason and of control; no logic inhibited their deeds and actions. The sufferers were overwhelmingly women. 'Attacks upon licentiousness and drunkenness became thinly veiled attacks on male behaviour in other areas.'[36] It is interesting in this context to note that when Elizabeth Whitehead married liquor merchant Frank Malleson who worked for Fearon and Company, her place in the movement was unaffected. Feminist women were less inclined to meld husband and wife into one, and appeared rather less judgemental in their social contacts for the most part.

One of the most striking ways in which, retrospectively, we can appreciate just how central such issues had become within the feminist struggle in the years following vocal anti Contagious Diseases Acts campaigning is by noting the extent of the overlap between activists in this moral arena and those in other campaigns. Even women like Millicent Garrett Fawcett, who had chosen to distance herself from active involvement in the prostitution issue for fear of bringing disrepute to her suffrage work, was, none the less, active and increasingly vocal in a variety of moral campaigns. The McLaren women divided their activities between Contagious Diseases repeal agitation, suffrage activism and women's local government work, as well as being supporters of the temperance movement in the later years of the century. They had connections, too, with the feminist periodical press of the period and were active in other social purity areas as well. Patricia Hollis has noted the overlap between Women's Guardian Society members and – amongst others – members of the National Vigilance Association, the Ladies' National Association for the Repeal of the Contagious Diseases Acts (LNA) and numerous suffrage societies.[37] Judith Walkowitz's exhaustive study of the LNA has demonstrated the connections between its committee personnel and women in other feminist activities. In the active Bristol LNA branch the Priestman family were prominent, as they were in the suffrage cause and in the temperance movement. Margaret Tanner, née Priestman, was treasurer of the national LNA and active in other women's campaigns as well. The executive committee of the National Society for Women's Suffrage – one of the most prominent of the large metropolitan suffrage societies – included Laura Ormiston Chant (who was also active in regulation agitation and in local government work as well as an early pioneer of women's rights to preach), Henrietta Müller of the *Women's Penny Paper*, and one of the Priestman sisters, whilst Dr

Elizabeth Blackwell was one of the organization's Vice-Presidents. Priscilla McLaren was on the executive of the National Union of Women's Suffrage Societies (NUWSS), and Josephine Butler on the council of the Women's Franchise League. Early in the twentieth century, the NUWSS commissioned the suffragist doctor, Louisa Martindale, to write a book on venereal disease; *Under the Surface* was published in 1908.[38] The commissioning of a medical text on sexual infection by an organization devoted to the extension of the franchise is, in this context, a highly revealing action.

This overlap signifies two important points – one, that single issue feminism did indeed feed into a more cohesive and consuming perspective on women's rights, and second, that women were now conceptualizing and vocalizing palpable connections between these various campaigns in a concrete manner.

The signatories to the initial Ladies' Petition of March 1870, which was the first significant salvo fired against the regulation of prostitution, call to mind a myriad of other feminist activities. Lydia Becker of the Manchester suffrage movement; Clementia Taylor, one of the *grandes dames* of London feminism; the Bright women from Lancashire; Elizabeth Malleson; the Ashurst sisters; and Harriet Martineau were amongst the signatories, women whose association with feminism was indisputable and whose energies were claimed by any number of related campaigns. These were women for whom the fight over prostitution and moral matters was a logical consequence of their work in the more obviously and traditionally political fields. The *Women's Suffrage Journal*, founded by Lydia Becker in 1870, constantly pointed out, as an earlier citation reveals, that solid political representation of women in the governmental process would serve to stem the legitimation of this gendered double standard.

The debates around sexuality which attracted feminist attention in this period crystallize some of the pragmatic and tactical as well as theoretical problems which plagued a political movement, the very existence of which presupposed a challenge to existing forms of political dissent. Both the repeal agitation of the 1870s and subsequent campaigns initiated by social purity groups relied markedly on the intervention of the state as a moral arbiter, although in the case of regulation the thrust of the campaign was to take issue with the state's condoning of untenable conduct on the part of men. This belief in the need for the state to play an active role in promoting behavioural and attitudinal change via legislatively-declared sanction marked a transition within feminist politics from more classical liberal preferences which held that the state's role should be as confined as possible, to a new and growing belief in utilizing its powers in positive ways. To a large extent, and whatever the resistance, that changing focus was an inevitable outcome of the political demands of the movement. Even in the 1850s, women had accepted the power of, and the need for, legislative action both symbolically and practically. None the less, their new acceptance of the state's right to intervene in issues generally classified as within the domain of the private (age of consent, seemingly consensual sex and the like) was an important signal of new forces within the movement.

Most commentators have argued that the LNA's attempts to force the abandonment of the regulation of prostitution rested squarely on a libertarian conviction of the priority of non-intervention. In practice, what feminists, both in the LNA and in subsequent social purity organizations, were demanding of government was their intervention as agents of moral change and not as champions of the double standard. The relationship that authors such as Paul McHugh have found amongst feminists, between an attachment to non-intervention campaigns such as anti-vaccination and prostitution regulation, is somewhat misplaced.[39] Martin Durham comes close to seeing this move away from a liberal-influenced hostility to the state in his observation that 'the women's movement was crucial in activating the disintegration of nineteenth century liberalism . . . [and] though feminism continued to be expressed most frequently in the language of radical liberalism, as a movement it spanned and cut across the full range of existing political forces'.[40]

In practice, what both the Contagious Diseases (CD) agitation and subsequent campaigning to see laws not repealed but rather enacted or strengthened reveals, is a new, if not always a wholly consistent, attitude to the state. Whilst many feminists of both Conservative and Liberal persuasion had long espoused a policy of philanthropic and private enterprise over the work of state agencies, their new and highly critical understanding of the depth of the two spheres of public and private began fundamentally to erode that position. With the growing rejection of separate sphere ideology as a tenable social and sexual construction that their actions implied, and the emphasis laid on the multiple ramifications of political (viz., public) disability, attitudes to the state as a vehicle for effecting or encouraging action and change underwent profound reassessment. The regulation of prostitution was certainly attacked, at least in part, through an enunciation of the inappropriate-ness of such palpably and grossly hypocritical state intervention, but from that time on, in practice, feminists looked more and more to the state to implement the legislative changes they felt were a necessary component of genuine liberation.

We cannot, on the one hand, note the feminist agitation for the state to intervene on such issues as child prostitution or relief from marital violence, and on the other, argue convincingly that they remained wholly committed to a liberal individualism anathematic to such state policy. And if the state continually failed them, as it did in passing legislation that continued to disservice all women, we should not mistake the state's failure for a failure of imagination or principle on the part of those who would capture and change its ideological position.

Ironically, feminists in this respect were in step with more general political trends, and at times came dangerously close to emulating or supporting some of the more repressive practices increasingly visible in late nineteenth-century English society. As sexual and social concerns came even closer together in this period (perhaps an ironic result of women's persistent challenge to separate sphere ideology), the closing years of the century demonstrated what Jeffrey Weeks has identified as an 'intensification of legal concern with sexual peccadilloes'.[41] The paradox of this palpable change in the manifestation of separate sphere ideology and of state intervention needs to be understood in the context not only of the dovetailing of women's concerns with those of moral and social conservatives, but also with the ability of feminists to capture the public imagination and determine the terms of the debates.

In effect, what we are witnessing in the outrage over the Contagious Diseases legislation in the 1870s is less a dissatisfaction with the principles of state intervention than with the philosophy which informed this particular chapter of legislation. It was the opinion of feminist women that the state needed to be 'feminized' – by the inclusion of women representatives, by a consideration of issues outside the traditionally public realm – rather than claiming to remain aloof from social and sexual issues. Many feminists pointed to the benefits that would accrue from female influence in politics. Florence Fenwick Miller promoted women's suffrage in part 'because there is a great deal of moral power amongst [women] . . . which they ought to be called upon to exercise for the good of our common country'.[42] In enumerating 'Sixteen reasons for women's suffrage' in 1871, the *Women's Suffrage Journal* argued revealingly, 'Because the admission of women into greater political influence would tend to soften our ferocities and purify our whole state. Female influence, if allowed due scope, would especially repress our two worst curses – drunkenness and prostitution.'[43]

The passage is interesting, not only in making explicit connections between political power and moral issues, but further in explicating that those moral issues rested on distorted and ferocious values. The arguments that anti-vivisectionists employed rested similarly on a critical interpretation of the legitimation of male brutality and on a plea for feminized humanism. The International Association for the Total Suppresion of Vivisection issued an open letter to the Prime Minister in 1881 – probably authored by the feminist Frances Power Cobbe – in which male force and female humanity were rhetorically juxtaposed to dramatic effect.

The sole element in Existence is force . . . Consisting of force only, intellectual or physical, humanity is fully represented by the man . . . The head is all, the heart is nothing; sense is all, conscience nothing; intellect is all, character or disposition nothing; consequences are all, means nothing . . . [44]

The letter was significantly titled '"The Woman" and The Age' and, indeed, in its condemnation of male-defined brutalization, reads as if it were a specific text of the feminist movement as much as a document denouncing the practice of vivisection.

The Contagious Diseases Acts thus ironically acted as a watershed, with feminist women thereafter recognizing in practical politics as in theoretical terms, just what the effects of state legislation – for and against their cause – could be.

This change in principles was not without its problems, and engendered a good deal of contradiction and bewilderment for many women. Millicent Fawcett was for some time an office-holder in the National Vigilance Association, an organization which constantly found fault with the inadequate protection offered young women by the Criminal Law Amendment Act of 1885, wishing to see its net widened and its provisions strengthened. At the same time, Fawcett was a strong and active Liberal whose attitude to state intervention was thus a strained one. As was so often the case for women who chose feminism as their principal political endeavour, its analysis served to negate many of their other beliefs, determining the uniqueness, and indeed the difficulties, of the feminist position and highlighting its necessary distance from existing political ideologies which it undermined.

It was not, however, merely in the stretching of other loyalties that feminists realized the complexities of their position. Attention to sexual and moral questions – and those solutions which the movement came consensually to favour – exposed women to attack as social conservatives of a deep order. In historical and political texts, the late nineteenth- and early twentieth-century feminist movement, as we have already seen, has been frequently deemed as repressive, authoritarian and prudish. The high profile involvement of women in social purity organizations and temperance societies, their rejection of male homosexuality, of pornography and 'adult' entertainment, their stand on raising the age of sexual consent have all been taken as signs of an encroaching moral authoritarianism vested in governmental power.

Their reliance both on Christian precepts and on the state have further fuelled these verdicts as has their silence on matters such as contraception. Superficially, the libertarianism which characterized the anti-state stance of the mid-century appears to have been submerged by this more authoritarian stand. That women's new belief in state intervention should coincide, too, with changes in the political culture that deemed it applicable for the state to impose normative private behaviours on its citizenry is significant. Clearly the changing climate of opinion was influential in determining that shift but it would not be disingenuous to suggest that feminists were both responding to these changes and attempting to manipulate them in directions more positive for women. Thus, by adopting the tactics of an acceptable public rhetoric, they could successfully expose, denounce and even seek changes to the legitimation of a double standard which had for so long and so severely disadvantaged women, and with astounding legal impunity.

The language and ethics of a militant Christianity were important factors in shaping the ethical and moral stand of the last quarter of the century.[45] Just as was the case with feminist campaigners overall, radical dissenting faiths were well represented in the moral fields. The LNA was almost wholly run by the Bristol Quakers, and the organization's founder, Josephine Butler, put considerable emphasis on prayer in her campaigning. Religion thus acted both as a liberating conduit through which women could derive a source of strength, of credibility and of rectitude, and simultaneously as a clear rein on the limits of their analysis, apportioning it an uncomfortably close association with actively repressive forces.

This seeming coalescence of religious conservatism and a radically conceived feminism points up both some of the contradictions which dogged women in this period and also some of the more innovative, and perhaps less well understood, aspects of feminist thinking. Gayle Rubin has argued that the 1880s in Britain was a watershed decade in the politics of sex, a time when social-sexual practice and ideology underwent profound and far-reaching re-assessment.[46] Other authors have named that watershed as the coming of a more narrowly codified area of acceptability.[47] Peter Gay has attempted to find the reasons for this diminishing freedom in the well-mapped crisis of Victorian intellectualism: 'evasiveness, cant, prudishness, hypocrisy were cultural defense mechanisms in a time of upheaval, a search for safety'.[48] Whilst the absurd delicacies which pervaded some of the upper echelons of Victorian society were all too obviously manifestations of a silence borne of discomfort, his explanation cannot fully account for the quotidian realities of Victorian life, of the public spectacle of prostitution, of the constant, conscious and public discussions and displays of sex without which our understanding of this period would not be complete.

The parallel focus on state responsibility and an ethics grounded in religious ideology was further consolidated by the continued emphasis government laid on its own foundation in a Christian ethics. Though divorce decisions were transferred from ecclesiastical to secular jurisdiction in 1857, the Act 'combined a new "moral economy" of sexual regulation, while largely maintaining the earlier moral and ideological configurations which had been developed under an ecclesiastical tradition'.[49] In short, the construction of a civil code in no sense implied the abandonment of Christian imperatives, merely their further absorption into the cultural and political mainstream.

For feminists, the recognition that it was possible for men to speak publicly of sex – in parliament, in medical texts, in the pulpit, as well as in less formal settings – and thus to define it, strengthened their determination to use all the forces at their disposal to challenge the disparity of power that the legal fiction of public and private served to bolster.

To some extent, and perhaps even more than in other areas of protest, they underestimated the strength of the opposition they faced. Their ability to yoke feminist interpretation to the Christian tradition in redefining an acceptable and equitable moral standard spelled somewhat a dilution of their principles; what had begun, in the heady days of the LNA and at the start of the social purity movement as a direct questioning of male-imposed inequity was recaptured and co-opted back into male-dominated conservatism. The changing membership patterns of the social purity organizations demonstrate the rapid loss of feminist supremacy in the sexual arena exactly at the point when legislative activity began to address these questions with vigour. Feminists quickly joined – and as quickly abandoned – the National Vigilance Association as its politics became more fully articulated. It is significant that even the Moral Reform Union, which Sheila Jeffreys has called the 'most overtly and determinedly feminist wing of the social purity movement'[50] and which boasted Elizabeth Blackwell, Helen Taylor and Henrietta Müller amongst its earliest members, had a mixed sex membership rather than, as earlier campaign organizations had favoured, a male figure-head but a female decision-making rank-and-file.

In 1888, *The Dawn* – another of the periodicals which Josephine Butler had set up – issued 'A Warning' to its readers. *The Dawn* was the organ of the British, Continental and General Federation for the Abolition of State Regulation of Vice. It cautioned its members against another of the social purity organizations of the time, the Social Purity League, whose policies it regarded as short-sighted and inhuman. Its programme, warned Butler, 'is chiefly a systematized crusade against houses of ill-fame, and for driving women off the streets; an illogical combination ... and withal a dangerous one, to say nothing of its unkindness to the most homeless and weakest of sinners. For, the houses prosecuted and closed, consequently the women living in them are turned out, to go *where?*[51]

Butler had worked too long on the streets of London and Liverpool not to appreciate the circular link between poverty and prostitution. Her highly moralistic view was thus tempered by a strong and practical social consciousness, a characteristic which, in general, set feminist campaigners apart from many others in the social purity arena.

In essence, this was an area so critical and so sensitive that the barriers to progress were far more heavily guarded. Women activists were subjected to attack whatever their position. In 1895, Canon Samuel Barnett personally withdrew an invitation that Lady Emilia Dilke had accepted to lecture at East London's Toynbee Hall. The correspondence which ensued in the wake of his withdrawal speaks volumes for the backlash of conservatism which feminist questioning had, in part, invoked. Challenged by Alice Westlake about his decision, Barnett was obdurate. 'I know nothing of her or her work but I cannot admit the wife of Sir C Dilke to a place for which I am responsible to the public.'[52]

Lady Dilke had married her second husband Charles in the wake of a divorce scandal in which he was cited and which irreparably damaged his political ascendancy. Adding insult to injury – and as a textbook instance of shame-ridden silence – Barnett was anxious that his rejected lecturer offer 'illness [as] a pretext, not for postponing, but for abandoning her engagement'.[53] For a man of Christian principles, this resort to untruth was hardly a noble gesture.

Unfortunately, there were also some painful occasions on which similar incidents scarred the normally supportive enclaves of feminist action. Lady Dilke seemed especially vulnerable. Writing to a male acquaintance, Millicent Garrett Fawcett had no hesitation in asserting that 'many ladies feel very strongly against associating their names with that of Lady Dilke'.[54]

Fawcett had made known her concerns over propriety earlier in the period when she had urged the pregnant but only latterly wedded Elizabeth Wolstenholme Elmy to resign the secretaryship of the Married Women's Property Committee for having offended Victorian sensibilities with her 'marriage and what took place previous to it'.[55] Elmy, despite the moral effrontery which Fawcett experienced, none the less retained her position within the movement as did Emelia Dilke, a comment as much on the resilience of the movement as on their own fortitude.

The parallel development at this time of a professionalized medical body amongst whose number was a fast-growing fraternity of gynaecologists further complicated the debates. Much of the new expertise lent weight to justifications of the double standard, finding scientific rationales to the determination of sex differentials in behavioural and psychological contexts. The women's movement rapidly developed a hostility to the new authority claimed by medical practitioners; when the implementation of the Acts in British India raised protests in the 1890s Elizabeth Wolstenholme Elmy – who had a long history of anti-regulation activism – was clear as to whose impetus lay behind their enactment there. 'That the desire and determination of the medical priestcraft is to restore the Acts in their most degrading and brutalizing form . . . no-one . . . can for one moment doubt.'[56] And one modern historian has roundly asserted that doctors were more than 'merely passive in their anti-feminism: their conduct and attitude actively reinforced the male assault on movements for women's emancipation'.[57]

The medical role in the creation of a new, or at least more closely defined, sexual standard dividing men and women, and the manner in which that role concretely translated into practical political action, need to be seen in the context of women's attempts to break the monopoly of male medical practice. For the early women doctors – licensed during the furore over the regulation of prostitution in the 1870s – the path was a thorny one. Despite her record of strong feminist activity, in this instance the recently qualified Elizabeth Garrett decided to side rather with her profession than with feminist interests, not only sanctioning the existence and necessity of the Contagious Diseases Acts but lending her name to those desirous of their extension into the civilian population. Much of her justification rested on the question of professionalism. 'This is strictly a professional question, upon which the opinion of trustworthy medical witnesses ought to be accepted as final. It is enough that unprofessional persons know what that opinion is.'[58]

Doctors cognizant of the new social and intellectual standing of their work saw social and sexual proscription as appropriate areas of political intervention and as a means of asserting their new professional and political status. The medical lobby supporting the introduction and extension of regulation was a powerful one[59] which rapidly crossed the boundary of medical necessity and entered that of moral stricture. Ironically, the moral element made it all the more tempting for female doctors to promote regulation. Women's access to medical education and licensing had, as Susan Kingsley Kent points out, assumed the characteristics of a moral crusade.[60] There was a certain bitter symmetry to their adoption of this less salubrious but morally-presented stand.

The rise of gynaecology as a fashionable and also a lucrative sub-speciality within medicine had an interesting pathology of its own. The vigorous interest which medical practitioners displayed in female sexuality and in the definition of sex roles was a new and unmapped terrain. Just as the politics of empire sought to understand and thus govern unknown and exotic lands, so the politics of medicine sought to control the potentially explosive area of sexuality, and particularly of female sexuality. The colonization of the body, the colonization of potential sources of unrest, the colonization of foreigners in their own lands was a metaphor for and a mark of triumph, of domination, of stability. Ironically, it was not only feminists who saw the dangers inherent in sexuality.

Sexual politics represent the bedrock of that enmeshing of the political and the private that came more and more to characterize and distinguish women's politics and views in this period. It was not possible, in the wake of the agitation over prostitution in the 1870s, to divorce sexuality from other political and public demands. The state itself had tripped on the contradictions of its own ideology and given feminists the connecting factor that made sense of their overall views. The paradigmatic centrality of prostitution as the site of the economic, social, political and sexual powerlessness of women enabled the parallels with the disabilities of 'respectable' women to be drawn with powerful efficacy. Attempts at controlling the dark continent of sexuality and morality, and thus of women, lent far more credence and far more edge, in the final analysis, to feminist understanding than it did to the successful imposition or maintenance of the dominant ideology.

6

Breaking the Male Monopoly: Politics, Law and Feminism

Under exclusively man-made laws women have been reduced to the most abject condition of legal slavery in which it is possible for human beings to be held. In property, in work, in person, in the affection which they bore for their children, in reputation, in their claims to right themselves before the law when wronged, in every respect that can possibly be thought of, a course of unchecked man-making of the laws reduced women to the most enslaved and the most helpless position in which it is conceivable for human beings to be placed, under the arbitrary domination of another's will, and dependent for decent treatment exclusively on the goodness of heart of the individual master.[1]

Speaking as the last decade of the nineteenth century began, activist Florence Fenwick Miller passionately argued that without legal changes to the status of women, their cause could make little realistic headway in freeing women from the bonds legitimized by law-makers and judiciary alike.

Throughout the second half of the century, issues of legal inequity remained a strong concern within feminism, whether focused on formal recognition of women's status as responsible adults or in more diffused dissatisfactions with the substantiating of the double standard in Britain's laws.

In the ensuing historical debate over nineteenth-century feminism, a commonly critical theme has been the limitations and the unimaginativeness that a concentration on formal legal issues displays, its straitening of the movement into narrowly class-defined parameters and its incapacity to see the failings of a reliance on abstract notions of equal justice.

Certainly, legal issues were, for the feminist movement, chronologically primary. The injustices which re-activated organizational efforts in the late 1850s centred on attempts to challenge the doctrine of coverture and establish a separate legal identity for married women apart from their husbands. In the years prior to the debates over sexuality which surfaced vocally only in the 1870s, legal concerns were clearly regarded as critical. Alongside attempts to win for married women rights over property they brought into their marriage, and to secure more equitable grounds for the dissolution of marriage, feminists also had recourse to the English courts in matters pertaining to other campaigns. Indeed, throughout this period, definition and the admission of contradiction were constantly forced upon lawyers and law-makers by women cognizant of the law's failures in justice and in consistency.

In facing the multitude of legal barriers which prevented them from achieving their aspirations, women were simultaneously challenging two of the most powerful and entrenched decision-making bodies of the establishment. When Frances Power Cobbe remarked in 1881 that 'men give us most rarely that which we really want, not favour but – Justice', there is no question about whom she is thus identifying.[2]

The legal and judicial battles in which women campaigners became so deeply embroiled signify more, however, than a simple belief in the efficacy of legal changes. There is no doubt that, at one level, feminists were prepared to channel their energies into fighting the strength of coverture, that legal device which subsumed women under the spousal authority and identity of their husbands.[3] In this respect, their campaigns were practical, pragmatic and narrow in focus. And yet, at the same time, the critique that women offered of these manifestations of the body politic touched on far deeper beliefs. The legal claims which they enjoined demonstrated, individually and collectively, their understanding that laws were neither arbitrary nor neutral in foundation or in application.

When Harriet Taylor and John Stuart Mill pointed out that 'women, whenever tried, are tried by male judges and a male jury', the resonance of their statement was far-reaching.[4] The claims made by English law to be both fair and representative (evidenced by national pride in the very concept of a 'common' law) were under attack, and though not for the first time, the growing acceptance of an ever broader fourth estate meant that women were able to exploit the extended contradictions thus developing.

At the simplest level, women were anxious to fight those concrete barriers, enshrined in the legal tradition of precedent, that disallowed them a public persona, but their intent and the articulation of grievances did not stop there. Their faith lay not in forcing, or even enforcing, equitable statutory provision but in combining that necessary symbol of conceded political identity with a redefinition of politics. Their pursuit of legislation designed to secure the property rights of married women or the representation of women in national and local government should not obscure our appreciation of their attack on the ideology informing the legal conditions that disabled them. As Sachs and Wilson have demonstrated, English common law provided 'the main intellectual justification for the avowed and formal subordination of women'.[5]

The Victorian era can be characterized in part by the tensions that arose between an acknowledged need for widespread political and social reform and a bewilderment, if not a reluctance, on the part of successive governments over their precise role in initiating, pursuing and overseeing that reform. In consequence, many of the reforms of this period failed outright or were limited either by the inability of politicians to predict the full range of their implications, or by government's failure to pursue thoroughly projects approved by Parliament. The legal reforms of the period, though attracting less retrospective attention than some other more controversial areas, display this ideological bewilderment as fully as chapters of social and political reform. Over the centuries, and as a response to the inadequacies of the common law to represent even the desires of the wealthy, a parallel law of equity challenging the decisions in common law judgments had grown up. In the following pages we shall explore one specific example of this dual legal system, tracing the contest over married women's property rights in this period.

Every aspect of women's lives was in some way regulated by legislation in the creation of which they had had no part: the lack of educational establishments open to them, the work they might undertake, the property they might own, their marital choices – in short, their capacity to exercise adult choices in all and any walks of life. The class specificity on which they seized – and for which latter-day critics have castigated them – only served to strengthen their attack; the liberal individualism which the state espoused (though practised rather less often) was limited in its application, not merely in class but critically in gender terms. In exposing the second tier of contradiction that this demonstrated – not just distinguishing rights by sex but dividing classes too – women tactically strengthened their position. Whilst a concentration on formal issues thus necessarily involved a tussle with mainstream middle-class concerns, it was also a subtle way of establishing and holding onto a direct exposé of the coherence of law, politics and public policy, a rejection of any belief in neutral justice.[6]

Women's recourse to the legal structures of their society for remedy can thus be read in a number of ways. Over and over again, feminists pointed to the inadequacies and unfairnesses of laws promulgated and interpreted by an all-male establishment. They none the less pursued precisely those areas whose failed claims to neutrality so irked them. Was it a faith in the underlying stability of those institutions or a direct challenge to their spurious universalism that spurred feminist attention to them? Few, if any, nineteenth-century feminists declared a belief in the wholesale abandonment of the institutional structures of their society. They did, however, call clearly for their fundamental redefinition. Both in classifying their contradictions and in seeking a feminization of the state and its agencies, women were pursuing a thorough regrounding of the political and legal process, and importantly, holding on to an appreciation of the inextricable links between the two. Albie Sachs and Joan Hoff Wilson have reiterated the important point that it was Parliament and not the judiciary who removed the formal barrier to women's participation in the public sphere.[7] It is interesting to note their identification of the 1919 Sex Disqualification Removal Act as the pivot of that reforming process; that Act was passed by a Parliament which, far more than its nineteenth-century predecessors, included a substantial number of lawyers amongst its members, a trend which had become more and more visible in politics in the early years of the twentieth century.[8] The 1919 Act, was, moreover, the first which granted women the right to practise law. In the nineteenth century, while other interests still dominated Parliament and the connections between law and politics were perhaps less demonstrable, or at least quantifiable, feminists did not doubt – and had no hesitation in articulating – that these two wings of the state were neither separable nor at odds in their attitude to feminist criticism. Women's firm belief in the gains of feminizing political values, as opposed to masculinizing women to fit them for public office, is critically important in understanding not only their critique of formal politico-legal inequity, but in demonstrating the tactical use which governed their attitude to separate sphere ideology.

These were, in many ways, the bread-and-butter issues of the movement, and if they lack the mystique and 'thrill' which sensationalism lent to the sexual and moral crusades of feminists, they offer us none the less a clear sense of the range and sophistication of the feminist challenge.

The legal areas in which feminists chose to highlight that challenge were varied, though necessarily related. In many instances, their legal work spilled over into other areas of campaigning, just as the memberships of the various committees and societies devoted to feminist politics resembled one another so closely. In essence, the various different legal strategies formed a seamless web of campaigning which constantly drew together the various claims voiced by activists. The central connecting theme was, as it was also in the debates around sexuality, marriage. Marital status, as so many writers have recognized, was the defining feature which shaped the lives of women, willy-nilly, from cradle to grave. Its social and sexual character was amplified by its legal ramifications: law after law, and governmental Act after governmental Act structured women's lives in accordance with their marital identity. As Rachel Harrison and Frank Mort comment, 'legislation governing marriage and divorce and the sexual division of property, stands in a[n] . . . immediate relation to the wider economic, politico-legal and ideological developments of the period.'[9]

The first major campaign of the organized feminist activity of the period was that relating to the laws of married women's property, begun at a time when new laws relating to divorce were being enunciated by Parliament in the late 1850s.[10] In addition to the status of married women, which was the backbone shaping the married women's property campaign, and some – albeit limited – expressions of dissatisfaction with inequities in the divorce laws, it was also in this period that child custody, marital assault and marriage to a deceased wife's sister received both governmental and feminist attention. Thus in a myriad of ways, marriage retained the strength of its hold over the defining of woman's place in Victorian England.

The other principal legal area in which feminists were heavily active was in claiming their rights to exercise the franchise, both at national and at local level. Here too, the marriage question was to be of considerable – and sometimes disagreeable – significance as a determinant of qualifications to exercise political choice. Campaigns to secure women's voting power in both municipal and national elections often foundered on disagreements over the acceptability – politically, ethically and pragmatically – of distinguishing the rights of single and of married women. It was in this area, perhaps more than in any other, that contention divided the movement, resulting in hostility and unhappiness. It was also the formal area in which overall success was slowest to come; although single women won the right to vote in municipal contests in 1869, few further gains in governmental access were captured before the end of the century. Women's presence on local government bodies, which grew substantially in the years following the reform, continued to disrupt the political harmony of single-sex bodies, and women seeking office in the more prominent municipal bodies sometimes found themselves involved in courtroom wrangles over the precise definitional boundaries of the rights they thus sought to exercise.

Thus whilst the early concentration on seizing the limited prizes offered by formal legal equality – whether within a governmental or a judicial context – may superficially appear a cautious and moderate course of action, we need to remember both that the weight of formal oppression was burdensome and, indeed, growing at this time, and that the individual victories which women were able to wrest from these institutions had enormous symbolic value as proofs of their successful challenge to the contradictory conservatism of venerated bodies. One modern historical interpretation even suggests that so oppressive was the array of legal handicaps women faced in the nineteenth century that, if anything, they 'served as a catalyst to a unified movement of resistance'.[11] Even the reforms instituted by the Judicature Act of 1873, whilst accepting the need to conciliate the clashes between common law and equity, did little to remedy the legitimation of women's inferior status.

The capacity of feminists to retain an appreciation of the connections between such mainstream campaigns on the one hand, and other areas in which concern engendered active efforts, is a striking illustration of the holistic character of nineteenth-century feminist activity. The same women who pursued the fate of reforming legislation or traipsed through the courtrooms in quest of justice also undertook the work of campaigning on education and employment, and on sexuality, and maintained the close links between activists up and down the country. The level of their support for different campaigns necessarily varied but, as we have seen elsewhere, for most the logic was a simple one. Women no more sank the full quotient of their trust in the potential of formal legal equality than they did in equal educational access or in the destruction of a double moral standard; the separate components of their activity cohered in a unified perspective. Catherine Winkworth, for example, was thus to be found attending women's franchise meetings and congresses of women workers alongside her committee work in women's education in Bristol and the west of England. Many, if not most, of the members of the Kensington Society were also supporters of the suffrage campaign, lending their name and often contributing financially to the various organizations fighting the issue. Many gave support, too, to the burgeoning efforts of women's local government activists as the century wore on.

Assessing the impressive career of Cheltenham Ladies' College headmistress, Dorothea Beale, Janet Courtney remarked that 'she was too much of her period not to be convinced of her right to vote, but she was so wrapped up in her school that she concerned herself little with current politics'.[12] Andrew Rosen makes a similar point about Emily Davies.[13] These were women whose range of activities were legion but who recognized that their potential could be more productive if more narrowly channelled. It was not that they turned their back on such activities or underwent a drastic change of heart. It was more that with the successful integration of a feminist perspective that saw a connective web linking a host of critical issues, their energies became increasingly focused. Many were like Davies and Beale, choosing an area in which to concentrate their overall beliefs to maximum effect, but in no sense rejecting the other and connected areas. Indeed, the implication is rather that the formal legal rights were so fundamental and obvious a step in the struggles of women, so much a touchstone, that there was no need to question the necessity of campaigns such as the suffrage.

Olive Banks asserts that almost all the feminist activists in her sample had links to the suffrage movement, whatever the other areas on which they chose to concentrate.[14] In the biographical data sample pertinent to this study, 52 per cent of the women had active ties to suffrage compared with a known 24 per cent in local government and 22 per cent in married women's property campaigns. In some respects the figures are misleading because, though suffrage activism spanned the entire period under consideration, committees seeking changes to the laws on married women's property were disbanded after 1882, whilst local government activity was really only just blossoming organizationally at that time. Thus it may be that what the consistency of suffrage activity in fact represents is more an expression of the continuum sustaining the feminist perspective than the cherished nub of the movement.

The dual existence of campaigns aimed severally at the formal symbols of male power, and simultaneously at the 'fine tuning', suggests that feminists in this period retained reservations about how effective a panacea the winning of legal and political rights of representation would, in fact, be, choosing rather to see them as necessary but by no means sufficient conditions of liberation.

The symbolic, rather than the specific, invocation of the rule of law, which historians and legal theorists alike have seen as a characteristic locus of power in modern capitalist states, thus led its challengers to an appreciation of how they, too, might yoke such symbolic value to their defiance.[15] It is interesting to contrast both the methods of protest employed and the state response paralleling them. Nineteenth-century feminists, whilst increasingly outspoken about their dissatisfactions, chose the verbal arena as their principal and strongest weapon. When, in the early twentieth century, the suffragette grouping (albeit always a minority within the wider feminist community) employed physical battle tactics ranging from passive resistance to more aggressive attacks on property, the responses from the state rapidly matched those changes. Redolent with symbolism as such actions were, they also moved the focus from debate – however abusive – to a literally more corporeal form. Thus whilst for the feminists of the nineteenth century, law impinged on them in formal and often indirect ways, their successors were determined to unmask the reality of physical force that they felt lay behind the complex vocabulary.

Even in the nineteenth century, however, legal and parliamentary challenges took on meanings that extended well beyond the gaining of voting or property rights *per se*. In many instances, women's recourse to the courts was a practice milked principally for its rhetorical potential to illuminate contradiction, hypocrisy and confusion. The celebrated paper-chase initiated by Sophia Jex-Blake and her associates in 1873 when the University of Edinburgh withdrew its agreements to qualify women for medical practice, is one such example. The Edinburgh case careered from court to court and though the women finally lost their case on appeal, the details of the judgment demonstrate well the slippage between legal claims of impartiality and the interpretative overlay of custom. The margin of judgment which awarded the university the right to exclude the women students was a narrow one (seven to five) and reached only after additional judges had been brought in to augment the original eight, whose opinion had been divided four:four. That the women lost their case is not surprising, nor were the arguments employed in the decision, which focused primarily on interpreting the parameters of the existing constitution of the university, and ignored the real and immediate questions raised by the women's presence.[16] In focusing attention on so many formal and substantive issues simultaneously, women were able implicitly to highlight the role of law in their subjugation and to demonstrate the contradictions which lay at the heart of that subjugation. Here was a case which raised, not only the educational disadvantages which continued to dog women, but their legitimation through a corresponding monopoly in the legal world. Women were not only excluded from that male monopoly but their potential redress also lay with men.

It is not without significance that in these spheres, as in others, women were cautious about the assistance of men in the organization of their politics. Given the membership and make-up of institutions such as Parliament, it was clear that change would be likely to involve the need to win over supporters who could lay claim to a voice in such institutions; the laying of bills before Parliament relied upon the sympathies of concerned men, and feminists framed much of their work around accommodating this tactical reality without too far compromising their own newly-found agency.

At an organizational level, women welcomed and encouraged the help of male sympathizers, and specifically of parliamentarians. Although John Stuart Mill has been lauded as the central male figure of the women's cause in the House of Commons, other men were also as deeply involved. The legal expertise of the Davenport Hill men was brought to bear upon the issue of married women's property. The radical Richard Pankhurst, the liberal Russell Gurney (after some initial hesitation: see below) and even the Conservative Faithfull Begg regularly reminded their fellow politicians of feminist claims. And yet, importantly, few of the women's organizations devoted to parliamentary and judicial lobbying ceded men any substantial decision-making powers. As we have seen elsewhere, their use as figure-heads was seldom contested, nor their potential to influence legislative decisions. Within the committees and societies of the movement, however, women remained firmly in control. In the National Union of Women's Suffrage Societies, an all-women executive considered the advice of parliamentary counsellors, and though men could take out rank-and-file membership in the organization, leadership was provided by the women. On the Council of the Women's Franchise League in the late 1880s, women outnumbered men two to one; of the sixteen men serving on the council, seven were husbands of women members.

This tactical but limited inclusion of aid that only men could provide displays the pragmatic concerns and strategies of the movement in its quest for solid achievement and, though perhaps more implicitly than openly, the keen sense women had of the importance of self-determined action. The tentacles of the movement were demonstrably and needfully so far-reaching that tactical considerations were in no sense a luxury but a sometimes compromising means of securing progress and movement. Questions such as the timing of campaigns, priorities in negotiation, means of accomplishment, were constantly and consciously explored in the legal and judicial area with interesting results.

Women fighting for the extension of the franchise had at the outset, according to early twentieth-century feminist S. J. Tanner, anticipated a swift and successful campaign.[17] Ironically, this proved to be one of the toughest, most entrenched and most divisive struggles fought, not least because the claims of working men were construed as competing directly with those of wealthier, propertied women. The protracted length of this battle is also one of the reasons why it for so long dominated the historiography of feminism. Inevitably another factor explaining its supposed primacy was the privileged position later historians accorded to constitutional matters.

For the feminists of the 1860s, however, one tactic actually involved reducing the issue from such elevated (and thus protected) heights to one merely of consistent legal interpretation, in short, attempting a 'back-door' entrance to representation for a limited group of women. The Manchester National Society for Women's Suffrage found no 'constitutional restraint of the political functions of women' to exist.[18] They duly chose, in 1867 and 1868, rather to seek the implementation of precise voter registration than to petition Westminster for legislative action. Their encouragement to qualified women to register to vote, in accordance with regulations empowered by the parliamentary reforms of 1867, led finally to a series of court cases which came in time to be dubbed the 'persons' cases. In deflecting attention away from Parliament itself to the decisions of barristers responsible for supervising electoral registration, women drew concrete parallels between political and legal functions which they saw as dually responsible for their condition. In 1868, National Society for Women's Suffrage committees in Manchester, London, Bristol and Birmingham co-ordinated a strategy of claiming registration rights for women ratepayers and by the autumn of that year more than twenty overseeing barristers had capitulated to their demands. The rejection of the claim in Manchester led the issue into the courts where a rash of conflicting judgments caused legal interpreters some considerable confusion. Though the recourse to an appeal in the Court of Common Pleas did not satisfy the high hopes of this well co-ordinated strategy, *Chorlton* v. *Lings* at least publicized the linguistic injustice of assuming the terms 'man' and 'person' to be coterminous, demonstrating the judicial ramifications of governmental action. Women thus employed tactics of direct legal involvement to make a point about the body politic.

The adoption of particular strategies was an important consideration, and perhaps most obviously so in this area where women's observable disabilities were so severe. Feminists were faced with the stark choice between working within existing frameworks or boycotting them. They chose largely to attempt change from within, structuring their plans and priorities accordingly, seizing advantages and exploiting constitutional and judicial channels wherever possible. It led, inevitably, to some curious decisions, some of which are unpalatable to modern tastes. Frances Power Cobbe's resentment of the 'rabble of illiterates' admitted to the franchise in preference to 'the mothers and daughters and sisters of those who already exercise it' does not sit well with twentieth-century libertarianism to be sure, but it was a tactic of considerable force in a society so wedded to the external trappings of class respectability.[19] The anxieties of many suffrage workers – John Stuart Mill among them – over the simultaneity of high profile sexual campaigning against the Contagious Diseases Acts (see chapter 5) and attempts to establish the basis of women's suffrage display a similar interplay of tactics and ideology. When the Women's Emancipation Union spoke, in the 1890s, of moving 'steadily along the line of least resistance to the destined goal' their tactics displayed a combination of pragmatism and optimism.[20]

The specific campaigns in which feminist involvement highlighted the degree and extent of female disability in political and judicial areas met with varying degrees of success. Reform from within was piecemeal and often grudging, but the symbolic importance of formal victory should none the less not be underestimated. In a sense, moreover, failure – like the fact of oppression – was not infrequently a catalyst to unity or action in related areas; we cannot separate out a plethora of single-issue campaigns and hope to understand a feminist coherence. Victory and failure were linked in a curious symbiosis, feeding one another and constantly pointing to the connections between elements of the feminist struggle.

At the heart of the various campaign issues, and central in some way to them all, was the question of women's status upon marriage. In addition to raising questions about the nature of the marriage contract itself, it was a central theme in debates about both property and political rights, and about women's role in society. Julia Brophy and Carol Smart have even declared that 'it is possible to argue that the primary focus of the earliest women's movement in the nineteenth century was law.'[21] In similar vein, Steven Spitzer has argued with some force that we must, in understanding the nature of law, acknowledge 'the essential embeddedness of the legal order in everyday life'.[22] Legislation, whether wholly effective or not, thus articulates a specific set of social relations which centrally affected these women's lives; their struggles, whether successful or not, equally demonstrate their challenge to the construction of a social formation which subordinated their interests to those of men.

Marriage was central to all women's lives, and as such was one of the most important and far-reaching sites of the feminist battle. As we have seen in chapter 3, the institution of marriage itself was never, in this period, rejected wholesale by women claiming a feminist commitment, a large proportion of whom succeeded in combining fruitful marriages and political action.[23] Nonetheless, they still raised – both personally and in more general ways – the legal and contractual problems wedlock posed for women. Their individual efforts to alter their own marriage contracts or retain their pre-marital identity through retaining their names suggests not only their resistance to the forms of authority posed by marriage but a deeper challenge to the idea that somehow contract was synonymous with consent.[24] In the alterations they made to standard legal practice in this way, they were rejecting the ultimate authority of a partisan law and specifying its non-neutrality.

At one level, prevailing judicial authority took a stern view of the range of contractual obligations involved in marriage but, as Mary Shanley has pointed out, in practice 'sexual relationships and the legitimacy of a man's offspring were the basic considerations of the marriage contract', a fact which governed the determination of the success or the dissolution of marital ties.[25] That assumption placed the burden of obligation far more squarely on wifely behaviour than on any other element of the union. It invoked the supremacy of motherhood, the necessity of fidelity and, silently, the dangers inherent in the 'feminine'. In stirring that spectre, it shifted the legal form subtly from consent to coercion. The doctrine of coverture, which deemed a married woman the secondary part of the fictive unity of husband and wife, had far-reaching consequences and implications, preventing women not only from maintaining a legal identity of their own but forcing upon them an economic dependence which made mockery of the very notion of consent. Though coverture had its roots in a social order based on land-holding, property issues remained paramount under capitalism. Coverture invoked a relationship of protector and protected (baron and feme) which, in practice, allowed for the protection not of the woman but of male rights to property. As Norma Basch has pointed out, 'the distribution of property was inextricably connected to the allocation of power.'[26] Women's lack of property and of rights to property as well as their *becoming* property thus defined and exacerbated their powerlessness. (See chapter 8 for a further discussion of the relationship between contract and power.)

In consequence, feminist activity did not seek to limit itself to a single arena, whether marital disputes, property rights or any other. Organizations and individuals alike constantly reiterated their fundamental connectedness. Elizabeth Wolstenholme Elmy – whose own marital history, as we have seen, was a source of some perturbation in the movement – was secretary of the married women's property committee but she attacked, too, the inequity of the divorce law, and of the highly partial granting of child custody, as well as other related issues. Millicent Garrett Fawcett, lecturing to a Bristol audience on 'why women require the franchise', suggested in a flourish of rhetoric that 'the first article of the stock in trade of the female thief must henceforth be a husband. Under the shadow of his authority she may hoodwink justice and commit the foulest crimes with impunity.'[27]

The problems associated with marriage were amongst the first to be systematically contested when new feminist organizations began to emerge in the late 1850s and early 1860s. A decade later, feminist analyses of marriage had incorporated a host of issues raised by it which pursued the public implications of a contract designated private.

The earliest of the organized campaigns – in which steering committees drafted pamphlets and leaflets, lobbied Parliament and arranged public meetings – concentrated primarily on the rights of married women to own and maintain ownership of property. The early days of this campaign coincided with the deliberations of a Royal Commission appointed in the early 1850s to review the laws of matrimony and dissolution; despite their clear dissatisfaction with the provisions of the 1857 Matrimonial Causes Act, feminists none the less still chose to focus principally on property rights at this time.

It should not surprise us that the issue of women's rights to own property after marriage was of considerable concern to feminists of this period. In the first place, it pointed unequivocally to the gendered double standard in lending men an additional economic advantage in a context where property already conferred privilege. Further, it was also an area where enormous and confusing contradiction prevailed between the parallel systems of common law and equity.

At the point at which the early married women's property committees were founded in Manchester and in London, women gave their property as well as their legal identity over to their husbands upon marriage. Under the common law, husbands acquired absolute control over a woman's personal property, including earnings, any leasehold properties she might own (though if still in original possession a wife surviving her husband assumed possession of them once again on his death) and a good deal of control over her real property. Although a husband could neither sell his wife's real estate nor influence its succession, control and income were otherwise his absolutely.

The parallel system of legal equity relied on judicial discretion as a means to mitigate common law disabilities. In the area of married women's property its effects were palpable but limited to that small class of wealthy women whose properties were substantial enough for the introduction of trustees to be financially viable and profitable. This separate estate, however, whilst it protected a woman's property from her husband, entitled her only to maintain possession.[28] Control of the estates in question was vested in the trustees, more often than not lawyers, and exclusively men. Thus, though some leeway could be claimed by wealthier women, the whole system of property and control still rested in male hands and, as feminists pointed out, with no real guarantee on their part of obligation to subordinate women.

When all that a woman possesses in the present and future is handed over unreservedly by the law to her husband, is there the smallest attempt at obtaining security that he on his part *can* fulfil that obligation which is always paraded as the equivalent, namely, the obligation to support her for the rest of her life?[29]

Cobbe's point here was that, as the means of economic security accorded a woman, marriage had grave risks. In addition to abandoning her legal persona and property to her husband, a woman might find herself wedded to a man who found himself unable to fulfil the conditions of her economic dependency. That the divorce courts were not full of women petitioning on grounds of economic abandonment suggests more that such legal recourse was unobtainable than that men were honouring their duty.

The feminist fight for married women's property rights was a pivotal one for the movement, both in terms of shaping the tactics upon which successive campaigns would draw, and of achieving *relative* success in a *reasonably* short period of time, in contrast to comparable claims in the political or the professional arena.

In tactical terms, this was a campaign which drew both on existing political principles and on a gradual reshaping of the symbiotic impact of class and gender upon one another. A number of 'non-feminist' arguments in favour of the measure were used as tools of logic and as a persuasive means of guaranteeing the campaign supporters in Parliament. The first feminist moves to secure more equitable marital property arrangements coincided with a period of more general critical overhaul of the judicial system. With the growing self-consciousness of legal personnel as professionals, and the keenly felt contradictions between common law and equity, many legal reformers were urging the need to overhaul the system and reassess the conflicting judgments emerging out of their dual existence. The earliest efforts of feminists coincided exactly with the matrimonial changes of the 1850s and, indeed, their parallel introduction into Parliament in the session of 1857 was an ill-timed error. As Mary Shanley has pointed out, their simultaneity alerted conservative alarm to this tide of feminist demands.[30] Moreover, the provision in the Matrimonial Causes Act of 1857 for allowing a wife access to her property in cases of separation and desertion diluted the arguments for a thorough review of the whole issue of married women's property rights.[31]

At the same time, the women could argue – as did their political champions – that their demands represented little more than the logical conclusion to those principles of individualism which were so prevalent and powerful a force in British politics in this period. After all, Palmerstonian rhetoric was at this very time proclaiming the sanctity and the glory of British freedoms with considerable flourish. In capturing the essence of contemporary political sentiment in this manner, women campaigners could realistically hope to secure some greater measure of success.

However, this 'mainstreaming' approach to the securing of their ends constituted neither the complete feminist perspective nor the whole intention of these campaigns. Feminists maintained both a sense of the class inequities that paralleled those resting on sex and, more surprisingly, a critical view of the overarching sanctity of property. Women frequently pointed to the connections between men's reverence of property and their treatment of women. Writing in 1885, after the passing of the second of the two Married Women's Property Acts had secured married women some legal standing of their own, Mary Ashton Dilke, a suffrage activist, made the point in a novel way.

The high importance attached by men to property is apparent in the fact that they have shown themselves much quicker and more eager to remedy the injustice of the laws of married women's property, than any other grievance.[32]

The centrality of property she invokes was seen as explicitly oppressive by many feminists. In her analysis of marital assault, Frances Power Cobbe argued the connection between property rights and physical brutality in a cogent and dramatic fashion.[33] The identification by feminists of values imposed upon women led them ever closer to a critique of the political structure, access to which they none the less sought to attain.

It was the same women who argued for the rights of married women to maintain their own property, and who drew the links between their aspirations in this direction and other areas of campaigning, who also argued so vigorously in favour of women's suffrage, local government and the variety of campaigns which feminists opened up. The constant references to the property campaigns in the *Women's Suffrage Journal*, which reported their meetings and subscriptions, and which routinely and critically reviewed the relevant court cases involving married women, displays this connection vividly. The make-up of Married Women's Property Committees, throughout the campaign's approximately twenty-seven-year history from 1855 to 1882, similarly demonstrates this overlap – various of the Ashurst sisters, Clementia Taylor, Lydia Becker – are among the prominent names alongside the supportive husbands of a number of feminists. Though in 1866 Emelie Gurney's husband Russell had shrunk 'from identifying himself with our movement just at the beginning of his parliamentary life', he none the less kept his word that, once secure in his political career, he would venture to express publicly his support.[34] Pamphlets and booklets on married women's property rights issued by the various committees often included speeches from the floor of the House made by sympathetic husbands and friends such as Gurney, Arthur Arnold, Lord Goldsmid or Peter Taylor. In the two years preceding the successful passage of the 1870 Married Women's Property Act, activists issued an incredible 35,000 pamphlets, sent 142 petitions to the House of Commons and a further seventy to the House of Lords, on which they had collectively secured over 100,000 signatures.

These figures attest not merely to the intensity of political activity amongst this determined group of women but to the level of interest they could arouse for their cause, and over a substantial period of time. The passing in 1870 of the first of the two laws addressing this question served, if anything, to strengthen the women's determination to win this early battle. The wholly inadequate nature of the first Act was widely criticized by activists and did little to mollify them. Elizabeth Wolstenholme, long-time secretary of the Manchester Married Women's Property Committee, roundly condemned the act as 'a measure which seems carefully designed to give to women as little security, and to impose upon them as great liabilities, as could be made consistent with an appearance of giving relief'.[35] Wolstenholme's assessment was not an unreasonable one for the measure was half-hearted and inconsistent. In designating only certain categories of property allowable exclusively to a wife, the act was guaranteed to come under fire. Between the time of its passing and the successful conclusion of the campaign in 1882, when the second Act became law, a further four politicians sought an extension of its provisions and faced, in consequence, the gamut of hostile parliamentary tactics from delay to negative voting.

Feminists maintained their complaints, refusing to rest contented with so palpable a compromise, and constantly drawing more closely together the various strands of their campaigns in related areas. In particular, the period between the two Acts saw an escalation in feminist attention to that other area of abuse within marriage, physical violence. The fact of women's economic dependence within wedlock, and its impact on their vulnerability to physical assault, was an important connecting point in the development of an overarching feminist perspective.

The second and final Act of 1882 was received with considerably more cheer than its predecessor and was, undoubtedly, substantially more far-reaching in its principle of entitling married women to a separate legal identity independent of their husbands. Even so, commentators at the time, as well as more modern assessors of the legislation, have acknowledged its failings. In many ways its importance remained more symbolic than actual, as was the case with so many of the judicial and legal victories enjoyed by women in this period. Not only did the promulgation of this Act fail to alter significantly the daily existence of most women, or really affect men's attitudes to feminist claims, but the Acts addressed only a narrow issue. The legislation was concerned only with property itself and not with the mechanism of its acquisition, or with women's lack of access to the expertise that necessarily accompanied success in its management or disposal.[36] Susan Atkins and Brenda Hoggett have pointed out that these Acts 'coincided with the entrenchment of housewife marriage across all sections of society'.[37] As a symbol of women's challenge to total dependency and of women's capacity to win rights through formal channels, the passing of the Acts cannot be underestimated; whether they served in practice to relieve the harshness of individual lives is a separate question.

The issue of marital status and its impact on women spilled over into other areas of legal and judicial concern where the central challenge was not the institution of marriage itself but the political representation of women. In the twin areas of local and national franchise (and civic and political participation), a woman's marital status was to become a difficult and often bitterly divisive strategic tool.

The substantive campaign to achieve women's rights *vis-à-vis* parliamentary elections dates from early in our period, gaining much enthusiasm and hope when, in 1869, the municipal electorate was widened to embrace single women rate-payers. Henceforth, throughout the remaining third of the century, women activists fought both to capture the parliamentary vote and to increase the female presence in local government. More and more women stood for election in School Board and Poor Law Guardian ballots, carving out the rights of women to enjoy the fruits of representation and to participate publicly in the electoral race and in municipal politics thereafter. Their tactics ranged from the more established forms of parliamentary lobbying, public addresses and mass demonstrations up and down the country, to direct courtroom confrontation over judicial interpretation. The rejection of special needs, of what Harriet Taylor and John Stuart Mill dubbed a 'sort of sentimental priesthood' in their 1851 article on the women's franchise,[38] was an important and integral core of the various suffrage campaigns; though women's presence and their perspective certainly altered the substance of political action and debate, they rarely, if ever, claimed advantages on grounds of sex, preferring to invoke the call of equality – symbolically and actually – for the most part.

Both local and national politics received a substantial degree of feminist attention throughout this time, and often from the same women, active in other areas as well, as we have seen. Women such as Helen Taylor, Henrietta Müller, the McLaren women, Elizabeth Garrett and Elizabeth Wolstenholme all involved themselves prominently in suffrage and in local government work, often standing for election and tackling the arduous and unremunerated committee work of local administration in a hostile and unrelenting environment, and risking simultaneously their social standing. Arthur Munby was surprised to find his sensibilities unoffended by public declaration of feminist principles by his radical women friends.

I went, at 5 [o'clock], to a meeting of the Women's Suffrage Society at the Hanover Square Rooms. The large room was full: the audience was chiefly well drest women, old and young, whose carriages filled the square outside; but on the platform were many men . . . in the chair was my friend Mrs Taylor [Clementia

Taylor] herself. I had thought it would seem strange, but it seemed quite natural, to see that gentle earnest ladylike woman acting as chairman of a public meeting, and to see other ladies standing up on the platform and making speeches. There was nothing bold or 'unfeminine' in their words or manner.[39]

Such reservations aside, the presence of women in various local government positions, and the consistency of their clamour for the national franchise, served to reshape in critical ways the behaviour and practice of late nineteenth-century politics. Although the intrusion of party politics worked on occasion to the detriment of a feminist perspective, women's presence in these areas of 'hard' politics was a declaration of major change.[40]

These two areas of campaigning were intimately linked, not only as the most governmentally centred of all feminist challenges, but also in sharing a similar galaxy of personnel. Though they operated independently of one another for the pragmatic purposes of achievement, their aims and aspirations clearly converged. Though experience in local government was never explicitly enunciated as a nursery in which to train women for national political office, the clear parallels between local and parliamentary representation and participation were perhaps too obvious to be drawn.

Both concerns commanded a substantial and widespread presence throughout the land; where other campaigns had had a mere handful of recognizable centres of activity in their early years – centring initially on the well-to-do urban areas of London, Manchester and Bristol – these two were able rapidly to extend their force far wider. By the end of the century, the umbrella National Union of Women's Suffrage Societies embraced as many as seventeen local organizations in rural as well as in urban areas and women were competing successfully for positions on School Boards and as Poor Law Guardians. Moreover, as Patricia Hollis found, women electors in local elections took their franchise as, if not more, seriously than male electors. In areas where the women's movement had a strong presence, women's voting rates often outstripped those of men.[41]

The presence and impact of women in and on local government closely mirrored the general tenor of feminist action and philosophy current at this time, suggesting strongly the growing and unified coherence of that perspective. At one level, the work women undertook as municipal officials – concerned principally with education and the relief of poverty – echoed their participation in a host of philanthropic organizations throughout the nineteenth century. There was, too, some inevitable tendency to underscore the peculiarly appropriate nature of the tasks. London activist Margaret Nevinson thought that 'the work of Guardians is so essentially housekeeping on a large scale, that we who have spent years working at matters of the house, cooking, cleaning, babies, sick folk, clothing and linen are manifestly better fitted for such things than men.'[42]

In a sense Nevinson was correct, although few of the early women Guardians (or those in other municipal posts) had directly undertaken the tasks she describes, being rather employers of domestic labour. None the less, as administrators of households their experience was undeniable. It was a clever tactic too; the seeming acknowledgement of a sexual essentialism was also an implicit criticism of male domination. Men not only submitted women to their power but did so in areas where they should have conceded 'rightful' authority. It was a subtle statement, a condemnation of greed, of men's own failure to practise the dicta of their own ideological construct.

In practice, it led often not to a substantiation of traditional femininity as such but to a successful humanitarian restatement of aims. Working in this context, women activists could implement progressive changes unhampered by party belief. Helen Taylor and Honnor Morten were outspoken in their opposition to corporal punishment in schools, Eva Müller instituted the practice of calling children by their name and not by a number. These changes heralded what Patricia Hollis has called a new and 'strikingly child-centred' approach which served the needs both of pupils and staff.[43] Care replaced cash in their assessments of educational benefit. In similar vein, Florence Davenport Hill was, according to Hollis, one of the leading proponents of those who wished to substitute the word 'person' for the commonly used 'pauper' in official documents.[44]

This concrete and determined process of humanization which so characterized the feminist input at the level of local government in no sense compromised the capacity or the willingness of feminists to face and challenge the hostility they continued to meet. Not only in these more subtle ways did women seek to introduce the principles of their politics into the mainstream, but they were fully prepared, too, to do battle in enemy territory. The use of judicial means to challenge political inequity spilled over into the political arena proper; alongside the public lobbying, activists in both local and national campaigns faced the courtroom.

In the wake of the Parliamentary Reform Act of 1867, which had enfranchised a larger proportion of British citizenry than ever before – though still limited by property assessments – suffrage activists decided to test the judicial waters. A massive campaign, begun in and centred around the Manchester area, encouraged women qualified other than by sex to seek voter registration. A series of judgments, culminating in the 1870 *Chorlton* v. *Lings* decision in which the exclusion of women was finally upheld, debated the issue in large and small towns where women had come forward as prospective voters on the basis of their household or property qualification. In some few cases, the barristers responsible for revising the registers after the 1867 Act had not queried the women's rights; thus Lily Maxwell in Manchester and Lady Scaris-brick and twenty-seven of her women tenant farmers in south-west Lancashire had cast their anomalous votes in the general election of 1868 before *Chorlton* v. *Lings* once more shut the door on them.

Some twenty years later, it was the turn of the municipal activists to face judicial opposition to their presence. *Beresford Hope* v. *Sandhurst* reached the Appeal Court in May 1889, where the hopes of the women were dashed. Lady Sandhurst was unseated from her newly-won place on the London County Council, where she had enjoyed a resounding electoral victory over her male opponent, Beresford Hope. The judges concluded that being a woman meant automatic disqualification from the necessary definition of a 'fit person'.[45] Sandhurst's loss was a serious blow for the movement and Jane Cobden, who had been elected at the same time, held on to her seat only because her opponent desisted from legal action. Along with Emma Cons, who had been elected an Alder-man, she now found herself in a strikingly anomalous position. The Sandhurst case had prejudiced women running for office again but legal technicalities prevented Cobden and Cons from summary dismissal. The law declared that if no challenge to an invalid election was laid within a year, validity would ensue for the remainder of the term. The feminist movement and sympathetic legal advisers counselled remaining nominally on the council but declining participation in committee work until the year was up. Though in practice the women did involve themselves substantially in council work during their first year in office, it was only thereafter that they publicly re-emerged as active committee workers. Immediately, a councillor opposed to their presence filed writs. *De Souza* v. *Cobden* dragged on, reaching the Court of Appeal in 1891 and resulting in a decision which, whilst damaging to women's participa-tion in the political arena, demonstrated the partiality of the law to the full. The judges in the case found Cobden's membership of the council valid but her participation in that council invalid and subject to financial penalty or imprisonment. The situation was not a good one but feminists could turn grim tidings to advantage in revealing not merely injustice but judicial confusion in matters of substantial importance.

The confusion they uncovered was, of course, and as they frequently declared, an outcrop of the double standard which operated not just in the areas of morality and family but at every point in people's lives. In a pamphlet released in 1889, Caroline Ashurst Biggs pointed to a classic instance of the double standard, confusion in the political arena. 'While competent to instruct voters in their duties, [women] are pronounced incompetent to give a vote themselves.'[46]

It was not only the hostility of men towards determined political activism that served to limit the march of female participation, however. The whole political structure of nineteenth-century Britain was geared to reward and maintain the rights of property and the propertied as we have seen. As a consequence, election to political office relied heavily on personal financial means, both in spearheading the necessary campaign and in sustaining oneself upon election, and in securing unpaid time for the enactment of duties.[47] Florence Fenwick Miller's second term on the London School Board had been threatened by her lack of personal financial resources; though she was not prepared to accept financial assistance either from a Commonwealth Club subscription list or from her feminist colleague on the Board, Helen Taylor, she took the money offered by educationalist William Ellis and was subsequently re-elected.[48] Fenwick Miller's case raises not only the issue of wealth and thus, inevitably of class, but, further, of marital status. Given the prevailing attitudes which determined married women to have no concrete separate identity, their role in the political process was a question of some considerable intensity for the movement, as we have seen.

There were, however, among single and married women alike a significant number who, for the sake of a foot in the political door, were willing to accept parliamentary measures which would enfranchise only single propertied women. Disagreements over this tactic signal some of the most divisive moments within the history of the movement. From the earliest days of the suffrage campaign, dissension on this point threatened the more usual harmony with which women conducted their political struggles and disagreements. In 1869 Helen Taylor was adamant that the exclusion of married women from suffrage demands would compromise her stepfather John Stuart Mill's beliefs beyond the acceptable. Almost three decades later, Elizabeth Wolstenholme Elmy was still alarmed by the prospect of a Spinster and Widow bill being introduced into Parliament with feminist assent. ' . . . to propose *now* a Spinster and Widow suffrage after last session's success and Mr Balfour's declaration that the enfranchisement of the married woman for local purposes implied their enfranchisement for imperial purposes . . . would at once be a blunder and a crime of the first magnitude.'[49]

By the 1890s it must have been obvious that the abandonment of the claims of married women was, in reality, affecting the success of suffrage not at all.

Meanwhile, other schisms rocked the mutuality of feminist activity. The National Society of Women's Suffrage, founded as a centralizing suffrage organization in 1872, weathered a minor break only to be reunified in 1877. In 1888, however, a more serious disagreement emerged over the principle of admitting to membership on equal terms societies sympathetic to the cause but with a specific political angle grounded in mainstream politics. Opposed to their admission was a fascinating mix of women from all points on the political compass – the liberals Garrett Fawcett and Ashurst Biggs, conservatives Power Cobbe and Boucherett and the more radical Ashworth Hallett – whose feminist commitment overrode their party ties. It was to be 1897 before unity in the suffrage movement was once more successfully negotiated with the founding, under Fawcett's leadership, of the National Union of Women's Suffrage Societies, and even then, the harmony was to be short-lived.

The furore over the admission of more party-oriented organizations as equal members in the suffrage campaign was similar to the earlier discussions over the precise role that men could or should play in such campaigns; in both cases, the real concern was the dilution of feminist principles through subjugation to an agenda formulated in a political mould fundamentally anathematic to its demands and location. In the summer of 1866, Helen Taylor had broached this subject in some detail in a lengthy letter to Barbara Bodichon. Pointing to the insinuations in the press that the suffrage petition presented by her stepfather on the women's behalf to the House of Commons was, in fact, penned by a man, she concluded that it was thus wiser to maintain the highest possible female profile. ' . . . to admit men into the governing body is merely to give over the whole credit into their hands – all the women concerned will merely be considered to take their usual and proper subordinate position.'[50]

It was in the same vein that the *Women's Suffrage Journal* could counsel its readers 'to disregard the ordinary political parties, and to vote for the man who favours justice to women, be his political creed, in other respects, what it may'.[51] Such opinions represent not an apolitical ignorance but a challenge to the existing boundaries drawn around political definition which so wholly excluded the concerns and interests which formed the basis of an alternative feminist politics.

It has been the contention of many writers assessing the feminism of this period that suffrage activity came to condense the definition and to dominate the exercise of feminist politics. Olive Banks has dubbed suffrage 'the central core of "first wave" feminism',[52] Brian Harrison, while rightly stressing the breadth of Victorian feminism, none the less sees a narrowing preoccupation with parliamentary politics,[53] and Patricia Hollis has gone so far as to suggest that, for women in organizations such as the Langham Place Circle and the Kensington Society, suffrage was, by the 1860s, the 'over-arching' issue with which they were concerned.[54] Andrea Nye is unequivocal in her estimation of its centrality. 'In the first great wave of feminist activity in the nineteenth century, the primary issue was suffrage.'[55]

This apparent concentration on Parliament as the cynosure which would bring succour has been seen as demonstrating the cautious conservatism of late nineteenth-century feminism. Whilst it is true that political representation and participation remained critical issues of feminist struggle, we should not forget that they did so partly because men offered so very much more resistance to demands in this area. At the same time, however, few women were so engrossed by suffrage activity that they were not severally involved in other areas and in developing a more far-reaching feminist perspective which perhaps saw voting rights as symbolically central to full citizenship, but which never represented them as a total panacea. In a gloomily pessimistic letter to her friend Harriet McIlquham in 1896, Elizabeth Wolstenholme Elmy wrote that 'without the Suffrage we win nothing, no matter what painful effort we put forth'.[56]

After thirty years of setback, women were unlikely not to invest this particular campaign with some significance. In those decades they had established at least partial rights in a host of important areas, and against substantial and vocal opposition. Linda Nicholson has argued that an emphasis on suffrage was, for early feminists, a means to achieving 'a self-identity not based on family relationships'.[57] Lydia Becker enunciated the principle more pithily in the form of a fable.

The venerable phrase 'Women have no business with politics', was once uttered as a reproach in the hearing of a witty Frenchwoman during the period of the Revolution, and called forth the ready reply, that in a land where women were liable to have their heads cut off for political offences, they liked to know the reason why.[58]

7

Invading the Public Sphere: Employment, Education and the Middle-Class Woman

Paterfamilias at his office all day, and reading his newspaper all the evening; Materfamilias fuming about her servants; the young brothers all driven away to seek some less tiresome spot, and four or five hapless young women, from twenty to forty, without profession or pursuits, or freedom of time or money, and with only a few miserable make-believe accomplishments of pseudo-music, pseudo-art, pseudo-reading to 'improve the shining hours'; – truly it is a hateful sight! Only two things could be much worse for them; namely being bronzed and lacquered into Girls of the Period, or deluded into the withering precincts wherein Starrs and Saurins are shrivelled from women into nuns.[1]

Frances Power Cobbe's scathing condemnation of enforced female idleness and its consequences was a common feminist theme, piecing together the threads connecting education and employment. The neglect in female education, and the frustrations experienced by adult women, were part of a continuum of ennui perfectly encapsulated by Cobbe's cameo of the middle-class Victorian family and women's experiences within it. Feminists consistently yoked education and employment together as necessarily linked aims, even though the campaigns in these areas were usually initiated separately.

In Victorian England, new occupations in the non-manual sector – clerical, commercial and service jobs – grew out of the rapidly changing structure of the economy, many of the more prestigious acquiring the cachet of professionalism. Education was a prerequisite for professional status and was thus the first hurdle – both psychological and practical – in the battle for middle-class women's employment.

Women were certainly not absent from the paid work-force at this time. Indeed, the successes enjoyed by the earliest generations of industrialists had frequently relied on large armies of cheap female labour. Women's participation in the work-force had hitherto been confined largely to domestic and other manual labour, but it was with opportunities in the non-manual sector that early feminists were primarily concerned.

The class-specific nature of the campaigns is immediately obvious. Feminist attempts to broaden women's employment opportunities continually stressed concern with the encouragement of that which Jane Lewis dubbed the 'white blouse' sector,[2] non-manual work far removed from the grime and noise and physicality of the manual labour that was commonly the lot of working-class women. The concentration in educational circles on establishing women's secondary and tertiary institutions of learning, rather than promoting elementary schooling, suggests similar aspirations.[3] The increasing emphasis on academic attainment – to which few working-class girls would ever have had access – suggests the narrow class base targeted in these campaigns. This should, however, hardly surprise us. Feminist articulations of frustration first surfaced in a middle-class environment, not only because non-working women had the leisure hours in which to explore such ideas, but also because their class was both the originator and the focus of the ideology entrapping women.

This clear class location has been the source for considerable criticism of feminist activities in these areas. In concentrating attention on the provision of jobs for single and widowed women, feminists have been accused of avoiding discussion of the ethics of married women's paid work.[4] Women's educational campaigns have been similarly condemned for what is seen as their conservative failure to challenge the existing sexual division of labour, enhancing rather the traditional role and capacities of domestic womanhood.[5] Education certainly could become the key to improved wifehood, both in emphasizing the refinement of domestic skills and expertise and by providing women with the education necessary to understand better the interests and activities of their husbands. This idea that women campaigners, in fact, reinforced traditional notions of sex-specific suitability, has been pursued by various historians; their criticisms will be important considerations in our revisionary understanding.

Changes in women's educational and employment patterns at this time are not, of course, wholly attributable to the efforts of feminist campaigners. Protective legislation and the burgeoning need for a wide-ranging bureaucracy as well as a gradually decreasing market for domestic service contributed to these changes. Peter Gay has asserted that 'it was not feminism that brought girls flocking to the lower echelons of sales forces or bureau employees, to posts where both pay and prestige were low; it was the rational, complex, modern capitalist economy.'[6]

Gay strengthens his argument by focusing on the specific areas of retail and office employment. Feminist champions of employment, however, concentrated their energies in other, and often less 'feminine', areas of employment. None the less both his general contention, and the stress laid by many historians on the conservatism of early women reformers in these two areas, prompt an examination of how we might effectively measure the specifically feminist input into these campaigns.

One way in which we can begin to approach the problem is by examining the personnel. Were they also participants in, or known supporters of, other issues which spearheaded the broader fight for women's rights, or were they women who consciously dissociated themselves from other struggles, which might have tainted those involvements or indeed their personal reputations?

What emerges from an examination of the principal players in these two dramas is their commitment to a range of women's issues and to a life constructed around feminist principles. The well-known names – Josephine Butler, Emily Davies, Barbara Bodichon, Bessie Parkes – need little introduction. All these women had, as we have seen elsewhere, significant connections across the range of feminist activities. Butler was President of the North of England Council for Promoting the Higher Education of Women and of the Ladies' National Association which organized protests against the implementation of the Contagious Diseases Acts. Parkes helped establish the first feminist periodical of her day, was active in London suffrage circles and in agitation for the extension of married women's property rights, and was also an early member of the Society for Promoting the Employment of Women.

Emily Davies and Frances Buss, the founder and proprietress of the North London Collegiate School for Girls, first met through a contact in the Durham and Northumberland branch of the Society for Promoting the Employment of Women, which Emily had helped found before moving to London with her mother.[7] It is a contact that amplifies further the cross-campaign connections which drew these fields so close together, the two educationalists meeting in the employment context!

Clara Collett, who made the Board of Trade wake up to the facts of women's industrial labour around the turn of the century, was also active in educational feminism. She was a governor of Bedford College, one of the very earliest of the new female institutions founded in 1849. She was also the first woman Fellow of University College London. Before taking up her work at the Department of Labour, Collett had spent seven years teaching in a Leicester girls' school. She was one of the many prominent women who sat on the seventy-two-member committee of the Frances Buss Memorial established after Buss's death in 1894.

Their multiple associations could, on occasion, cause women problems of political strategy. In late 1866, when she was drafting the first proposals for her women's college at Cambridge, Emily Davies resorted to a shrewd tactical invisibility. Along with Harriet Cook (who, incidentally, shared a house during this period with medical activist Elizabeth Garrett and with Jane Crow from the Society for Promoting the Employment of Women), she was the architect of a women's franchise petition, convinced that 'the immediate business on hand however was Women's Suffrage'.[8] She insisted, none the less, on maintaining a low profile in that arena, 'to avoid the risk of damaging my work in the education field by its being associated with the agitation for the Franchise'.[9] In 1867, pressured by her educational work, she ceased to be *active* in suffrage activities but none the less kept up her feminist connections, social and organizational.

Feminists, generally, laid far more importance on their work than on any personal kudos. Davies's reticence in claiming personal recognition for her franchise work was not an isolated example. Kate Amberley donated £50 to the fund for Davies's nascent women's college at Cambridge in 1869, even though her radical connections made Emily refrain from inviting her to join the organizing Committee.[10]

All of these women had a clear idea of why emancipation rested so fundamentally on the achievement of these twin objectives, and were convinced that education and employment had to be *politically* linked. They argued that, without access to education and training, women were, effectively and in the long term, disbarred from any equality of opportunity, that they were, in effect, disadvantaged at the first post.

The simultaneousness of the demand for industrial freedom and for higher education is based on a necessity. The education which most women need is one which will fit them for business in professions or in industries.[11]

Butler's pragmatism echoes a sentiment shared by many of her contemporaries. The number of activist women who undertook a rigorous programme of self-education, or who lobbied hard for permission to attend the new schools and colleges, suggests the considerable value they apportioned to the acquiring of knowledge. George Eliot wrote with passion to Barbara Bodichon that 'the better education of women is one of the objects about which I have *no doubt*.'[12] A glance at the female characters in her novels confirms the point: Dorothea in *Middlemarch*, Maggie Tulliver in *The Mill on the Floss*, and as a horrific moral fable, Gwendolen, the luckless bride of the cold Grandcourt in *Daniel Deronda* whose lack of a serious education, or indeed occupation, condemns her to this loveless match.

In her classic feminist statement *Aurora Leigh*, Elizabeth Barrett Browning acknowledged that power too, a power withheld from women.

Books, books, books!
I had found the secret of a garret-room
Piled high with cases in my father's name,
Piled high, packed large,—where, creeping in and out
Among the giant fossils of my past,
Like some small nimble mouse between the ribs
Of a mastodon, I nibbled here and there
At this or that box, pulling through the gap,
In heats of terror, haste, victorious joy,
The first book first. And how I felt it beat
Under my pillow, in the morning's dark,
An hour before the sun would let me read!
My books![13]

In a more prosaic vein Gertrude King, Secretary of the Society for Promoting the Employment of Women, when asked by members of the Taunton Commission on Secondary Education in 1866 whether 'the want of a good previous education is an obstacle to women obtaining employment that is useful to themselves', replied, 'Yes . . . Those that have had good training can always get employment with greater ease than those who have not'.[14]

Feminist campaigners wisely concentrated their efforts on those whose needs they saw as immediate, combining pragmatism, compassion and feminist outrage. And those areas which *did* see an increase in the number of women hired were precisely those areas which the feminist Society for the Promotion of the Employment of Women (SPEW) had targeted as appropriate avenues of potential female employment.

Changes in the classification system used in successive censuses makes accurate assessment of women's work – whether paid or un-paid – difficult, but it is clear that women benefited in some degree from the expansion in non-manual and non-domestic areas.[15] The growth in the white-collar sector noted by Peter Gay, which was a response to the growing sophistication of the economy, aided that process substantially. The ratio between women classified as 'gainfully occupied' and the total female population remained roughly the same throughout this period, but there does seem to have been some shift in the areas in which women actually found employment. The traditional female employments of domestic service and textile manufacture remained significant. Successive chapters of protective legislation served to whittle away women's industrial options, and domestic service openings gradually declined; it is in the non-manual sector that small though relevant changes can be charted.

Between 1861 and 1871 the number of women employed as commer-cial clerks and accountants rose more than tenfold, the number of women printers almost doubled and those involved in hairdressing almost trebled in number.[16] In all these cases, the numbers involved are tiny – no more than a few hundred women. The vast majority of working women remained concentrated in a small range of jobs which their middle-class sisters would never even have contemplated; middle-class women remained, for the most part, still trapped within the stuffy environs of home, both physically and ideologically. It was Emily Shirreff's considered opinion that the charitable endeavours with which they filled their hours were less the fruit of altruism than of a desperate need for occupation.[17] (See chapter 9.)

Education workers directed their energies primarily upwards to a narrow class constituency. In the wake of the pioneer independents – Queen's and Bedford Colleges in London in the late 1840s, North London Collegiate School and Cheltenham Ladies' College in the early 1850s – the second half of the nineteenth century saw the foundation of more than 200 endowed and proprietary schools for girls, many under the aegis of the Girls' Public Day School Company (GPDSC) founded by sisters Maria Grey and Emily Shirreff in 1871. The Elementary Education Act of 1870 meant that there was some expansion, too, in state funding for girls' education. At the tertiary level, women's colleges were established at both ancient universities (Oxford and Cambridge) well before the end of the century, though the actual granting of degrees was to be a rather more protracted battle there than at London or the new civic Victoria University in Manchester where women were granted degrees well before the end of the century.[18]

These, then, are the institutional and organizational criteria by which we may measure the success and the proof of a feminist input in educational advances. The recipients of all these advances were a predictable cross-section of the daughters of professional and business families.[19]

The mere existence of schools and colleges, or of women gradually ensconcing themselves in formerly closed work situations does not, however, serve to indicate whether such campaigns were indeed feminist. Some historians, as we have seen, contend that the new girls' schools did little to challenge the precepts which governed Victorian thinking about gender. It is certainly the case that they were initially hesitant in their promotion of new values; they had, after all, to attract a fee-paying clientele large enough to sustain the venture, given the paucity or complete absence of inaugural endowments.

Funding for girls' education could not command the same respect or standing as that for boys, which enjoyed, of course, a long and well-established history. In practice, many middle-class families could not easily have borne the cost of educating both sons and daughters. An editorial in *The Times* in 1894 stated the problem with typical Victorian prolixity:

What will the little stock of accumulations which paterfamilias can hope to leave behind him, after he has paid for his son's education, provided for his widow, and been aggregated by the Chancellor of the Exchequer yield his girls to live on, and what other sources have they got?[20]

For most families, the education of their sons was of far more importance than that of their daughters. The account books of the Hobhouse family, used by Barbara Caine in her study of the Potter family, show clearly how much more money parents were willing to expend on their sons.[21] Even where the provision of funding was non-specific, that preference dominated.

Where funds have been left for education without distinction of sex, girls have often been unfairly dealt with; as in the case of Christ's Hospital (the Blue-coat School) which was originally established for the purpose of maintaining a certain number of boys and girls. The funds of this school now amount to £42,000 a year; out of those funds one thousand two hundred boys are fed and clothed, and educated in such a manner as to fit them to proceed to the Universities, and nineteen girls are trained as domestic servants.[22]

And as Lady Stanley pointed out, the common fund-raising devices of subscription and donation which dominated charitable and private enterprise of this sort in Victorian England were hamstrung by the same thinking.

Large sums were required for boys; and, the claim of boys being admitted, the sums were always speedily forthcoming. Very modest demands were made in favour of girls; but, their claims not being admitted, purses remained closed, and the funds that have been raised have been raised generally within the same small circle of the earnest promoters of the cause.[23]

Even towards the end of the century, when the principle of academic provision for girls was better established, financial exigency continued to plague female education. Janet Howarth and Mark Curthoys show the marked variation in benefaction enjoyed by men's and women's educational institutions even from within such broadly sympathetic communities as that of Unitarianism and Quakerism.[24]

One of the most radical features of the new schools, as Joyce Pedersen has argued, was a marked decline in client control, which had as its corollary the rising professional and expert status of the schoolteacher and, perhaps more importantly, the woman schoolteacher. Parents could no longer wholly dictate the course of their daughter's education to servile teaching staff ever mindful of their lowly status. Reforming schoolmistresses continued to encounter some measure of parental suspicion, but their new prowess in general facilitated the steadily increasing encroachment of school life on girls' after-school hours.[25] None the less, Dorothea Beale at Cheltenham Ladies' College had to struggle to convince parents of the value of her educational philosophies. She was, according to one of her staff, 'obliged to postpone Euclid for fear of killing the school. She had a hard fight with the parents when she abolished afternoon school; still harder when she introduced mathematics. Some of them threatened to remove their girls for fear they should be turned into boys by studying the same subjects.'[26]

It was not only schoolmistresses who had to fight such traditional suspicions, but often the students themselves. Helena Swanwick, who early in the twentieth century was to become prominent in the feminist movement, recalled the resentment aroused in her by the distinction operating in her own family between her and her brothers' education. In 1878, she entered Notting Hill High School in London, the second of the foundations established by the Girls' Public Day School Company. Despite the homework doled out by the school which grew, she remembered 'to formidable proportions',[27] she was still expected – unlike her brothers – to participate in household chores

... whereas education was of importance for my brothers, it was of no account for me. I resented also that I was required to render them personal services which they need not reciprocate. When they had done their lessons, they went to play, but when I had done mine, I very often had to mend their clothes and sort their linen and wash their brushes and combs.[28]

Similarly, whilst Elizabeth Wolstenholme's only brother received the Cambridge education which was a virtual prerequisite for young men of his class, Elizabeth's modest desire to study at London's Bedford College was quashed by her guardians.

The provision of a new and more academically rigorous schooling for middle-class girls had implications well beyond the curriculum and the futures of the girls themselves; in employment terms, teaching was an area which offered educated women increasing and attractive opportunities for self-fulfilment and self-expression. Teaching had, in one way or another, long been a common means by which self-supporting women had attempted to sustain themselves, as governesses in private homes or as proprietresses of small and largely unremarkable girls' schools.

Though school-teaching in the nineteenth century had attracted little, if any, social cachet, Arnold's reforming methods at Rugby assured the gradual growth of its respectability.

For women teachers, their somewhat tenuous standing was far more acute than that experienced by their male colleagues. In the first instance, the simple fact of earning a living could be a socially embarrassing statement for women of bourgeois origin. Millicent Garrett Fawcett pointed out that, 'The vast majority of female teachers take up employment against their will, and unexpectedly'.[29] Women entering teaching frequently had neither training nor vocation for their chosen employment, and the regime they imposed in their ignorance or impatience was often remembered in later life with horror by their students. Frances Power Cobbe was openly critical of the select girls' school in Sussex to which her wealthy parents packed her off in the 1830s. 'Nobody dreamed that any one of us could in later life be more or less than an "Ornament of Society" . . . Everything was taught us in the inverse ratio of its true importance.'[30]

Anna Swanwick echoed Cobbe's scorn; the education offered at her equally exclusive Liverpool girls' school 'was so meagre that I felt like the Peri excluded from Paradise'.[31] The governess-educated girl seldom fared any better. Mary Paley (later Marshall) remembered the emphasis laid on deportment over and above learning. 'We repeated our lessons standing in a row with wooden trenchers on our heads . . . and I . . . had to lie flat on a reclining board whilst learning lessons.'[32] As Constance Maynard was to remark: 'Our real education lay outside the schoolroom.'[33]

Inevitably, the first generation of feminist schoolmistresses, and indeed of women academics – women who exercised a choice unknown to women of earlier generations – had little training available to them. As chapter 3 has shown, Anne Jemima Clough went from school-teaching which, like so many women of her social standing and generation, she had taken up on the failure of her father's business interests, to become the first Principal of Newnham College, Cambridge. Though her brothers had had a thorough schooling in the private sector and at Oxford, for Anne, the only daughter, education had been a more cursory affair. In consequence, she had no 'qualifications' either for teaching or for her subsequent university post, beyond her commitment and a strong practical humanism. The first generation of women principals at the Oxford and Cambridge women's colleges were all of the same ilk, often chosen more for their social standing or connections than for qualities commonly regarded as necessary in an 'academic' forum.

Circumstances were little different at the secondary level. Helena Swanwick's teachers at the Notting Hill High School which, as a GPDSC school prided itself on high academic standards, were apparently 'women who were, in many cases, themselves studying in their spare time (sadly little that was!) for degrees, and who had no training of any sort as teachers'.[34] And of Dorothea Beale, Janet Courtney commented, ' . . . her standards of scholarship had never been sufficiently tested . . . Neither her ethics nor her metaphysics would have stood the stern test of logical examination . . . On the other hand she was eminently practical. She was an organizer second to none.'[35]

Victorian women teachers came to their profession, for the most part, unequipped and untrained. In the state sector, little training existed beyond the elementary schools schemes where bright but poor pupils might find an apprenticeship as pupil-teachers. The greater number of women schoolmistresses in private institutions entered the profession as the simplest and most genteel means at their disposal of earning a living. 'Except by tuition, there is no way in which an ordinarily gifted gentlewoman can earn her own living.'[36] Margaret Nevinson maintained that it was unfortunate widows or the wives and daughters of bankrupts who set up such schools 'with no further preparation, poverty their only certificate'.[37] Her own attendance at such schools was prompted by her father's charitable consideration of the plight of such women. Whilst her brothers were sent to established schools, she passed from institution to institution, her outraged father removing her each time he discovered the paucity of the learning they offered, at least 'till the next poor woman was widowed or bankrupt'.[38]

Despite their own inadequate training, the new women teachers were determined to distance their methods and their values from those prevalent in older girls' schools where femininity was far more highly prized than scholarly achievement. The novel stress, in feminist schools, on academic attainment for girls, resulted on occasion in a replication of the ambience of the boys' public schools on which some consciously modelled themselves. As a result, they contrasted even more starkly with the traditional girls' schools where a commercial if amateur ethos necessarily prevailed, and where the accent was on the public display of good breeding and genteel conversation rather more than sound learning. Significantly, women in the feminist academies signalled their determination to entrench their new-found professionalism by the founding of professional bodies such as the London Schoolmistresses' Association and the Association of Head Mistresses.

The new schools and colleges were 'public' in a host of ways and the curriculum they collectively favoured – despite the scarcity of suitable staff – showed a marked attachment to the values of the male academic establishment. Emily Davies rigidly insisted upon her Girton students following the same courses and sitting the same examinations as their male contemporaries, whilst the new secondary institutions stressed the value of academic attainment over and above domestic skills. Indeed, the Girls' Public Day School Company imposed entrance requirements for prospective pupils, regardless of whether their parents owned shares in the company. In her fight to establish that boys and girls sat the same papers in the Cambridge Local Examinations, Emily Davies argued that 'exclusively female tests have no well-known recognized value . . . All they can assert is that the holders of them are a little less superficially taught than other girls.'[39] She was convinced that separating out the intellectual aptitudes of the sexes could only be detrimental to the cause of women's education.

In the case of the state schools established in this period, Davies proved wisely prophetic. The home economy syllabus which came to characterize the state's provision for girls' education was never a prominent feature of the curriculum in the fee-paying schools. At one level, this pruning of the syllabus might indicate that well-born girls would never sully their hands with such tasks beyond the supervision of their own domestics, but at the same time the rejection of domestic schooling was consonant, too, with the new public status of such institutions.

Sheila Fletcher has pointed out that in the wake of the report of the Taunton Commission on education in the 1860s, it was government rather than feminists who actually pioneered the establishment of new girls' schools, but that their initiative failed to expand beyond the initial gesture of establishing new schools.[40] Fletcher is correct in the strictest chronological sense, and a one-dimensional reading of the situation might lead us to applaud their volition. However, the limited monies which government then expended on providing for female education, as well as the specifically domestic curriculum they put in place, suggests at the very least a certain tokenism in their actions. We might then question their motives for even including girls' education within their remit; not surprisingly, the Commission had had no intention at first of examining female educational provision. It was the lobbying of feminists which persuaded its members even to acknowledge that it might be an area worthy of their attention.

It was precisely the feminist input – from women like Frances Buss and Dorothea Beale, Emily Davies and the Shirreff sisters, all of whom espoused a greater philosophy of women's rights alongside their specific commitment to educational reform – which determined the intrusion into the public sphere which is the peculiarly feminist legacy of these developments. As early as the 1860s, Frances Buss's North London Collegiate School had introduced science subjects into its curriculum, whilst at the James Allen school in South London, sciences were offered from the school's inception in 1882.[41] Physical education, too, was encouraged, from callisthenics to lacrosse.[42]

In contrast, Margaret Bondfield, one of the few feminists of the period to have been board-school educated, remembered the learning with which she and her fellow pupils were equipped. 'In the girls' school we were taught reading, writing and arithmetic, and needlework – no geography, no history except the dates of kings.'[43]

The needlework, cookery and laundry classes to which generations of state school girls were to be subjected remained a minor consideration in the curricula of the private feminist-influenced girls' schools. Feminists could have little direct effect on the syllabus promoted in government schools but in the institutions they had helped found and fund, a largely meritocratic system prevailed, notwithstanding the restrictive basis imposed by private education.

Inevitably, the recipients of this new academic education were almost exclusively girls from comfortable middle-class backgrounds. The Girls' Public Day School Company, as well as more expensive institutions such as Roedean, were keen to dispel the idea that they catered exclusively for the wealthy and the GPDSC stated categorically that 'no qualification as to social rank is thought of'. Helena Swanwick remembered sitting 'between the daughter of a publican and the daughter of a laundress at Notting Hill High'.[44]

It was predominantly from the ranks of the middle class that such schools acquired their intake. Before the introduction of compulsory elementary schooling the children of poor families, whether boys or girls, would have been too important a source of potential income for long-term schooling to be a major consideration. Though supporters denied that schools like Roedean turned their back on the daughters of the poor, they did none the less acknowledge that 'the daughters of parents of very limited means' were apt in practice to be overlooked.[45]

The class basis on which the new feminist education was thus built was also a factor in determining why its stress lay with secondary and tertiary schooling. Many of the feminists of this period would doubtless have employed nannies and tutors to deal with the earliest years of their childrens' lives. In consequence, the nursery provision which would have been so liberating for poorer women was largely, though not completely, neglected; Emily Faithfull certainly recognized the value of the kindergarten, lecturing on its merits when she toured America.[46]

In their emphasis on academic attainment the new schools were bowing, of course, to male criteria of scholarship and importance though their reasons were cogent and well-founded. The Taunton Commissioners had eagerly questioned their women witnesses as to differences in the educational capacities of the sexes, a question to which Emily Davies, in particular, had given much attention. Equality of opportunity was undoubtedly one of the most influential of feminist educational tenets at this period.

> .... neither the enlightened ladies nor the London University know what the intellectual differences between men and women may be, but what I argue from this is, that *therefore* existing examinations having already a recognized standing, had better be thrown open without reservation and let us see what comes of it. The moment you begin to offer special things, you claim to know what the special aptitudes are.[47]

In the context of the period it was a shrewd argument. The inclination of the Newnham founders to accept special and, inevitably, less academically ambitious examination papers for women would, Emily argued, do little to promote the cause of women's education in the long term. The argument needed to be couched in terms of women's capabilities, not in terms of their disadvantages and thus special needs. It was all too easy in the age of Darwinism for the special needs argument to be taken as a sign of weakness and inferiority, and Emily Davies's tough and unbending attitude to this question was the option most likely to succeed in such a context. As Frances Buss pointed out somewhat tartly to the Taunton Commissioners, 'it is rather difficult to ascertain what is the proper education for a boy'.[48] Emily Faithfull joined the debate too, writing frequent letters to *The Times* arguing for equal educational opportunities.[49]

And in championing an equal education for the sexes, feminists were not always wholly disparaging of the virtues of a domestic education. Laying the foundation stone for Manchester's fifth board school in 1877, Lydia Becker neatly turned the tables. 'She said she did not know why cooking was considered an exclusive subject for girls. If she had her own way every boy in Manchester would be taught to mend his own socks and cook his own chops.'[50]

At the same time as it pursued public recognition through academic excellence, the new women's educational movement began also to develop some distinctive features which none the less implied a keenly critical thinking about the methods current in boys' education. Asked about the value of a competitive learning system, Frances Martin – who taught in the lower school at Bedford College and who was instrumental in the setting up of the Working Women's College in London in the mid-1860s – was unequivocal in her condemnation of its effects. She told the Taunton Commissioners that 'it is injurious to boys just as much as to girls. I think it fosters vanity and self-will.'[51]

This disparagement of competition is a constantly recurring theme in the feminist debates of the period. At one level, it represents a capitulation to the concerns of Victorian propriety. Male arbiters thought it unseemly to publicize class lists ranking women's examination performances, and feminist activists were forever soothing the ruffled feelings of their male supporters on this front.

I hope you do not suspect our Committee of wishing for anything as repugnant as a 'neck and neck race between the sexes'. As far as I know, we should all dislike to see boys and girls racing with each other . . . Our idea is that women may learn and labour even in the same field as men without a thought of rivalry . . . It is not likely that they will ever want to be soldiers or sailors or navvies.[52]

The women's evaluation of the rivalry and competition encouraged in the education of men none the less exhibited a definite questioning of its utility. They rather embraced a sense of collectivity. It was different in kind from the quasi-familial ambience of some of the earlier girls' private schools and it still inclined in the direction of that guarantor of middle-class propriety, formality. It stopped well short, though, of pitting individuals against one another in the brutal manner of boys' schools, where the cultivation of masculinity all too frequently derived its definition from such harsh tenets.

The characteristically collective nature of Victorian feminism, where Conservative and Liberal women found amity, was successfully translated into their visions of female education. In 1861, Emily Davies attended a twice weekly class in physiology organized by a friend. 'Tho I did not care for the subject, I very much enjoyed being associated with others in learning anything.'[53] And though one of the early Girton girls later reminisced about the awesome academic formality Emily imposed upon her students, she was at the same time fully aware of the joys of collective freedom which Davies's determination had opened up to young women.[54] Emily wrote jovially to her friend Anna Richardson in 1867: 'I have a strong impression that we shall have to devise some appropriate forms of torture as a counterpoise to the exhilarating influences of the place.'[55] When the all-women's Westfield College in London proposed a move from its early home in a residential house in Hampstead's Maresfield Gardens to near-by Kidderpore Hall, their Girton-educated Principal Constance Maynard, had reservations about the new building. 'It is an institution . . . and so it does not suit.'[56]

It was that combination of academic rigour and of a humanizing influence which defined so precisely the feminist input, discernible in both secondary and tertiary education, as well as in the feminist medical campaigns around this time. This coalescence of the deeply demarcated values of public and private was the distinctly feminist contribution; when girls from Queen's College and North London Collegiate School failed the mathematics sections in the first Cambridge Local Examinations in late 1863, both schools immediately set about syllabus reforms to counteract the academic deficiencies the exam. had exposed.[57] At the same time, though, the human face of education was never discarded. Mary Paley, sitting those same exams as a young woman, found herself in some distress over a problem she could not tackle. 'Miss Clough came and comforted me when I was floored by the paper on Conic sections and was crying over it.'[58]

Alongside their belief in existing academic standards, there was none of the oppressive cruelty – psychological or physical – which so often accompanied the declared pursuit of excellence in boys' schools and colleges. Both the schools and the colleges founded within the feminist circle of influence upheld what might seem in retrospect a fairly conservative set of values – virtue, obedience, plainness, thrift. To some extent, these symbolized for Victorian feminists their rejection of idleness and frivolity as the determining characteristics of womanhood. At the same time, though, they were an *appropriation* of the values of Victorian ideology. The new women's institutions saw their function, as Joyce Pedersen has pointed out, as the training of women for public involvement, the direct female equivalent of the smarter boys' schools and colleges.[59] In order to achieve that breakthrough for women they needed, without doubt, some measure of conformity to wider values. They were able, though, to find interpretive means of yoking that acceptance to a reading which consistently saw gender as a critical motor of understanding. The rejection of feminine-associated vanity and levity and the need to negotiate for public space and recognition were prime motives for the high seriousness which, by the turn of the century, came to be associated with the academic education of women; it was part-caricature (the fun-lacking, bespectacled and maidenly blue-stocking), part-commitment and part-tactical. It was also highly effective. The report of the Bryce Commission on Education in 1894 may have been a little too prematurely smug in applauding the achievements in women's education (which, ironically, owed little to government initiative) but the terms of its approval demonstrate an interesting shift in attitude. 'The idea that a girl, like a boy, may be fitted by education to earn a livelihood, or, at any rate, to be a more useful member of society, has become more widely diffused.'[60]

Feminist activists were sensitive, too, to the opinions of a critical and watchful public. Elizabeth Garrett, fighting her lone battle to obtain medical qualifications in the early 1860s, was scrupulous in her attention to tactical detail. 'I am glad they cannot say I am masculine, it is a providence that I am small and unangular. For the same reason I am very careful to dress well habitually, rather more richly in fact than I should care to do if I were not in some sort defending the cause by doing so.'[61]

Her assessment of the ambiguities forced upon active women could scarcely have been more accurate. When, in 1862, the indefatigable Emily Davies organized a memorial protesting at Garrett's exclusion from the examinations at London University, many of the replies came back addressed to S. E. Davies Esq. On the advice of her niece and co-activist, Margaret Llewellyn Davies, Emily had deliberately omitted her Christian name in correspondence when garnering support for the petition – in case 'they'd think it was some horrid woman in spectacles'.[62] The result may have been predictable but it was also instructive!

In such circumstances, their overtures in the direction of sympathetic male patrons suggest a shrewd political consciousness rather more than a desire for male approval. From its foundation in 1849, Bedford College had attempted – if not always wholly successfully – to weight the decision-making bodies in favour of the women who formed the majority on the College's governing Committee. Its original trustees had been men – not unrealistic given the legal status of women in financial matters at this juncture – but founder Elizabeth Reid, was careful to leave the greater part of her property in trust to three single women for 'the elevation of the moral and intellectual character of Women'. And her reasons? 'I think it better to confine it to Ladies for ever, and I am certain that if Two Men are chosen it will become a job and a sinecure.'[63] She insisted, too, cognizant of the legal incapacity of the married woman to hold on to independent ownership of property, that were any of these original women trustees to marry, they would be required to relinquish their trusteeship.[64]

We should not, therefore, underestimate the impact and success of the feminist voice, both in the flowering of a new philosophy of women's education and in an increase in its availability. It is true that the state's new acceptance of its role in overall educational provision did result in a greater number of girls receiving at least some education, but it was in the state schools, more than anywhere else, that girls were trained principally to motherhood and domestic acquirements. This emphasis on domestic training represented an interesting contradiction of the dominant ideology which saw, or at least proclaimed, that gender roles were somehow innate. Schooling girls in their 'natural' attributes suggests some degree of anxiety on the part of the status quo. Moreover without organized lobbying from the feminist movement, there seems little doubt that the Taunton Commission which catalysed these changes in secondary education would have confined its attention entirely to boys' schools.

At the tertiary level, government was markedly less active. The reforming Oxford and Cambridge Commissions of 1850 failed even to touch upon the question of admitting women, despite their stated and much debated concern over the narrow social basis of undergraduate admission. Nor did the second chapter of enquiry in the 1870s consider the subject. Agitation for women's higher education was almost exclusively a feminist province. The initial impetus derived largely from the efforts of Emily Davies, whose first encounter with the authorities of the University of Cambridge had been in 1862, when she had successfully lobbied for the inclusion of girls in the new Local Examinations administered by the university.[65]

The first women's college opened, not in Cambridge itself but in nearby Hitchin in 1869, moving to Cambridge three years later when a suitable site was secured. Davies's efforts in establishing what became before long Girton College paved the way for many similar foundations, both at Cambridge and elsewhere. The women's movement turned its attention to tertiary education not only in the university towns of Oxford and Cambridge but in London and Manchester as well. Whatever the driving force behind the foundation of the colleges – and their emphases and beliefs did differ considerably on issues as diverse as religion and educational philosophy – they were all characteristically serious about the education they offered aspiring young women. Elizabeth Wordsworth, first Principal of Oxford's Lady Margaret Hall, recalled some of the early misconceptions which so amused the educationalists.

How anxiously we 'counted heads' as the new applications from students came in! Some times these were very amusing; the enclosed may serve as a specimen: 'I should be delighted', says my correspondent, 'to place her under your care for a time. She is seventeen; she can draw and play on the piano nicely; she knows French pretty well, and can also make pastry and useful puddings, or a plum or plain cake; and so she would be useful, and it would be good for her to be amongst a few ladies of her own age and standing'. I fear we turned a deaf ear to this appeal.[66]

The women who did take up the challenge of so novel and reviled a path found themselves inevitably under considerable pressure. 'We worked very hard, for we were pioneers and we had to do credit to the Cause.'[67] They were subject to criticism from all sides; there were those who saw women's femininity imperilled by study and those who, conversely, saw that very femininity as a barrier to effective study. 'We were like the bat in the fable, neither birds nor beasts, but shunned by both.'[68] Margaret Nevinson's mother had forbidden her father, Timothy, to continue coaching his daughter in Greek, mindful that 'no one would ever marry a girl who read Greek'.[69] In the Meinertzhagen family to whom Beatrice Webb was an aunt, the standard family threat with which to counter infant high spirits was 'if you're naughty, you'll have to go to Girton'.[70]

Indeed, the derogatory epithet 'strong-minded' bandied around at this time did not entirely miss the truth. The strains to which early college women were liable were such that without a strength of spirit and conviction, their lives would have been miserable.

They all felt the responsibility of the new effort and were discreet and very quiet in public. But amongst ourselves the ferment worked vigorously. Everyone had come to College by her own strong desire, everyone had come in the face of a little laughter, that could hardly be dignified with the name of opposition, and the atmosphere was charged with electricity.[71]

There was a constant tension for the early women students between the needs of propriety and their hunger for the traditional life of the student. Endless small dilemmas clouded their judgement over and above the hostility – whether expressed openly or in the sniggering which Maynard recalled – which dogged their very existence as students. The life of the student was seldom consonant with the maintenance of femininity, a disjunction manifesting itself in a trail of minor crises. Janet Courtney went through agonies of indecision when her chaperon for a lecture at New College, Oxford failed her.

The audience had all gone in, they had seen me waiting outside, the lecture had begun – was I to turn tail and go cravenly home? Greatly daring, I went in, half expecting the heavens to fall. Mr Robinson paused, looked paternally at me over his spectacles, remarked impersonally, 'The subject of this Lecture is Property in Land', and the incident closed. But when I recounted the event at Lady Margaret Hall, there were purists who held that I ought not to have gone in unaccompanied.[72]

These problems of etiquette and gentility were by no means confined to the colleges of Oxford and Cambridge. At Owen's College, Manchester, the forerunner of the city's university, even after the full academic admission of women, the sexes were segregated in ways that hampered the women's work severely. The women students were not permitted to enter the library, a prohibition which could not fail to disadvantage them. The system devised for the fetching of library materials for them was both cumbersome and highly instructive of the class divide which separated even these disadvantaged women from their less wealthy and well-placed sisters.

We had to 'fill up a voucher', and a dear little maid-of-all-work, aged about thirteen, went to the library with it. If we were not quite sure of the volume we required, she might have to make the journey ten times, but it was never suggested that she should be chaperoned.[73]

In effect, the function of the chaperon was one of de-radicalization. One of the singular and most revolutionary features which the new colleges offered quite specifically was the opportunity for young unmarried women to live away from home. Without the provision of some supervision few parents would have been willing to allow their daughters to attend.

The need for women students to be chaperoned was not restricted to the lecture-hall and tutorial where they were thrown together with male students who, more often than not, were hostile. Even where single-sex tuition was conducted, a chaperon was necessary given that the lecturers were invariably men. For the chaperon herself, it could be a tedious task. 'Poor Miss Clough, having to do a good deal of this work, some-times . . . went to sleep. At the end of a long economic argument she once woke up with, "Would you mind saying that over again Mr Marshall, it is so difficult", and he meekly obeyed.'[74]

Even outside the class-room, women students were supervised. Mary Paley recalled the weekly visit of the Newnham students to the town gymnasium accompanied by an agile Millicent Garrett Fawcett who was 'always the best climber of the long rope and could look out at the top window'.[75] Here was a chaperon with novel abilities![76]

The initially small intakes of the colleges doubtless exacerbated these problems by ensuring that the women stood out. Numbers at Newnham began very modestly; in its first term as a hall of residence before it became a fully-fledged college in October 1871, there were five students. By its third term, the numbers had risen to eight. In 1884, the situation was far healthier with ninety students in residence.[77] Four hundred and sixty-seven women passed through Girton in the years between its foundation and the summer of 1893, whilst the same period at Newnham saw a total population of 720 students.[78]

The initial intakes of these early institutions spanned an enormous age range: women from sixteen to thirty-one years came as students. The entrance into the colleges of women well beyond the usual student age is a significant comment on the need that the colleges fulfilled. No such opportunities had existed for women earlier; adult women hungering for an education were unconcerned with age barriers. Uncomfortable with their inexperience and often resentful – as we have seen – of the privileges showered on their brothers, many of the first generation of activists sought out whatever training they could find, however meagre. The twenty-two-year-old Frances Buss enrolled at Queen's College, Harley Street, to improve her teaching skills whilst Fanny Metcalfe founded her girls' school only after seeking out a training abroad in Germany. The first crop of teachers at the St. Leonard's School in Scotland – Louisa Lumsden, Jane Dove, Constance Maynard and Rachel Cook – were all early Girton products. In effect, and though it took time for the real fruits of this labour to emerge in the class-rooms and lecture halls of schools and colleges, feminist educational institutions provided a crucial first step towards the creation of an ethos of professional excellence and adequate training. Feminism was not incidental to the women's education movement, as others have argued, but rather a central and effective body of thought and activity.

At the same time, the presence of older women as students throws an interesting – and an ironic – light on the issue of chaperonage and the sheer dead-weight which the needs of propriety imposed even on grown women. Mary Paley thought that, 'Perhaps in those days Miss Clough was rather inclined to treat us like school girls.'[79] Poor Anne Clough was hardly able to act otherwise if the college were to guard its closely monitored respectability.

Students at all the colleges shared a common purpose and determination, and yet both publicly and privately, important differences between the various institutions, and most obviously between women reformers at the two ancient universities, were acknowledged. Oxford was, in many ways, the exception to the feminist norm in the agitation for women's access to higher education. Most of the women active in Oxford explicitly disavowed any attachment to feminist principles. Though their campaigns were broadly similar in aim to those which had been conducted at Cambridge, and indeed fed off those experiences, women such as Annie Rogers and Bertha Johnson avoided public involvement whenever they felt their male supporters and co-workers could act on their behalf. They constantly reiterated their rejection of other current women's rights issues.

Both the earliest of the two Oxford colleges – Somerville and Lady Margaret Hall – though differing from one another in many respects, served to allay the fears of conservative Oxford by the genteel manner in which they conducted their business. It is interesting to find members of both these colleges parading the specifically non-feminist influence they exerted over students. Of Madeleine Shaw Lefevre, first Principal of Somerville College, Lilian M. Faithfull remarked, 'It was the spirit of unobtrusive receptivity and deference to University traditions and prejudices rather than a demand for rights which [she] took pains to instil into the first students.'[80]

Elizabeth Wordsworth similarly posed no threat, for though 'Oxford was very fearful of the new venture . . . who could seriously contemplate unfeminine behaviour in a handful of girls living in a white villa under the chaperonage of a lady of such unexceptionable antecendents?'[81] Indeed, Wordsworth's influence was such that this same student felt that under her supervision, 'it would have been impossible to grow up a feminist'.[82]

Oxford, significantly, witnessed none of the struggles engendered by Emily Davies's refusals to compromise at Cambridge. For many years, the university at Oxford virtually ignored the existence of the women's colleges, granting them no institutional recognition but according them in practice a rather curious *de facto* right whereby women students could study and sit for university examinations but their colleges remained wholly separate entities outside the jurisdiction of the university. The willingness of the Oxford women to achieve their aim in this most passive and unchallenging manner offers a clue to understanding the *feminist* force of other campaigns which deliberately pitted women's interests against these more traditionally 'feminine' means of victory. The reasons for their stand on this issue are complex certainly, and derive not only from their reluctance to be seen as a wing of feminism but also from a critique they shared with a large number of Oxford men, as with the Clough camp at Cambridge, as to the bankruptcy of the dominant educational philosophy which they were anxious not to replicate.

Girton was the acknowledged pioneer in promoting tertiary access to education for women, and Emily Davies thus found herself a frequent target of varied and considerable criticism 'among those who thought the method itself little worthy of imitation in days of modern progress, and among those who deprecated for women all emulation with men'.[83]

Criticism of existing curricular arrangements was by no means the exclusive province of feminists. Many men were as dubious of the wisdom of preserving the traditional methods and concerns of the ancient universities, and fought vigorously for syllabus reform.[84] Many also supported the women's cause and urged on feminist activists the need to reject and rebuild their educational programmes.

Despite the distinct tactical as well as educational differences which divided women at the two ancient strongholds of male learning, they none the less maintained amicable relations with one another. When Lady Margaret Hall was struggling to establish the foundations of a college library in its earliest days, a donation of books from Newnham College – hardly a wealthy institution itself – was gratefully received.[85]

And there was clearly some value in the coexistence of the different philosophies they espoused. Janet Courtney was much relieved by the impeccable social character of Oxford's Lady Margaret Hall. 'I should have had small hope of being allowed to go to Girton or Newnham, centres as they were then thought to be of "advanced" and therefore "dangerous" notions.'[86] Elsewhere, however, the feminist input was marked. In the mid-1860s, when a trickle of doughty women took on the medical establishment and fought for their right to train as doctors, Emily Davies was in no doubt that the trend was a feminist one. In a letter to Anna Richardson describing one of these pioneers, a Miss Colborne, she dubbed her one of 'the present generation of "Women's Righters"'.[87] The emphatically public profile which women active in such campaigns necessarily adopted was in itself a direct challenge to separate sphere ideology. The confrontation and antagonism they faced and which they so vividly described in letter after letter constantly tested the limits of their commitment and determination. They ran the gamut of public hostility for their involvement, and by stepping so radically out of the confines of acceptable domesticity and into the public eye, they automatically acquired a feminist label.

At the same time, though on a much smaller scale, a number of feminist women and radical men became interested in the provision of evening education for working women. In 1864, the Working Women's College was set up in London's Bloomsbury. It offered a coffee room and a reading room in addition to a range of classes. Non-sectarian in character, it attracted an impressive initial enrolment of 157 women.[88]

It was staffed by women such as Elizabeth Whitehead Malleson, Clementia Taylor and Frances Martin, assisted by men like Frederick Denison Maurice (founder of the Working Men's College which had served as a model for the women's institute), Arthur Munby and John Westlake, the lawyer husband of prominent feminist Alice Westlake. Arthur Munby recalled the newly qualified Elizabeth Garrett demons-trating with confidence the dissection of a frog to the women students.[89] His own Latin classes were, according to his diary, well attended by women 'behaving with quiet frankness; not giggling, nor yet too grave'.[90] The experiment was as instructive for the male tutors as for the women themselves. Munby tells a touching tale of a young working woman and her enthusiasm for joining his class in 1867. She was employed at a London glassworks firm painting Latin inscriptions on church windows and wanted to be able to translate them.[91] An interest in education was certainly not in any sense a middle-class monopoly. None the less, in the feminist efforts of the period, attention to working-class needs was essentially no more than a tributary of the mainstream push to achieve widespread educational opportunities for middle-class girls.

The middle-class nature of all this campaigning is, of course, un-questionable and if we look at women's employment we find a similar emphasis there too. In the later decades of the century, the revival of the protective legislation debate brought middle-class feminists to a greater consideration of the class issue (see chapter 8) but earlier in the period, their attention had focused primarily on the problems encountered by the independent middle-class woman, and it was this area which dominated the campaigns of the 1860s and early 1870s. Work in this area was prompted not only by the genuine and growing problem of potentially destitute women who had neither husband, father nor brother on whom to rely financially, but also by the boredom and frustration which characterized middle-class women's daily lives. As Frances Power Cobbe so descriptively put it, 'scores of fathers in the higher ranks, give their daughters diamonds when they crave for education and twist round their necks the serpents of idle luxury and pleasure when they ask for wholesome employment.'[92]

The links with education are obvious in this context; education was a route out of boredom and at the same time offered at least the prospect of useful and interesting occupation.

Until it is recognized that education means neither a cramming of facts nor a smattering of accomplishments, but a preparation for *life*, and for the demands which life makes upon every woman, whether married or single, these sad consequences of deliberate incapacity and helplessness must abound. Whilst parents persist in venturing their daughter's welfare on the single chance of a successful marriage, a chance which by circumstances not under her control, is daily being removed further from certainty, misery of mind and body must be the fate of many.[93]

Louisa Hubbard's uncompromising statement of the problem high-lighted the need for women to take control of their own lives. The injustice of falling victim to situations outside their control was a constant and sharp threat which women endured – desertion, wido-whood or a family financial crisis, for instance, or, more pressingly, the decision made on their behalf, and ignorant of their actual needs, that their wages be secondary to those of men.

This fact more than anything else accounts for the immense difficulties of introducing order and humanity into the field of women's labour; for obviously, if the woman worker is to acquire any form of economic independence she must be able to earn such a rate of wages as will enable her to maintain a decent standard of subsistence.[94]

It is in this context that we should assess the decision of earlier feminist activists to focus their work upon the employment prospects of single women. Few at this date disparaged the institution of marriage, but, aware of the economic traps it could pose, refused to see it as the sole avenue of female fulfilment. Josephine Butler, herself contentedly married, remarked, 'I cannot believe that it is every woman's duty to marry, in the eyes of the world.'[95]

Inevitably the question of women's employment brought in its wake discussion of the ramifications of such a move for the marital state. The leisured wife was one of the most striking symbols of male prosperity, even though the symbol was sometimes little more than a mask. Though the issue of married women's employment was never a central topic of feminist interest in this period, there was considerable reflection on whether the prospect of paid employment would, in fact, act as a disincentive for women to marry. Alice Gordon's figures on the post-university careers of the first generation of Oxbridge-educated women prompted her to conclude that such women 'do not seek to make marriage their career in life'.[96]

Feminists, however, remained adamant that the most pressing point about the whole issue of women and marriage was simply that a substantial minority of women would never have the option, and would, therefore, have little choice but to pursue paid labour. 'Those who argued in the face of facts that a woman's place was nowhere but by her own fireside, or the care of her children, were readily enough answered: the firesides were not always to be had, and for every governesses's situation there were fifty applicants.'[97]

Whether Victorian feminist statements were primarily asserting women's rights to marital choice or responding more to a situation in which numbers of single women were forced to find a means of independent subsistence, they still protested forcefully the consequences of male control of the labour market. The task was inevitably a more difficult one than that faced by educationalists; in the first instance, they were dealing with the stark urgency of untrained adult women needing paid work, and further, occupational change was so dependent upon the vagaries of the wider economy that they could effect only minor and not structural changes. As with the pattern established in the educational field, the hallmark of feminist activity was the individual private venture – the establishment of small companies and businesses employing, and often training, a handful of women in such trades as printing, plan-tracing for engineers or law-copying. Some particularly enterprising women set themselves up independently in trades. When cousins Agnes and Rhoda Garrett set up shop as house decorators, they found themselves much in demand. Working from their premises in London's Regent's Park, they designed and decorated the houses of many of their feminist contacts.

Most of the experiments in employment, though, were conducted under the auspices of the Society for Promoting the Employment of

Women (SPEW), founded in London in 1859 by women connected with the Langham Place Circle, and rapidly establishing branches up and down the country. Publicized through the *Englishwoman's Journal*, the society established classes to train women in marketable skills like bookkeeping, offered financial incentives to businesses prepared to employ women and set up a register of women seeking work. James Hammerton has pointed to the anxiety of feminists lest a potential collision of class interests erupt as 'ladies' increasingly competed for jobs with less 'genteel' women.[98] The perceived overcrowding in a narrow band of 'respectable' occupations persuaded activists – and those in the SPEW in particular – that the solution was to encourage women to experiment with non-traditional albeit still 'respectable' areas of employment.

The society was itself funded by donation, which confined its activities to a modest scale. None the less, it successfully placed a number of women in employment, albeit only a fraction of those who flocked there for succour. 'Of necessity the Society was more a centre of propaganda than a labour bureau.'[99]

The all-women establishments dating from this period, unusual as they were, were insistent upon the establishment of humane work practices for their employees. Whem Emily Faithfull founded the Victoria Printing Press (which rapidly became the in-house printer for feminist literature), she not only altered the tasks expected of the compositor to avoid the physical strains previously associated with the job, but paid close attention to working conditions, hours and wages. In encouraging needy women into the work-force, and, moreover, into a variety of jobs they would never have previously considered, feminists were careful not to adopt uncritically the labour practices prevalent in the waged sector. As with educational practices, it is that synthesis of dominant values and a critique of them which highlights the uniqueness of the feminist position.

And these were not ineffective ventures. Two years after the foundation of the Victoria Printing Press in 1861, the number of women printers in England and Wales was 419. Thirty years later that figure had expanded to more than 4500. In the clerical sector, the rise is even more impressive. From a mere 404 female commercial clerks and accountants recorded in the 1861 census, the numbers grew in that same timespan to 17,859 recorded in the 1891 census.[100]

A significant proportion of the women active in promoting women's employment themselves had experience of waged work, as we have seen. To reiterate, 46.4 per cent of the women in this sample are known to have had work experience. The overall number of constantly working women was smaller but many found writing, in one form or another, both lucrative and liberating. With the exception of teaching, it is writing women – poets, translators, novelists, journalists and the like – who make up the largest category of working feminists. The advantages of such a career for women have been rehearsed elsewhere; it was an unregimented area in which hours and attendance were flexible, and it could be undertaken at home and fitted to a domestic timetable. Alongside the many women who wrote under pseudonyms, there were as many who wrote under their own name and often in an explicitly feminist mode.[101] Whilst some 13 per cent of the women in the sample found their vocation in teaching, another 6 per cent in medicine, midwifery and nursing, a rather larger 32 per cent had books published.

There were also those, of course, who worked or considered work in the more recognizably disciplined context. When Emily Davies's father died in 1861 she

came to the conclusion that to follow E. Garrett was the only course to which I could see my way. The practice of medicine had no attraction for me, and I had no aptitude for the necessary study . . . but there seemed to be no other opening to any sort of career and I did not care to take up parish work as the business of my life.[102]

Fortunately for Emily the need was not pressing enough to force her to training or work for which she had neither aptitude nor taste. She remained wealthy enough to devote her life to her various feminist enterprises, though her brief period as editor of Emily Faithfull's *Victoria Magazine* was a salaried appointment.

Frances Power Cobbe attempted some version of the parish work which Davies was so anxious to avoid when, her father's estate having been ceded to her brother, she resisted the maiden aunt future mapped out for her by her male relatives. Cutting off her long hair in a symbolic gesture of defiance, she left her home in Ireland and after a year of solitary travelling in the Middle East joined Mary Carpenter in her slum work in Bristol, an arrangement whereby 'lady' volunteers such as herself were 'provided . . . all day long with abundant occupation'.[103] When that arrangement failed to satisfy either party, Cobbe began a successful and well-paid career as a journalist. Many others such as Bessie Rayner Parkes and Maria Rye, who ran the law-copying office associated with the Society for Promoting the Employment of Women and headed the Female Middle Class Emigration Society, were also sometime journalists. Governessing and teaching provided an obvious livelihood for many women activists at some stage in their lives – Anna Jameson, Mentia Taylor, Elizabeth Wolstenholme and Elizabeth Whitehead all had experience – long or short term – of such work.

As we have seen elsewhere, some worked for feminists and feminist organizations. Emma Smith (later Paterson) worked for the Working

Men's Club and Institute Union and then briefly and unsuccessfully for the London National Women's Suffrage Society. Isa Craig (later Knox) was secretary to the National Association for the Promotion of Social Science. Emily Davies, as we have noted, was briefly the paid editor of the *Victoria Magazine*. Emilie Venturi lasted rather longer, earning an annual salary of £150 for editing the journal of the Ladies' National Association for the Repeal of the Contagious Diseases Acts, *The Shield*, from 1870 to 1876. Jessie Craigen was also a paid agent for the organization.

In some cases, it was employment itself which brought women into the feminist movement, often via women's trade unions. Margaret Bondfield, Julia Varley and Sarah Dickenson were all women from working backgrounds whose feminism was concerned primarily with the unionization of women workers.

There was also a small handful of women who took up work in areas which had never before been accessible to women, and was now rendered possible largely through the efforts of feminist campaigners. Elizabeth Wolstenholme Elmy reported with some satisfaction to her friend Harriet McIlquham that there were, in 1898, seventy-nine women Registrars of Births and Deaths, another 370 women Deputy Registrars and at least nine women rate collectors in England and Wales.[104] Such women generally had close connections, themselves, with the women's movement and often saw themselves specifically as servants of the cause. The two most obvious areas opened up in this way in our period were medicine and the Home Office's employment of women in the Department of Labour.

A number of women followed the example of American-trained Elizabeth Blackwell and home-trained Elizabeth Garrett in entering the growing profession of medicine against overwhelming odds and massive hostility. Their training as much as their subsequent careers were the object of legal wrangles, occasional fisticuffs and a series of bureaucratic attempts to prevent their registration and recognition.

In the case of the women entering civil service employment in the 1890s, concentrated largely in the factory inspectorate, feminist trade unionists and working women had long recognized the need for a female inspectorate. The work to which the department directed them was less specialized than that of their male colleagues, but it was an occupation which saw them invading a whole range of previously male enclaves. Factory inspectors moved regularly around the country in and out of industrial premises and from there to the courtroom where they conducted prosecutions for infringements of the law. Thus, long before women had won the battle over legal training and employment (which did not occur until the 1920s), government women had established their role within the country's legal procedures. It is significant that such positions were filled by women like Adelaide Anderson and Hilda Martindale, recipients of the new feminist education. Anderson was a product of Queen's and Girton Colleges whilst Martindale's schooling had been stringently supervised by her feminist mother who visited and appraised the institutions to which she sent her two daughters.

The problems connected with women's entry into the labour force at this level did not cease, however, when they were able to find some form of paid work. Aside from the obvious social difficulties in which women often then found themselves, consigned to a thin line between maintaining respectability and keeping penury at bay, other issues surfaced too. Their intrusion into the public world was, after all, a literal physical intrusion not only within the workplace but, as David Rubinstein has shown, travelling to and from work, and finding both suitable accommodation and companionship.[105]

Their wages remained lower than those of men though their material needs did not differ radically. Rents were not, alas, gender-specific and there was the added complication for women of securing accommodation that was both safe and respectable. Working women did not win, alongside their right to work, rights to the ease and freedom of movement which men enjoyed. The process of socialization for a working woman was a difficult one. She was not an immediately acceptable social asset and could mix happily neither in genteel middle-class circles nor with working-class women. It was an isolating and often disheartening result of the piecemeal advances which marked the progress of the feminist cause. Even for women teachers in the new feminist academies, such problems were not immediately solved. Margaret Nevinson found that in her four years as a mistress at South Hampstead High School, 'I sometimes found my lodgings rather lonely'.[106]

When we speak of the middle-class preponderance in late nineteenth-century feminist circles, we should remember these facts. Feminist activists were not working in a vacuum. They were not ignorant of the sheer volume of the problems they tackled but they *were* forced to work within the parameters of their experience precisely because of the magnitude of the problems they faced. Bessie Rayner Parkes expressed their understanding of the dilemma when, in an address to the National Association for the Promotion of Social Science, she asked, are 'we trying to tide the female population of this country over a time of difficulty, or are we seeking to develop a new state of social life?'[107]

The realm of respectable employment created other difficulties besides for the naturalization of the separate spheres. The growing romanticization of nursing (and of its young recruits) in this period and after reveals the fracture necessary to maintain that ideology. The evocation of womanly service, sacrifice and calling which accompanied its status transformation created the possibility of attaching the professional ideal to women's work (although carefully rendered as auxiliary) and, in contradiction, denied the possibility of 'true' professionalism by identifying that work as a spiritual calling. Thus, whilst men were acknowledged as entering the professional male world for solidly material reasons – status, money, knowledge – women were permitted to do so only if the profession derived from a calling. In this way, women entering occupations which acquired the patina of professionalism could be accommodated without risking too far the position of professional men or the sturdiness of the prevailing ideology.

Feminists were not wholly blind to the needs of working-class women either. When the protective legislation debate resurfaced in the 1880s, feminists such as Clementina Black and Helen Blackburn, Josephine Butler and Millicent Garrett Fawcett supported working women who opposed the legislation as a threat to their livelihood. Feminist journals ran articles voicing their concern and opposing such measures.[108] (See chapter 8.) None the less, their principal target remained the injustice of a system which deemed marriage the ultimate and indeed sole ambition appropriate for women, especially within the middle class, but which could not or would not provide for women outside that institution. And if the immediate alleviation of some of that distress was the pragmatic expression of their concern, they never lost sight of the wider issue.

Passionate denunciations of that injustice abound in feminist writings, none more powerful, perhaps, than that of Josephine Butler in her introductory comments to *Woman's Work and Woman's Culture.*

I wish to say a word about that constantly reiterated assertion that 'Woman's sphere is the home.' The saying, as it is uttered now, in the face of the great facts of society as they lie confessed before us, is to a great extent wholly inapplicable, and assumes the character of a most ungentle irony . . . there remain both men and women who continue solemnly to inform the women who are striving for some work or calling which will save them from starvation and who have no human being save themselves to depend on, that their proper sphere is *home*, – that their proper function is to be wives and mothers, and their happiness is to be dependent on men! Alas! these women have learned a lesson which neither they, nor the generation which follows them, are likely to forget on the subject of dependence on men . . . Like Pharaoh, who commanded the Israelites to make bricks without the material to make them of, these moralizers command this multitude of enquiring women back to homes which are not, and which they have not the material to create. I trust that such mocking words as these will cease to be spoken.[109]

In their wake, the campaigns around education and employment threw up other relevant feminist concerns – wage parity, property ownership, women's physical and intellectual capacities, child-care – in short, a host of quotidian bread-and-butter issues. As feminists were to find, neither the provision of a humanist education nor that of worthwhile employment for women was a universal panacea for their subjugation, no more than the capture of parliamentary voting rights. Johann Handl has demonstrated that in the long term, 'no equality in occupational status' has yet followed from women's increased access to educational qualifications.[110]

In what ways, then, can these twin campaigns of late nineteenth-century feminist activity be said to have been successful? At an organization and institutional level, albeit on a small scale, both sets of campaigns enjoyed considerable success. Girls' schools and women's colleges propounding a radically new plan for female education ran the gamut of male suspicion and flourished. In the labour market, women gradually opened new fields of employment for future generations. Obviously, we must be wary of an over-enthusiastic representation of their successes in the latter context. This was, of course, an age in which former craft occupations rendered faster and simpler by technological improvement were de-skilled to become women's work with correspondingly low rates of pay, and in which women's wages in all areas continued to lag significantly behind those of men. Moreover, the tag of gentility became a password for exploitation in a number of industries. The status of gentility often replaced the reward of hard cash. Anna Davin quotes Gertrude Tuckwell's condemnation of practices which saw the woman office worker overworked and underpaid but never categorized properly as a sweated worker because 'the gentility of the occupation appears to lift it out of the category and to form its reward'.[111]

And what of the women coming through the new feminist educational movement? After all, the connection between education and employment had been a constantly reiterated theme in the feminist rhetoric of the period. At the same time, contemporary assessments have looked back to the timidity with which educationalists encouraged their students to a more independent existence. Marriage clearly remained, as Barbara Hutchins pointed out in 1909, 'the most important and extensively followed occupation for women', and that paid work, as opposed to the familial domestic work they undertook in their own homes, was often 'an episode of early life', a pre-marital experience.[112]

For women who received a tertiary education in the new Oxford and Cambridge colleges in the 1870s and 1880s, the figures are revealing. They were not, as we know, breaking into new areas of employment in significant numbers. A sprinkling of women – four from Girton and five from Newnham – entered the medical profession in the years before 1893. The majority did work, would appear not to have married – or at least not in the decade or so following their collegiate career – and found employment principally, and not surprisingly, in the teaching profession. Of the 720 students who had passed through Newnham College between 1871 and 1893, 374 were employed as teachers in 1893. Ten or so were married. Very few taught in the public sector; the majority were concentrated in proprietary girls' high schools. One hundred and twenty-three of Girton's 400 or so students in this same period were teaching as were 73 of Somerville's 173 graduates.[113]

The new colleges were successful in promoting a more confident female self-image which was undoubtedly a significant factor in the eminent success of many of their products. Women such as Henrietta Müller, Margaret Llewellyn Davies and Constance Maynard owed as much to their years as pioneer undergraduates as did the many women who had benefited from the courses offered by the London colleges, Bedford and Queen's – Sophie Bryant, Anna Swanwick, Sophia Jex-Blake, Louisa Twining and Dorothea Beale among them.

In small ways, feminist campaigns nurtured and supported significant changes in professional and skilled areas of work evidenced by the census returns. These are campaigns which have been belittled, indeed vilified, by historians in the past for their class-specific and narrow base, for their expediency and for their very obvious limitations. They have too often been stripped of their feminist character and moulded into examples of liberal reform, but if we look to the less institutional aspects, what emerges is unmistakably a feminist perspective. The cross-campaign connections of the bulk of these women suggests a wider feminist sympathy but at the same time a sense of decision as to where to invest their major energies. Their attachment to a women's culture which borrowed from and modified aspects of both the values deemed masculine and feminine by their society lent feminism a strength of purpose. The feminists had morality and respectability on their side, winning rallying calls in bourgeois English society.

They adhered, too, to an organizational autonomy in important respects. Male supporters were their figureheads, to be sure, and often fulfilled functions closed to the women, but wherever possible one sees the controlling hand of the feminists themselves in these campaigns. Questions of education and employment hit right at the heart of male dominance; women working in these areas invaded the public sphere – and more importantly, perhaps, largely on their own terms. These two campaigns, in particular, helped give voice to one of the dominant themes to emerge within the feminist movement at this time, the promotion of women's self-definition – through knowledge, through work, through the politics and the culture of feminism moving away from the constraining and stifling orthodoxy of the dominant ideology.

8

Nurturing the Sickly Plants: Women, Labour and Unionism

The organization of feminist activity in the latter half of the nineteenth century was, as we have seen, undertaken principally by women with access to education, financial security, the resources of leisure, and freedom from at least the manual portions of domestic drudgery. For women afflicted with the additional burdens of poverty and poor class status, the problems associated with gender were indubitably intensified.

By the middle of the century, though, poverty was not confined wholly by class status. The formation of such early women's organizations as the Society for the Promotion of the Employment of Women had been prompted in large part by the predicament of bourgeois women facing penury without support, and with few available options to mitigate its effects. These early efforts, though confined principally to the corridors of gentility in their scope and their interest, served to render to women a work-related language with which they might speak about and discover both the commonalities and differences affecting women of all classes.

In the campaigns to which feminist activists devoted their energies, the issue of class was, albeit sometimes clumsily, none the less frequently articulated. In the furore over the Contagious Diseases Acts, in the efforts to initiate changes in the legal status of married women, in various of the employment-related campaigns, feminist women of impeccably bourgeois background frequently invoked class as an important factor in discussing the subjugation of women. Many commentators have asserted that the issues which taxed feminist women in this period could have been little more than luxuries to women forced into the marketplace to earn their livelihood, but such criticism fails to recognize the simultaneous potential points of contact between women which parallel the obvious experiential divergence of working-class and middle-class women's lives. Clearly women whose daily lives were unburdened by pressing economic need and by arduous household duty were in a position of some considerable privilege and comfort, privilege which allowed them the space to develop their theoretical understanding of the gendered dislocation entrapping them. None the less, few issues of concern to feminists did not relate in direct ways to women of all class backgrounds, and it was this theoretical commonality that activists stressed. Although the 1870 and 1882 Married Women's Property Acts largely benefited wealthier women, they also enunciated at least the principle that a woman's wages were her own. Legislation of this kind made little concrete difference in the lives of most women but still served as an acknowledgement and recognition of the politics of gender.

In researching women, especially those of poorer or more obscure background, one of the many problems is deciding how to define, or indeed recognize, a woman's class position. It was certainly the case in the nineteenth century, and remains largely so today, that primary relationships with men ultimately determine a woman's class status, rather than any specific occupational or economic involvement of her own. Indeed, it may be that the way we think about class is itself not helpful in our determination of the status and position, the lifestyle and politics of women, precisely because it frequently has little bearing on their experiences and simply accords them associative rather than full and independent class status. Ironically, it is easier to identify *working* women than it is to separate out what constitutes the working class of women. Not all working-class women were employed in the paid labour force, though those involved principally in unpaid domestic pursuits were hardly leading lives of indolent leisure. Again, class remained a status conferred via male activity.

In this context, and given the consistently high rate of women's low-paid participation in the manufacturing work-force, the question of *industrial* organization was one of the earliest working women's issues to which the feminist movement of this period turned its attention; here, at least, was a visible group of women with a set of common problems effectively denied by separate sphere ideology. The founding of trade unions for and by women at a time when 'mainstream' (i.e. male) trade unionism was fiercely and vociferously antagonistic to the plight of women workers was a critical point of independent female organization.

The women's trade union movement took two basic forms in this period, and the degree to which we are able to reconstruct these two varieties of activism reveals much about the construction and tenacity of class privilege – and its relations with posterity. The individual occupation-specific unions formed throughout the period by women workers were generally short-lived ventures like their male counterparts; extant documentation of them is scarce and sparse. Alongside them were the umbrella organizations headed, funded and marshalled by middle-class feminists and designed to offer aid to the trade-identified unions and encourage their formation. The Women's Protective and Provident League (later the Women's Trade Union League) founded by Emma Paterson in 1874, the National Union of Women Workers also founded in 1874 and the Women's Industrial Council (1894), all fall under this broad heading and have attracted not only the historian's attention, their papers being more readily accessible, but also the radical's criticisms for their seeming conservatism and distance from the grass roots.[1]

Working women's organizations of whichever form cannot be readily contained within some constructed and fixed contemporary schema of feminist thought or action without our falling prey to precisely that definitional rigidity which for so long excluded feminist activities from consideration as political organizations. If these organizations fail to fit the ready-made categories by which we have for so long judged and defined political activity, we should consider the frequency with which women's politics have been belittled on precisely those grounds of definitional exclusion. These organizations, both those which operated specifically as unions within trades and those which sought to connect the disparate unions through the explicit recognition of gender as a category, are significant principally in their conscious autonomy from male control, and frequently from male definition. In that respect, in stating through action women's needs and abilities to organize separately as women in whatever class context, can we derive and detect a feminist awareness.

Just as we must be cautious of over-determining a feminist movement entirely stripped of class divisions, however, we must be equally and connectedly cognizant of the regional variation in organization as in personnel. Trade societies concentrated principally on bettering, or often simply maintaining, working conditions, wages, hours and the like. They were precariously situated within the mechanisms of a wildly fluctuating economy characterized by a cyclical procession of slumps and booms, often microregional in effect. The fate, if not the foundation, of individual trade unions rested as much on external economic factors as on effective organizing or sufficient militancy. Women's unions were certainly as, if not more, susceptible than their male counterparts to these oscillations, and their success was often thus restricted to those areas where their presence in the work-force was pronounced; it was in London and, even more, in provincial industrial towns that societies of women bookbinders, upholstresses, tailoresses and the like found small but sufficient numbers to organize.[2]

We know little of these individual unions in specific industries, beyond their obvious concentration in more artisanal areas of work where skill could, at least on a temporary basis, sometimes override the disadvantage of sex in the establishment of trade societies. As with male craft unions, numbers were small, and women workers faced sex-related stigmas additional to those experienced by men joining unions.

The data we have for the larger umbrella organizations based largely in London – where worker organization was often reasonably high and heavy industry low – is far more copious. These were committees run by women with considerable overall experience of feminist activism and significantly greater amounts of time to spend on such activities than the working women whose interests they attempted to represent. If their exhortations to activism sometimes resembled the language employed in more openly philanthropic arenas, we should not be surprised. An aura of social gentility and respectability frequently shrouded their practice in this, as in other areas, and indeed on occasion an echo of spiritualism even found its way into their language and practice. Emilia Dilke, who always exhibited a curious blend of divine asceticism and a distinctly worldly secularism described trade unionists as ' . . . soldiers of labour, who are fighting to preserve to the nation all that is noble in human life. They are fighting to deliver the sacred city of the spirit from captivity to the heathenish conditions of modern industry.'[3]

Whilst it has been argued that the impact of middle-class involvement in trade union organization served as a means of rendering putative militancy lukewarm and of conferring an often inappropriate respectabily, one might equally argue that in positing a solidarity premised on gender rather than on class, the feminist movement offered not conservatism but subtle subversion as its primary agenda.

At the same time, it is clear that division along class lines, with its inevitable experiential differentiation, was the cause of one of the most deeply felt rifts within the nineteenth-century women's movement. With the second spurt of protective legislation undertaken by government, which gathered momentum particularly in the last two decades of the century, many feminists chose to articulate their suspicion of state power and authority precisely in this context.[4] Though by 1893 when women factory inspectors were finally employed, the Women's Trade Union League (WTUL) had moved to an endorsement of such legislative measures, it had from its inception in 1874 (as the Women's Protective and Provident League) taken a strongly oppositional stance on any such implementation, as an obstacle to women's right to work.

In this respect it was consonant with the most commonly held views within the feminist movement, views which indubitably served to divide it sharply from the emergent socialist wing of English politics, though less markedly from working women whose jobs, after all, were under threat. James Schmiechen has noted, with some considerable justification, that 'there is little doubt that the impact of government reform was an unwelcome reality for many late Victorian and Edwardian working people.'[5] The issue was always and everywhere a complex one, though pragmatic assessment was almost invariably the practical victor in debate. Where for middle-class feminists, even when concerned with women's loss of earning capacity rather than a specific avocation of anti-state *laissez-faire* values, the issue remained an entirely theoretical principle, for working women the issue was clouded. For them, there were the questions of the unpleasantness and the danger of many of the jobs under scrutiny, the considerations of child care and other domestic concerns competing with the working day and, above all, the vital question of where the most money might be earned. It is, thus, not without substantive consideration that Jane Lewis writes that 'women in manual trades objected to the rigidity of the Factory Acts rather than the principle of protective legislation *per se*.'[6]

Even within the women's trade union movement itself, the implementation of protective legislation did not always meet with collective approbation.[7] Many feminist trade unionists enthusiastically endorsed a non-gendered reading of the principles behind such legislation, accepting the need for the state's role in the amelioration of working conditions. Indeed, ironically, and as Judith Baer has pointed out, where no trade organization exists (or where such organizations are too weak to exert pressure) 'legislation may be the only form of amelioration'.[8]

Feminists were quick to point out, too, the far-reaching ramifications which implementation of gendered protection would have. Jane Brownlow read a paper at the London Conference of the Women's Emancipation Union in October 1896 in which she couched her support for the principle of protective legislation in a trenchant critique of its gender-bound application.

Any law which places full-grown women in the position of a helpless, thoughtless, irresponsible child, who must be legislated for, has the effect of creating and fostering an opinion that women are helpless, irresponsible beings, incapable of taking care of their own interests – an opinion which, untrue though it be in the present day, is yet so deeply rooted that it forms the chief hindrance to the emancipation of women.[9]

It was Brownlow, too, who pointed out so cogently that the various pieces of legislation had to be read in partial terms, As she showed in her address to the conference, only certain areas of work were affected by the acts; not only were the female-dominated sweated trades certainly outside their scope but 'no legislator has yet attempted to make laws which shall prevent women from taking night work when nursing, or acting, or dancing. No one has yet proposed to restrict the number of hours given to her work overtime by the female teacher.'[10] Brownlow could have added that the vast bevy of female domestic servants hidden within the households of the legislators were another group wholly untouched by the factory-based restriction of this period.

For women whose stance was a wholesale opposition to any and all forms of protective legislation, contemporary historical judgement has frequently been unkind, assessing their position as derivable simply from a *laissez-faire* and class-specific antagonism to any form of state intervention. Their position has been found to represent a divorce of class and sex,[11] an exercise in the unnecessary polarization of issues,[12] and an alliance between feminists and employers.[13]

The reality of the feminist anti-protection position, whether one regards their various analyses of this area of legislation as correct or not, is considerably more complex and problematized than any of these dismissals, in fact, suggest. Jane Lewis has attempted a partial resuscitation of the stand taken by opponents of protective legislation by pointing out that their insistence on women's unqualified right to work challenged the growing idealization of motherhood which accompanied such legislation.[14]

Feminists opposing protective measures outright were often the products of an older political tradition deriving from a liberal ethic centred on the polarization of centralized authority and individual autonomy. Their belief in autonomy fed the need for female self-determination. At the same time, the actions of the state gave women no cause to think that it might act benevolently toward their claims. It was thus that within feminist thought the tensions between notions of individualism and of collectivism centred on the issue of individual versus state power and authority. The slow acceptance of statutory intervention amongst trade unionists and socialists perturbed many women who rather saw the combination of male interests served by such a partnership than a progressive alliance for change that would favour women's issues. Their experience of the male monopoly in trade unionism, the device of the family wage, the bare tolerance with which the Trade Union Congress greeted discussion of women's concerns, coupled with their experience of parliamentary activities in that context, was hardly likely to convince women already imbued with a suspicion of state control of the desirability of extending governmental authority over any farther aspect of women's lives.

The stand against protective legislation taken by prominent feminist activists like Millicent Garrett Fawcett, Jessie Boucherett and Helen Blackburn proved divisive for the movement as a whole. When, in the early 1890s, the WTUL under the guidance of its President Emilia Dilke, moved from almost two decades of opposition to a pro-legislation policy, it was not without cost. In emphatic opposition to its policy change, activist Ada Heather-Bigg founded the rival Women's Employment Defence League precisely to drum up support against the further implementation of such measures. Women such as Heather-Bigg subsequently found themselves – and have remained for many historians – branded as destructively bourgeois, unable to accept the positive potential of the state's role in curbing the excesses practised in the workplace.[15]

In their opposition to state intervention, feminist activists were neither careless of the conditions in which labouring people lived and worked nor hostile to the principle of unionism. Where they did attack trade unionism, it was precisely because unions had traditionally not only excluded women from the benefits and protection offered by membership but, in a plethora of ways, sought to exclude women as competitors on the job market. Equally, their suspicion of the state was certainly well grounded. It was not that the greater proportion of feminist activists *because* they hailed from materially comfortable backgrounds were thus unable or unwilling to revise their position to incorporate a class analysis, it was rather that their political understanding rested fundamentally on gender as a category of domination and power beyond class. Undeniably they blindly imposed values inimical or alien to the experience of working women on occasion; none the less, what they offered was an alternative and realistic solidarity amongst women. That the class divisions so effective in Victorian England made their vision untenable is a telling comment on the pervasive power of male political ordering.

The position on the state that feminist opponents of factory regulation assumed, though, was not always wholly consistent. Whilst their critique of the state's unwillingness and incompetence in legislating changes in the power structures of gender were as accurate as they were heartfelt, their attitudes were not always consonant across campaigns. Some of the same women who called for an end to state intervention were simultaneously active in post-Contagious Diseases social purity issues where the new moralism looked precisely to the state as a potential agency of amelioration. Although anti-CD activism had been explicit in its opposition to state intervention (drawing upon the specific débâcle of certification and regulation as a prime example of what occurs with the imposition of a centralized authority), subsequent campaigning in related areas often demanded that the state accept responsibility for legislating various moral positions, as chapter 5 has shown. None the less, we can discern some shadow of difference in feminist evaluations of the role of the state in the moral and the industrial arenas. In calling on the state to enunciate principles governing sexual conduct, feminists were essentially addressing the issue of behaviour and focusing largely on reforming men. Legislation which affected women's place in industry, however, impinged directly upon women's lives and most centrally on their capacity to earn a living. Thus, though the feminist position did not necessarily always cohere, the seeming positional inconsistency is not all that great. There was a concrete difference between the practical effects of these two theoretically similar areas of legislation that had specific resonances for women.

The problem for nineteenth-century feminists thus rested in large part on the issue of agency, on where to locate and fight for the desired changes in society, whether in the collective sphere or the individual, the public or the private arena. It was a tension which echoed, of course, that dichotomy which shaped and dictated their lives, and which was so often the target of feminist activity. To represent the feminism of this period as hopelessly entrenched in middle-class values, in anti-state liberalism, in evangelicalism is to deny the force of their specifically gendered analysis of the body politic. Functioning within a system designed precisely to deny their agency, the contradictions and oppositions crystallized by the divisions over support of protective legislation serves rather to clarify their specifically and cogently feminist, albeit not always sufficiently consistent, outlook and interpretation.

In consequence, and perhaps with some naivety, there was some tendency on the part of feminist activists to pursue the solidarity of sisterhood without due acknowledgement of the wedges driven through English society by the inescapable class system. These notions of a gendered bond overriding other and palpable areas of differentiation manifested themselves in a variety of ways. We can trace the connectedness of the various wings of the feminist movement, for instance, in the pages of the *Women's Union Journal*, organ of the WPPL.[16] Throughout its history, far more topics than simply those pertaining to union or even industrial matters were aired with frequency and liveliness. Leaders on the question of married women's property rights, discussions of rational dress and other feminist-related topics, all came under scrutiny – gaining considerable support – suggesting a consonance of interests between those activists writing for and reading the journal, and those active across a variety of other feminist campaigns.

Solidarity was not always and not necessarily expressed in consciously and openly feminist terms, a silence which has led Helen Jones to argue that the 'appointment of women [factory] inspectors should perhaps not be regarded as a victory for feminism, so much as a channelling of organized women's demands into material changes, which barely touched on fundamental power relations.'[17] Jones is absolutely correct in pointing out that little if no difference in the status quo transpired from the women's appointments. However, the very fact of their appointment, as well as her identification that it was catalysed by autonomous female demands, is itself significant. The new women inspectors saw themselves (as Jones points out)[18] as pioneers conducting their profession in ways tangibly different from their male colleagues. This separate identity evidences their sense of female identification, of commonality with the women whose working conditions it was their job to investigate, not at the level of class relations, but as women concerned with women's labour.

For the working women, the appointment of female factory inspectors had been an issue raised by them at the annual conferences of the TUC for some twenty years before the Home Office finally undertook implementation in the teeth of substantial male hostility. For both parties, the new female inspectorate and the women activists in trade union politics, the issues were the needs and the problems facing working women, a group disadvantaged by sex as much as by class. That realization and understanding critically affected their definition and articulation of the key elements of their feminist politics, a politics which, as we have seen, stressed gender over class solidarity.

The drive to initiate the appointment of women inspectors none the less never emerged as a central feminist campaign, though individual activists were generous with their support. The TUC, though endorsing the principle of such appointments, did little that was concrete in furthering its success. However, all those who advocated the demand, in however nugatory a fashion, agreed that the women appointed should be selected from amongst those with practical experience in the field and not from the usual middle-class pool of civil service recruits. Their pleas fell, not surprisingly, on deaf ears and the first appointees were, as noted in chapter 7, all women with no more experience of factory labour and working conditions than any of their male colleagues.[19]

In a recent book on women and radicalism, James Young argues that in Scotland the lack of a strong bourgeois feminist movement as precedent inhibited the development of feminism, resulting instead in a markedly militant female labour force with scant interest in women's issues.[20] In thus dividing feminist from industrial and related activities so starkly, Young reads feminism as a politics both reducible to and subsumed by class analysis, as have other contemporary writers. The constant attempt by feminist activists to connote women as a separate category (and often as a separate class), their reading of seemingly specifically working-class issues such as protective legislation in terms premised other than on class suggest that this common – and frequently fault-finding – analysis is a misreading insistent upon privileging the divisiveness of class over that of gender. As feminist activists never tired of pointing out – whether it was in their attempts to win the suffrage, to challenge the legislative double standard or to implement educational and occupational opportunities for women – all women, regardless of class, were subject to all men.

The issues thus raised by the articulation of a feminist position in this arena, issues which clustered firmly around the question of dependency, remained throughout this period, as they do today, tinged with an uneasy ambivalence. The issue of protection had far-ranging ramifications; it was a myth which feminists were determined to combat in every area of their concern. Where it clashed, as it did in this instance, with contesting claims of class solidarity, feminists were undeterred. For them, however mismanaged the interpretation might appear in retrospect, there was a direct genealogy of dependence encompassed as much by the family wage as by the implementation of restrictions on dangerous, unhealthy, and thus relatively well-remunerated, work.

Whatever the feminist position, however, the question still remains of how far we can determine an overlap between known feminism and the organization of working women during this period. It is Olive Banks's contention that, of all the activities in which feminist involvement is identifiable, trade unionism remained, throughout the century, the most isolated.[21] Its tentative relations with the nascent organizations of socialism served, if only latterly, to bring about a distinction between women who saw socialism as a means of achieving gender parity and those whose mistrust of political philosophies framed around what they saw as male interests embraced the socialist agenda alongside older political manifestos. The interpretation of this era of the women's movement as polarized into socialist (and hence working-class) feminism and bourgeois feminism replicates within an alternative political culture precisely those tenacious elements of the mainstream which the lifestyles and politics of these feminists intended to challenge.

It is indicative that few nineteenth-century English feminists had institutional and formal ties with labour or socialist organizations. Of the sample used to determine this study, 3 per cent were Labour party members, 2 per cent had connections with the Independent Labour Party and 1 per cent with Hyndman's Marxist Social Democratic Federation. In part, these figures reflect little more than chronology; these were organizations founded only in the closing years of the century. Some 19 per cent of this sample had Liberal affiliations, but the party had not only a far longer history (and we are thus counting affiliation over a longer stretch of time) and pedigree but a proven, if unsatisfactory, parliamentary record. Moreover, the great surge of support for governmental Liberalism was roughly coincident with the rise of this wave of feminist activity, dating from the late 1850s and 1860s. Their parallel gathering of activist momentum doubtless helped feed the connection in important ways; though women remained unrepresented in the electorate, the rise of a new and governmentally active political force was an important and heartening step, a potential repository of action.

Though specific political affiliation to labour and socialist organizations remained far lower than that to the Liberal party throughout this period, other quantifiable indices of support tell a slightly different story. Eleven per cent of the sample were engaged in specific trade union activity and 12 per cent belonged to the WPPL/WTUL. Four per cent were members of the Women's Co-operative Guild, which grew out of the Co-operative movement, again late in the period, in 1883. Thus women with an interest in what we might dub issues specific to working women often chose to become active in the women's movement in preference to affiliation with a particular party, even with a party which chose direct association with those issues. Women with a primary concern for the problems of women workers might thus be found in larger numbers in the various women's trade and trade union organizations than in the infant Labour party or similar cross-gender organizations.

In some respects the figures reflect, too, the overall difficulties female trade unionism faced in recruiting members. James Schmiechen has argued that the type of work common in the female labour force was such that it inhibited women from embracing unionism; by the last years of the century when mass trade unionism finally began to make inroads on the British political scene, many women workers (particularly married women) were concentrated in the sweated homework sector, driven out of factory industry by the powerful combination of separate sphere ideology and the increasing intensification of heavy industry. In Schmiechen's words, 'Because so many women worked in the home and not the factory, their work experience and value system remained largely traditional and pre-industrial.'[22] More obviously, of course, the individuation of paid work tasks into the private household and away from a collective workplace made effective organization virtually impossible.

None the less, the dual existence of both women's trade unions and feminist-associated broader organizations did aid in the growth and extension of the movement. In the 1890s, when unskilled male unionism began to flex its muscles, though still sporadically, not only were trade union and other working-class organizations gradually establishing and maintaining their political role in British society, but perhaps even more determinedly, so was the women's movement. In the 1890s, women activists had wrung considerably more victories out of successive and reluctant governments than had either trade unionists or adult suffragists. In this context, it is surprising that historians have chosen rather to credit 'new unionism' and working-class strength with encouraging working-class feminism than in seeing women's own gains in confidence, articulacy and political acumen as factors. After all, women of all classes continued to face an endless succession of exclusionary practices: from educational opportunity, from various manual trades and almost all professions, from political adulthood and from a host of organizations including those dedicated to the various modes of working-class representation. Whilst late nineteenth-century feminism certainly did not rank female union organization at the very peak of its priorities, there was still far more support for it there than from mainstream trade unionism.

The problems of female trade unionism were further exacerbated by the growing polarization of male and female work, particularly in the manual sector. Increasingly, women workers were less and less in the same trades as men, and concentrated increasingly in unskilled and semi-skilled areas of work. In many occupations, formal exclusion of women from unions was unnecessary because the work-force was an entirely male one. It was in traditionally and increasingly female areas of employment that unions found their least fertile ground, not least because they also seldom looked to those areas as potential sources of membership.

Just as trade unions found recruitment of working women a difficult task, feminist organizations encountered similar problems. Although almost half the sample had direct experience of paid employment, as we have already noted, few were locked into the less pleasant and most poorly paid sectors of labour where large numbers of working-class women were to be found. Only 6 per cent were engaged, at any point in their lives, in manual trades, amongst whom we find bookbinders, mill workers, shop assistants, watch engravers and ropemakers.[23]

It is difficult, given these figures, not to concur with Olive Banks that working-class women, even in areas such as trade unionism, remained a minority within the feminist movement throughout this period.[24] Banks also points out that the paucity of data – almost invariably a problem when researching on women – is most acute for working-class and for locally focused women.[25] Her assessment is an accurate one, but it should also be noted that the two categories overlap frequently. Whilst more leisured and wealthier women might be inclined to travel, and many were seasonally resident in the metropolis, working-class women were far likelier to be place-bound by economic and family ties to one locale. The dependencies around which women's lives clustered made mobility far less likely and local activism far more attractive to them.

Despite this, one of the most interesting aspects of the growing feminist interest in trade union and labour activity was its effect on the political geography of feminism. As this area of interest gathered strength in the later years of the century, so did feminism spread its regional wings, finding acceptance and interest in places other than those associated earlier with its following. The net result of this expansion was not only to enhance those areas which might be seen as strongholds of a feminist voice beyond the most obvious haunts of the urban *haute bourgeoisie* but to cross-fertilize further the various causes which severally made up the women's movement of this period.

As early as 1882, the *Women's Union Journal* proudly listed the areas in which the organization had had success. Though some were in the more predictable centres of feminist consciousness, such as Manchester and Bristol, there were also organizational successes in less immediately obvious environments. The introduction to the first issue of the journal for 1882 lists industrial centres such as Leicester, Liverpool and Nottingham, and also some rather more surprising sites such as Dewsbury and Folkestone.[26]

London, despite its magnetism as a centre of feminist activity, was slow to witness the growth of female unionism but then, much of the female labour force in London was involved in sweated industry, a large portion of it in the home.[27] Moreover, the radicalism that had fed other forms of unionism and militancy in London in earlier periods was almost wholly male in origin and exclusionary in practice. The divide between the specifically feminist and the specifically unionist contingent is nowhere more apparent than here; Ellen Mappen has shown that while the WPPL's membership was heavily concentrated in London, the organization none the less had little impact on the capital's female work-force.[28] It was not merely the failure of feminism that this discrepancy indicates; trade unionists overall found a more sympathetic environment elsewhere, more particularly in key industrial counties farther north.

A similar regional make-up can be seen in both the co-operative and the women's co-operative movement, both of which were inaugurated and found their sustaining membership in more northerly regions. The early strongholds of the Women's Co-operative Guild, formed in 1883, again with the help of metropolitan feminists such as Margaret Llewellyn Davies, were often in mill and factory towns.

The regional diversity to which working-class involvement, however small, committed the movement and the parallel concentration on working-class issues led also to a broadening of the scope of feminist interest, visible both in campaigning and in personnel. Despite the differing approaches to protective legislation which divided the movement and led on occasion to organizational upset, a broad sweep of activists prominent in other areas of campaigning also lent their support to issues of unionization and women's labour. Millicent Garrett Fawcett was an original trustee of the National Union of Women Workers. The Sturge sisters, Lilias Ashworth and one of the Misses Priestman sat on its earliest executive committee whilst Yorkshire feminist Alice Scatcherd was one of its corresponding members along with Elizabeth Wolstenholme Elmy's husband, Benjamin. Later in the century Frances Balfour, Louisa Hubbard and Dorothea Beale were committee members, with women such as Emily Davies, Augusta Leigh Brown and Ada Heather-Bigg representing various other women's organizations at the annual conference held in Nottingham in October 1895.[29]

Similarly, the WCG actively involved itself in compiling data for Clara Collett's ground-breaking work on women's employment as well as in collecting signatures for the 1893 national women's suffrage appeal. The organization actively sought links, too, with groups such as the Women's Trade Union Association and its successor the Women's Industrial Council. Individuals likewise crossed campaign boundaries with frequency. Emma Paterson (née Smith), founder of the WPPL, was immensely active in a host of feminist campaigns. Norbert Soldon has noted that aside from her trade union and related activities, Paterson acted as secretary to the Vigilance Association, was an active campaigner for women contesting elective municipal office and aided in the foundation of various co-operative societies.[30]

Those women who, when the renamed WPPL assumed a favourable attitude to protective legislation in the early 1890s, broke ranks and joined the Women's Employment Defence League, were equally comprehensive in their pursuits. Jessie Boucherett and Helen Blackburn were involved in many areas besides women's employment. By the time she began campaigning actively against protective legislation, Boucherett was a veteran of this era of feminism, having been active in the Langham Place Circle in the 1850s and 1860s.

The sheer breadth of Margaret Bondfield's acquaintances suggests some degree of and some potential for cross-over between differing political positions even at this juncture. Bondfield knew many of the active feminists of her day and mixed in their circles as well as in the trade union milieu in which she made her career. In addition, she had a wide acquaintance amongst socialist groups which included such prominent European women as Emma Goldman.

The overlap was tremendously beneficial to both parties, offering working women a practical outlet for feminist identification and some expertise in political strategy not derived from the traditional sources. For the feminists, it was an opportunity to embrace neglected areas of severe subordination, strengthening the identification of women's issues as an autonomous political cause.

None the less, it may be that we can still distinguish between women whose primary focus was trade unionism and those whose feminist principles could embrace a variety of connected issues. Certainly there was some tension within female unionism as to whether identification as members of the same trade or as women was paramount, a tension neither fully articulated nor wholly resolved in this period. It was a tension manifest explicitly in the organizational make-up of the movement; whilst the umbrella WPPL saw itself as an institution devoted to aiding women in the formation of an autonomous politics, individual unions necessarily identified as well on an occupational as on a gendered basis, a factor which rendered their political articulation distinct from explicit feminism. These differing characteristics were not, however, either necessarily static or monolithic; women such as Julia Varley and Emma Paterson straddled the two worlds with seeming ease, productive and active in both unionism and feminism.

In addition, it was seldom that for women political involvement would not be filtered through family and domestic identification. One of the principal difficulties in establishing a successful female trade unionism was the sheer invisibility of so much female labour; the inauguration of a role in trade unionism for women in itself made that invisibility no longer feasible.[31] Even though short-lived, women's unions, like the larger umbrella organizations attempting to nurture them, at least clarified the principle of women's involvement both in the labour force and in various organizing activities. The effect of this political involvement, both in the case of individuals and collectively for the feminist movement, was to expand the remit of feminist activity and mobilize, however sporadically, a potential amongst a far wider group of women than earlier campaigns, however well-intentioned, had been able to do. Even articulating the potential for a feminist configuration which could acknowledge the parameters of class but still argue rather for the centrality of gender identification, the slow and difficult growth of working-class feminism was crucial in expanding the language and consciousness of feminism in important ways.

The inseparability for women of home and workplace, whilst it complicated the tasks of feminism, also served to render its analysis both more comprehensive and more convincing. Whether it was because women so often took waged work within the setting of the home or because work settings in so many ways replicated the hierarchies organizing the private sphere,[32] it was almost impossible for women to escape the trap of this dichotomous reading of their lives. Feminist politics, whether focusing on trade unionism, women's labour, their sexuality or their legal status, fully recognized the implications of that polarization and in their formulation of a political philosophy rejected it through redefinition. In posing a politics and a strategy which brought private lives to bear on public issues and public attention to bear on private lives, feminists sought to collapse separate sphere ideology in its

dominant form. In the specific area of trade unionism, feminist organization of women workers challenged the lack of access to a work identity
which in fuelling the myth of domesticity, had rendered a vast female
work-force invisible. By highlighting and legislating women's activity in a
few high profile and traditionally masculine areas of work, protective
legislation similarly allowed the collective conscience to be salved whilst
enormous areas of female labour remained untouched and invisible.

With the gradual move of feminist activists towards protective legislation in the closing years of the century, we can trace a movement within
this corner of feminist thinking from a blanket individualism to an
acceptance of special needs.[33] Interestingly, this shift paralleled earlier
considerations in education campaigns when, in the 1860s and 1870s,
Emily Davies had bitterly opposed efforts to introduce a special needs
curriculum for women students at Cambridge. (See chapter 7.)

The dynamic between individualism and the collective identification
invoked in the special needs argument was central to the configuration of
feminism as a separate and alternative political identity at this time. As
earlier chapters have demonstrated, a substantial number of women
actively involved in campaigning throughout the second half of the
nineteenth century had learned their earliest political and tactical lessons
within an environment framed by liberalism and radical liberalism. The
stress on individual character, strength and rights which was so dominant a feature of English political rhetoric in this period was derived
heavily from that stance. For many women, their adult encounter with
feminism often challenged that position fundamentally. Carole Pateman
has argued powerfully that 'the "individual" is the bedrock from which
contractarian doctrine is constructed',[34] and it is significant that so great
a part of feminist and female concern over working women foundered
precisely on the unyielding rock of contractarianism. Rosemary Feurer
has recently asserted[35] that for nineteenth-century feminists the notion of
freedom of contract was their most complete and radical expression of
the call for independence in the sphere of labour. Yet contract was
something that feminists had for some time felt comfortable either
attacking or altering in many areas of their lives.

For the most part alteration in contract had been limited to women
who found the traditional marriage contract constraining when themselves on the verge of wedlock. The issue of the labour contract raised by
feminist interest in employment, however, introduced some interesting
means whereby women could explore the duplicitous applications of
separate sphere ideology.

The pervasiveness of contract as the appropriate means of ordering a
variety of social relations (labour, marriage, et al.) had implications for
the relative condition of the two sexes. The very existence of contracts

suggests a measure of organization. The contract to govern was seen as the basis of 'civil society'; in the case of employment, the labour market came to rest increasingly on the ability of trade unions to negotiate agreement with an employer. Contracts involving women – whether marital or occupational – were rarely organized[36] and seldom negotiable in this way, a further reason for the urgent need for autonomous female trade unionism. Organization and negotiation, like contract, were male prerogatives, inapplicable in the female sphere.

Whilst it was clear that marital arrangements represented a contractual area relating specifically to women although not controlled by them, employment contracts remained agreements between men; much of the non-feminist support for protective legislation rested precisely on an implacably dichotomized definition of who had the capacity to contract. Given that acceptance of the marriage contract effectively and formally ate into the already restricted freedoms of women, the notion that contract was a 'paradigm of free agreement'[37] made it even less available to unfree women in the employment context. Whilst men could contract their labour to an employer, women could contract theirs only to a husband; contract was a hierarchy of status built as much upon gender as upon class. Indeed, many pointed both to the gender and the class inequities embodied in its very principles.

It is objected that the State has no right to interfere with the individual who if of full age ought to be free to say how long and under what conditions he or she wishes to work. But this objection is entirely fallacious. If employer and employed could meet upon entirely equal terms it might be possible to reason thus. But they never do, for the worker, who has only his labour to live upon, has no other means of support while he is bargaining with an employer, so in order to subsist he is compelled to accept terms disadvantaged to himself.[38]

Brownlow's argument is an interesting one in a number of ways, not least in that she chooses to revert to a male example of unfreedom to make her point in this context, thereby intensifying the image of lack of freedom. In enquiring into how voluntary the contract is in reality, she implicitly draws on arguments which make clear the tensions in nineteenth-century England between individualism and notions of collective authority and agency. It was a dilemma which made manifest the need for feminists to reconcile their continued respect for individualism with their observable belief in the efficacy and power of collective sisterhood and action. Again, a traditional reading of individual and collective as polar points on the political terrain makes this feminist stance appear both confusing and inconsistent; it was, in fact, the genesis of a reformulation which radically challenged the existing definitional boundaries of politics. Women committed to a feminist lifestyle sought rather to merge a commitment to individual autonomy with an acknowledgement of the force of collective women's action. The nature of their campaigning, in these specific areas as in others, and their criticisms of existing structures surrounding the very principles of contractarianism, demonstrate their attempts at moving towards a feminist articulation of that melding of a damaging and dominant dichotomy. The necessarily collective definition of the inequalities and injustices arising from sexual identification which feminism forced upon individualism secured some distinct political relocation. Feminist opposition continued often to be cast in seemingly individualist terms – namely, the right to contract, to vote, to acquire citizenship – but the tenacity of these formal legal symbols long remained potent, challenging the inventiveness of feminist strategy.

The slow process whereby the needs and problems of the women from the poorer classes came to figure more and more in feminist perspectives further eroded the impact of traditional individualism. Its inadequacies in explaining their position or in offering amelioration became increasingly obvious. Millicent Garrett Fawcett, a staunch liberal, saw through the myth of the formal equality of individuals in the economic sphere, arguing that the exclusionary practices preventing women from equality in the workplace made the whole notion of equal pay a hollow one.[39] Her argument differs little in substance from that of Jane Brownlow in pointing out the gap between the principles of equality and the practice of inequality.

This gap between ideology and reality was a powerful and recurring motif in feminist rhetoric, a theme strengthened by the growing and concrete concentration later in the century on the plight of working and working-class women. The constant expansion of feminist interest of which this is a part led committed women inexorably to see the relentless interconnectedness of their varying concerns, and the senselessness of divorcing the different wings of feminist campaigning, except for tactical reasons. It was not, as some historians have argued, that women were 'detaching the question of women's rights from the basic social issues, by making it a separate question'.[40] That formulation subsumes 'women's rights' in a hierarchical assessment of the 'basic social issues' in similar ways to Anne Godwin's assessment of Emma Paterson as 'seem[ing] more feminist than trade unionist'.[41] In both cases, not only is there a forced and hierarchical separation of various political concerns but an unspoken assumption that feminism is a luxury, a tangent to more basic bread-and-butter issues.

In many ways, it was such judgements that nineteenth-century feminists faced when they turned their attention to areas of working-class concern from the 1870s on. The movement had certainly taken root, predictably perhaps, among leisured, educated and, on occasion, already politicized women whose attempts to straddle class boundaries were often naive and clumsy, and sometimes disastrous. Their intention, though, was consistent with the reformulation of political culture upon which their feminist perspective was premised. It offered an analysis of domination centred primarily upon sex rather than upon class, though acknowledging its further mediation through that socio-economic filter. Feminists proposed a solution rooted in the bringing together of public and private spheres apparent in the cross-over between their own personal and political lives.

Clearly, for working-class women whose aspirations and whose daily lives differed starkly from those of their wealthier sisters, lifestyle changes were less feasible. However, the very notion of an organizational autonomy coupled with an acknowledgement of their presence in the labour force was a distinctive contribution to the political arena. It was not that women championed their own right to work in uncongenial jobs as a principle; dire economic reality governed that 'choice' far more often than an urge to independence. None the less, given their presence and numbers in the workforce – and the constant threat to their livelihood from legislation, from trade unionism and from the reclassification of skills – this more positive attitude to an often grim situation represented a unique articulation of women's role and rights in this tough and hostile arena.

9

Organizing Principles: Re-reading the Political Genealogy of Feminism

Nineteenth-century English feminism was far more vigorous, diverse and prescient a movement than we might at first perceive. Though it culled its personnel largely, though by no means exclusively, from women born into material comfort, its concerns demonstrated the primacy of gender as the motor of oppression. As a movement cognizant of the effects of class stratification but attempting to understand that within a more comprehensive framework structured by the imposed binary opposition of female and male, nineteenth-century feminism distanced itself from other contemporary movements. Its determined concentration on noting diversity of circumstance contained within a wider collective experience of womanhood had a significant influence on its political practice and philosophy. Despite its relative homogeneity of class position, the emphasis on collective experience and action, the rejection of heroization and the meshing of public and private, moves the feminism of this period beyond the confines of traditional political practice.

It would be easy to represent the feminist movement of this period as a vanguard of awareness and of practice amongst women. And yet to do so would be to return to a traditional reckoning in which both collective and individual agency become submerged in a dualist reading reserving power to the *cognoscenti* and arrogating to them the 'correct' forms of resistance. Notions of vanguard implicitly place the favoured group beyond ideology, beyond discourse, outside their culture. Whilst feminists at this time were clear in their articulation of the gendered ills of their society, they were still within its grasp as both constructors and consumers of their culture.[1] They were neither victims without recourse to challenge nor bold agents of a change that others were too victimized to see. Feminists working through a variety of positions at this time, and embracing the need for a changing perspective through both experience and circumstance, claimed no such role. To do so, would have been to replicate exactly those structures of domination that their campaigns sought – if not always successfully – to undermine. Joan Scott's contention that 'political movements develop tactically not logically . . . from a mélange . . . of interpretations and programs'[2] is an excellent summary of the flux and inconsistency that typify such movements, read too often as static in their prescriptions.

The idea of a vanguard has further implications, too, for feminist scholars. Vanguard theory necessarily evokes an evolutionary teleology and a hierarchically ordered assessment which forces us as commentators to pass judgement as if from a more 'advanced' position. The frequent use of the term '"first wave" feminism' to describe the activities of this period entrenches that position, as well as imposing a static starting date on a movement with rather longer antecedents. When does '"first wave" feminism' begin? If the Langham Place years are its foundation, then what can we say about Mary Wollstonecraft, Anna Wheeler and a host of other earlier women activists? If Wollstonecraft is the touchstone of this proclivity to periodize, then what of Katherine Philips, Margaret Cavendish, Mary Collier or Mary Astell? And so on. The exercise is a fruitless one but it draws attention to the absurdity, and indeed the impossibility, of pigeon-holing these activities inside an artifice of chronology. The 'first wave' epithet now employed so commonly to describe an extraodinary range of nineteenth-century women implicitly decontextualizes by hinting at a comparison with the modern movement. Invoking ancestry all too often involves spotlighting earlier misjudgements as a means of improving the contemporary profile.

The common parallels drawn between feminism and the common exercise of philanthropy, in which so many middle-class women were involved at this time, are similarly untenable.[3] The idea that women learned the techniques of organization and an independence of action through their unpaid charity work is highly misleading. So, too, is the less optimistic notion that the class-based patterns of power inherent in such activities were necessarily imprinted on relations between middle- and working-class feminists. The practices and principles informing nineteenth-century feminism are distinguishable from those central to the philanthropic enterprise, because they markedly undercut the idea of dually-conceived social relations. Whilst the basis of philanthropy frequently devolved on rendering inequality acceptable, feminists explored those relations, questioning their polarized basis in economic, political, social and sexual terms. When feminist educationalists looked askance at reproducing the existing curricular arrangements of male education or the same methods of discipline, when feminist employers offered working conditions intentionally better than other employers, when 'respectable', women publicly voiced their disapproval of the sexual double standard, they were rewriting the political script in fundamental ways. It was a radical project of redefinition.

Many of the campaigns demonstrate the capacity such women developed to capitalize on inconsistencies and confusions in their society, to seize – ironically enough – on the vulnerabilities within the system. These were moments of pragmatic triumph when women could demonstrate the ideological failures of that system in its own terms. Activists pointed to the partial class-rendered sensibilities of male chivalry and courtesy, to the sharp schizophrenia of passive and active sexuality, to the massive gaps in protective legislation which left innumerable working women unattended. Bob Connell has singled out the franchise campaigners as capturing that vulnerability. The campaign, he says, 'was not a diversion from "social" issues . . . ; it seized on the major contradiction that the development of the state at that point had exposed.'[4] Their exposure of inconsistency and injustice did not always, nor ever very rapidly, culminate in successful capitulation, but that is hardly the point. It would be foolish to attempt to measure the movement's success specifically in terms of formal victories.

This period certainly witnessed some changes – expansion in educational provision, changes in the laws of married women's property, changes in municipal franchise qualification amongst them. Some important differences also separate them. Whilst the improvements in educational practice and availability were almost wholly secured by feminist action in the non-governmental sphere, the other rights ceded came necessarily from parliamentary decision, namely, from male concession. It is interesting to note how very much more far-reaching were the changes implemented solely by feminist action than those reliant on government.

Feminists thus spread their activities across a wide-ranging landscape, ensuring that they were neither wholly dependent upon securing the ear of the establishment nor entirely removed from the powerful symbolism of formal equality. In treading this path, it is clear that far more was at stake than winning a role in parliamentary politics, or in gaining entrance to the male clubs of privilege. To measure and judge feminism by that yardstick would be to misunderstand and misrepresent not only its motives but the very complexities of power and ideology themselves. Power and authority were not then, nor can be, contained exclusively within the state or in any other single site, but are rather dispersed, visibly and invisibly, in gendered social institutions, in formal legal, political and economic structures.[5] When we piece together the variety of means and the sites of attack which feminists chose to pursue in the nineteenth century their overall perspective becomes clearer. How else to contest multiply experienced and perceived structures of power than with similarly multiple ways and means?

The contradictions[6] which such diverse, incremental and layered authority displayed lent feminists a powerful weapon but have also sometimes diffused our understanding of their matching strategies. Feminists did not displace their energies by severing their politics into an abundance of single issue campaigns, but rather used those several campaigning questions to demonstrate the hydra-headed nature of the beast they confronted.

Seeking to effect equality or justice in formal legal terms was certainly an important feature of feminist activity at this time, a public declaration of visibility. It needs, though, to be seen as just one means of contesting authority within the full spectrum of feminist activity as it confronted the entrenched permeation of patriarchal power in a plurality of ways. These were women who consistently and determinedly yoked public to private and private to public. They made public their private lives in politicizing both marriage and singlehood and in questioning the double standard. They made private their public lives by demonstrating the importance and longevity of feminist friendships forged through action in the political arena.

Feminism informed their decision making at every step. It shaped their marital choices, their child rearing, their social calendars and contacts. It coloured their understanding of political issues, their assessment of politicians and political groupings and their choice of activities.

Above all, a feminist perspective offered women more than a glimmer of autonomy, the chance to consider their lives apart from male authority. The overwhelming level of entrenched patriarchal power at this juncture, and the inequities and iniquities of the class system, were immense barriers to the achievement of that goal. That some women consistently sustained a critique which saw the twisted ramifications of gender in such clear terms is a far greater index of 'achievement' than a list of legal and institutional victories, however long.

Notes

CHAPTER 1 CONFIGURING FEMINISM HISTORICALLY

1 Mary Poovey, *Uneven Developments. The Ideological Work of Gender in Mid Victorian England* (1988) p. 6.
2 Nancy Cott, *The Grounding of Modern Feminism* (1987) pp. 3–4.
3 Ibid. p. 3. In his 'Discourse, desire and sexual deviance: some problems in the history of homosexuality' (in ed. Kenneth Plummer, *The Making of the Modern Homosexual* (1981) pp. 76–111), Jeffrey Weeks argues strongly that the adoption of the neologism 'homosexuality' was a distinctive mark of changes in attitude and assumption (p. 82). Whilst his argument is a strong one, we should also be wary of the implicit teleology that might result from an over-zealous attachment to such an argument. In the feminist context, moreover, it might be more useful to see the adoption of the neologism as marking a new attitude to separate spheres but not necessarily a more thorough or more sophisticated appraoch to problems that had been addressed for some considerable time.
4 For a useful Europe-wide overview, see Karen Offen, 'Defining feminism: a comparative historical approach', *Signs* 14 (1988) 1, pp. 119–57.
5 Linda Gordon, 'What's new in women's history', in ed. Teresa de Lauretis, *Feminist Studies/Critical Studies* (1986) p. 29.
6 Alice S. Rossi, *The Feminist Papers: From Adams to de Beauvoir* (1973).
7 Kathleen McCrone, 'The assertion of women's rights in mid-Victorian England', *Canadian Historical Association Historical Papers* (1972), pp. 39–53.
8 Ray Strachey, *The Cause* (1928).
9 Judith R. Walkowitz, *Prostitution and Victorian Society. Women, Class and the State* (1980); Jane Rendall, *The Origins of Modern Feminism. Women in Britain, France and the United States 1780–1860* (1985).
10 For information on male sympathizers, see the work of Olive Banks. A chapter in her *Becoming A Feminist. The Social Origins of 'First Wave' Feminism* (1986) is devoted to men, and many of the entries in her *Biographical Dictionary of British Feminists* (1985) are for men.

11 The exclusion of Welsh feminism reflects my inadequacies and not those of Welsh feminism.

12 Linda Nicholson's discussion of the precise relationship between class and gender in her *Gender and History. The Limits of Social Theory in the Age of the Family* (1986) – especially pp. 195–6 – is illuminating.

13 E. M. Sturge, *On Women's Suffrage*. (1872) p. 3.

14 Poovey, op. cit, p. 20. See, too, her 'Feminism and Deconstruction', *Feminist Studies* 14 (1988) 1, pp. 51–65 which warms the hearts of 'those of us who' – like her – 'are convinced . . . that real historical women do exist and share certain experiences.' (pp. 52–3).

15 Janet Todd, *Feminist Literary History* (1988) p. 14. See, too, Alice Jardine's discussion of French female theorists' antipathy to feminism in her *Gynesis. Configurations of Women and Modernity* (1985).

16 See Gordon, loc. cit. p. 30.

17 See Nancy Hewitt's excellent and provocative critique of the concept of sisterhood in 'Beyond the search for sisterhood: American women's history in the 1980s', *Social History* 10 (1985) 3, pp. 299–321.

18 Dorothy Hammond and Alta Jablow, 'Gilgamesh and the Sundance Kid: the myth of male friendship', in ed. Harry Brod, *The Making of Masculinities. The New Men's Studies* (1987) pp. 241–58.

19 It should also be noted that these women routinely formed strong and loving marriages as well. See my article, '"So few prizes and so many blanks": marriage and feminism in later nineteenth-century England', *Journal of British Studies* 28 (1989) 2, pp. 150–74.

20 Mary Maynard, 'Privilege and patriarchy: feminist thought in the nineteenth century', in eds. Susan Mendus and Jane Rendall, *Sexuality and Subordination. Interdisciplinary Studies of Gender in the Nineteenth Century* (1989) p. 225.

21 Teresa Brennan and Carole Pateman, '"Mere auxiliaries to the Commonwealth": women and the origins of liberalism', *Political Studies* XXVII (1979) p. 199.

22 Fawcett Library, London. Autograph Letter Collection. Women's Suffrage. 1895–1898. Letter of F. P. Cobbe to Millicent Garrett Fawcett, 7 December 1895.

23 Marilyn Lake, 'The politics of respectability: identifying the masculinist context', *Historical Studies* 22 (1986) 86, p. 127.

24 The equality-difference debate in modern feminist scholarship has not been touched upon here. For a recent discussion, see Joan W. Scott, 'Deconstructing equality-versus-difference: or, The uses of poststructuralist theory for feminism', *Feminist Studies* 14 (1988) 1, pp. 33–50.

CHAPTER 2 FAMILY, FAITH AND POLITICS

1 Noel Annan, 'The intellectual aristocracy', in ed. J. H. Plumb, *Studies in Social History. A Tribute to G. M. Trevelyan* (1955) pp. 243–87.
2 Girton College, Cambridge. Bessie Rayner Parkes Collection. MS Box I. Item 4. Diary, August to December 1849 (incomplete fragment) f.1.
3 Isabel Petrie Mills, *From Tinder Box to the "Larger" Light. Threads from the Life of John Mills, Banker (Author of 'Vox Humana'): Interwoven with some early century Recollections by his Wife* (1899) p. 9.
4 Jacqui Matthews, 'Barbara Bodichon: integrity in diversity (1827–91)', in ed. Dale Spender, *Feminist Theorists: Three Centuries of Women's Intellectual Traditions* (1983) pp. 92–3.
5 Steven Mintz asserts in his *A Prison of Expectations. The Family in Victorian Culture* (1983) that 'conflicts within specific Victorian households embodied and reflected broader historical tensions within Victorian culture.' (p. 5).
6 I am indebted to June Hannam of Bristol Polytechnic for this information.
7 Brian Harrison, 'A genealogy of reform in modern Britain', in eds Christine Bolt and Seymour Drescher, *Anti-Slavery, Religion and Reform: Essays in Memory of Roger Anstey* (1980) p. 135.
8 Bertha Mason, *The Story of the Women's Suffrage Movement* (1912) p. 25.
9 Edward W. Ellsworth, *Liberators of the Female Mind. The Shirreff Sisters, Educational Reform and the Women's Movement* (1979) p. 5.
10 Ibid. p. 13.
11 Olive Banks, *Becoming A Feminist. The Social Origins of 'First Wave' Feminism* (1986) p. 33.
12 Blanche Glassman Hersh, *The Slavery of Sex: Feminist-Abolitionists in America* (1978); Gerda Lerner, *The Grimké Sisters from South Carolina: Pioneers for Women's Rights and Abolition* (1971); James Walvin, *Slavery and British Society 1776–1846* (1982).
13 Brian Harrison, loc. cit. p. 125.
14 Lady Frances Balfour, *Ne Obliviscaris. Dinna Forget* (1930) p. 114.
15 Ibid. p. 128.
16 Brian Harrison, *Prudent Revolutionaries. Portraits of British Feminists between the Wars* (1987) p. 129.
17 Margaret Wynne Nevinson, *Life's Fitful Fever. A Volume of Memories* (1926) p. 17.
18 Banks, op. cit. p. 26.
19 M. Jeanne Peterson, 'No angel in the house: the Victorian myth and the Paget women', *American Historical Review* 89 (1984) 3, 677–708, p. 701.
20 Patricia Jalland, *Women, Marriage and Politics 1860–1914* (1986) p. 34.
21 Barbara Caine, *Destined To Be Wives. The Sisters of Beatrice Webb* (1986) p. 32; Olive Banks, op. cit. p. 26; 28–9; Peterson, loc. cit.
22 Hilda Martindale, *From One Generation to Another. 1839–1944. A Book of Memoirs* (1944).

23 Bodleian Library, Oxford. Pearson Collection. MS Eng. lett. d. 187, f. 168. Millicent Garrett Fawcett to Charles Pearson, 5 September 1890.
24 Fawcett Library, London. Letters of Millicent Garrett Fawcett: Box 89, f. 16. 13 June 1890.
25 Frances Power Cobbe, *Life of Frances Power Cobbe* (1894) I. 99.
26 Jalland, op. cit. pp. 33–35.
27 eds Bertrand and Patricia Russell, *The Amberley Papers* (1937) II. 343. 2 June 1870.
28 Ibid. p. 17.
29 Ibid. p. 325.
30 Helena M. Swanwick, *I Have Been Young* (1935) p. 84.
31 Carroll Smith-Rosenberg, 'The female world of love and ritual: relations between women in nineteenth-century America', *Signs* 1 (1975) 1–29, pp. 15–19.
32 Bodleian Library, Oxford. Pattison Papers. MS Pattison 140, ff. 37–8. 23 November 1881.
33 S. J. Tanner, *How the Women's Suffrage Movement Began in Bristol Fifty Years Ago* (1918) p. 6.
34 Tallahassee, Florida. Papers of Barbara Bodichon in the possession of Barbara S. McCrimmon. Florence D. Hill to Barbara Leigh Smith, 20 August 1854.
35 Davenport was only appended to the family name of Hill after the death of Matthew, father of the feminist sisterhood. They were both establishing a memorial to their father and at the same time distinguishing themselves from another reforming Hill family (that of sisters Octavia and Miranda Hill) in adding Davenport to the family name.
36 Frances Power Cobbe, op. cit. I. 345.
37 In her 'Victorian reform as family business: the Hill Family', in ed. Anthony S. Wohl, *The Victorian Family. Structure and Stresses* (1978) pp. 119–47, Deborah Gorham effectively delineates this strong familial urge to good works.
38 Diana M. C. Worzala, 'The Langham Place Circle: The beginnings of the organized women's movement in England 1854–70,' unpublished PhD thesis, University of Wisconson-Madison 1982, p. 54. This has also been a common theme in much of Harrison's work; see, for instance, his 'A genealogy of reform in modern Britain', loc. cit. 1980, p. 135.
39 For a different interpretation of the links between radical reform and feminism, see Olive Banks, op. cit. p. 135.
40 Ibid. p. 106.
41 See Eugene L. Rasor's entry on Eliza Ashurst in the *Dictionary of British Radicals* (1984) I. 13–15.
42 The notion of a 'sisterhood' does not necessarily connote an attachment to feminist ideas, of course. Barbara Caine's work on the Potter sisters, op.cit., shows how sisters, however diverse their temperaments and their lifestyles, might still constitute and perceive themselves, in important ways, as a sisterhood.

43 Elizabeth Garrett Anderson Papers. Jersey, 12 April 1864. My thanks to David Rubinstein for this material.
44 David Rubinstein, *Before the Suffragettes. Women's Emancipation in the 1890s* (1986) p. 139.
45 Elizabeth Sturge, *Reminiscences of my life* (1928) p. 63.
46 Caine, op.cit. p. 215.
47 Quoted in Ray Strachey, *Millicent Garrett Fawcett* (1931) p. 27. 24 October 1866. Barbara Leigh Smith Bodichon and Miss Crowe (Jane or Annie) were prominent women with whom the Garrett sisters were associated principally through the Langham Place Circle.
48 Millicent Garrett Fawcett, *What I Remember* (1924) pp. 51; 53. Mill had strong feminist support in his bid for Parliament.
49 Seymour Drescher, 'Two variants of anti-slavery: religious organization and social mobilization in Britain and France, 1780–1870', in Bolt and Drescher, loc. cit. p. 45.
50 Catherine Hall, 'The early formation of Victorian domestic ideology', in ed. S. Burman, *Fit Work for Women* (1979) pp. 15–32.
51 Leonore Davidoff and Catherine Hall, 'The architecture of public and private life: English middle class society in a provincial town 1780–1850', in eds Derek Fraser and Anthony Sutcliffe, *The Pursuit of Urban History* (1983) pp. 327–45; Alex Tyrrell, '"Woman's mission" and pressure group politics in Britain (1825–60)', *Bulletin of the John Rylands University Library of Manchester* 63 (1980) 1, pp. 194–230.
52 Amongst the minority religions were Judaism which numbered three adherents – Lady Goldsmid who was active in the foundation of Girton College, Hertha Ayrton (born Phoebe Sarah Marks) who became a beneficiary of Goldsmid's activities in 1876, and Bradford feminist, Fanny Hertz; and Methodism, which included two women whose lives are discussed in the text, Isabel Petrie Mills and Elizabeth Wolstenhome Elmy.
53 In her *Becoming A Feminist*, Olive Banks used a series of categories which measured levels of religious belief rather than specific choice of worship. Her three categories – freethinkers, positive religious affiliation, no known affiliation (p. 14) – measure a slightly different problem than that tackled here, showing a greater concern for belief than for doctrinal preference. Additionally, Banks believes that denomination is secondary to evangelicalism in influencing feminist thought. This study, whilst accepting her premise that religious belief was of itself an index, goes a stage further in seeking to determine the nature of that religious belief and its possible significance.
54 Elizabeth Isichei, *Victorian Quakers* (1970) p. 252.
55 ed. Margaret J. Shaen, *Memorials of Two Sisters. Susannah and Catherine Winkworth* (1908) p. 25.
56 Frances Power Cobbe, op. cit. I. 105.
57 Isabel Petrie Mills, op.cit. p. 14.
58 Nancy Hewitt, 'Feminist friends: agrarian Quakers and the emergence of woman's rights in America', *Feminist Studies* 12 (1986) 1, p. 29.
59 Jane Marcus, 'Transatlantic sisterhood: labor and suffrage links in the letters of Elizabeth Robins and Emmeline Pankhurst', *Signs* 3 (1978) p. 744.

60 Gail Malmgreen, 'Introduction', in ed. Gail Malmgreen, *Religion in the Lives of English Women, 1760–1930* (1986) p. 7.

61 Catherine Hall, 'The early formation of Victorian domestic ideology', loc. cit; Davidoff and Hall, 'The architecture of public and private life', loc. cit.

62 Davidoff and Hall, ibid. p. 329.

63 Brian Harrison, 'State intervention and moral reform in nineteenth century England', in ed. Patricia Hollis, *Pressure from Without in Early Victorian England* (1974) p. 297.

64 Girton College, Cambridge. Emily Davies Papers. Family Chronicle, op.cit. f. 66.

65 Elizabeth Isichei identified London, Birmingham, Bristol, Lancashire, West Riding, Norwich, Banbury and Kendal as Quaker strongholds in the Victorian period (op. cit. p. 16), most of which were also areas of strong feminism.

66 Douglas Charles Stange, *British Unitarians against American Slavery 1833–65* (1984) p. 85.

67 Mills, op. cit. pp. 77; 158.

68 Diana Worzala, The Langham Place Circle, op. cit. p. 314.

69 Malmgreen, loc. cit. p. 6.

70 Quoted in Barbara Stephen, *Emily Davies and Girton College* (1927) p. 366.

71 British Library, London. Add. MS. 43946. Dilke Papers, loc. cit. p. 14.

72 Sheila Herstein, *A Mid-Victorian Feminist, Barbara Leigh Smith Bodichon* (1985) p. 16.

73 Millicent Garrett Fawcett, op. cit. p. 126.

74 Tallahassee, Florida. Bodichon manuscripts of Barbara S. McCrimmon. Elizabeth Whitehead to Barbara Leigh Smith, undated, 20 July 1851 or 1852.

75. Harrison, *Prudent Revolutionaries*, p. 130.

76 E. F. Richards, *Mazzini's Letters to an English Family* (1920) I. (1844–54) 32.

77 Elie Halevy, *A History of the English People in the Nineteenth Century* Vol. III, 2nd edn (1952) p. 509; Carol Dyhouse, *Girls Growing Up In Late Victorian and Edwardian England* (1981) p. 72.

78 Olive Banks, in *Becoming A Feminist* (op.cit. pp. 16–18) shows the increasing incidence of a socialist outlook in the later cohorts of her sample.

79 Indeed, Olive Banks is perhaps rather too generous when, in her analysis (ibid. p. 159), she remarks, 'By the end of the nineteenth century, however, feminism found its main political expression through the various sections of the Labour movement since the Marxist variety of socialism has in general been unsympathetic in practice if not in theory.' In terms of earlier Marxist movements in Britain, the thorough-going mysogyny of H. M. Hyndman (founder of Britain's first Marxist party, the Democratic Federation), upholds Banks's point in one respect at least. A letter written by Elizabeth Wolstenholme Elmy to Harriet McIlquham in mid-1897 suggests that continental Socialism was little better in this respect. 'At Naples and Rome . . . the chief opposition . . . seems to be from the Socialist men, who

denounce our British women's suffrage movement as bourgeois and designed to serve a class and party only.'

80 Martin Pugh, *The Tories and the People, 1880–1935* (1985) p. 48.

81 For a different reading, see Patricia Hollis, *Ladies Elect. Women in English Local Government 1865–1914* (1987) p. 140.

82 Brian Harrison, 'State intervention and moral reform in nineteenth century England', in Hollis, *Pressure from Without in Early Victorian England*, p. 291; 'A genealogy of reform in modern Britain', in Bolt and Drescher, loc. cit. p. 125.

83 Banks, op. cit. p. 135.

84 See Ruth Bordin, *Woman and Temperance. The Quest for Power and Liberty, 1873–1900* (1981); Brian Harrison, 'The British prohibitionists 1853–72. A biographical analysis', *International Review of Social History* XV (1970) 3, 375–467; Alex Tyrrell, loc. cit.

85 *'The Woman' and the Age: A Letter Addressed to the Rt. Hon. W. E. Gladstone by Sundry Members, Clerical, Medical and Lay of the International Association for the Total Suppression of Vivisection* (1881) p. 18.

86 Fawcett, op. cit. p. 40.

87 Stephen op. cit. p. 2.

88 Quoted in ibid. p. 206. Davies to Barbara Bodichon, 23 November 1868.

89 For an excellent discussion of the implications of these differences in the Edwardian era, see Tricia Davis, Martin Durham, Catharine Hall, Mary Langan and David Sutton, '"The public face of feminism": early twentieth century writings on women's suffrage', in eds. R. Johnson, G. McLennan, B. Schwarz, D. Sutton, *Making Histories. Studies in History-writing and Politics* (1982) pp. 302–324.

90 Frances Power Cobbe, op. cit. II. 97.

91 Quoted in David Rubinstein, op. cit. p. 140. British Library Add. MS. 47451, f.222. Elmy to McIlquham, 29 June 1898.

CHAPTER 3 REAPPROPRIATING ADULTHOOD

1 Patricia Jalland, *Women, Marriage and Politics 1860–1914* (1986) p. 222.

2 Olive Banks, *Becoming A Feminist. The Social Origins of 'First Wave' Feminism* (1986) p. 36.

3 Patricia Jalland, 'Victorian spinsters: dutiful daughters, desperate rebels and the transition to the new women', in ed. Patricia Crawford, *Exploring Women's Past* (1983) pp. 129–70 (pp. 130–31).

4 Blanche Athena Clough, *A Memoir of Anne Jemima Clough* (1897) p. 25. Quotation from Clough's journal, dated 1840.

5 Margaret Wynne Nevinson, *Life's Fitful Fever. A Volume of Memories* (1926) p. 45.

6 Brian Harrison, *Prudent Revolutionaries. Portraits of British Feminists between the Wars* (1987) p. 128.

7 Nancy Hewitt, 'Feminist friends: agrarian Quakers and the emergence of woman's rights in America', *Feminist Studies* 12 (1986) 1, pp. 27–49 (p. 31).

8 M. F. Cusack, *Women's Work in Modern Society* (1894) p. 8.

9 Bodleian Library, Oxford. Papers of Mark Pattison. MS Pattison 118, f.36. 22 January 1880, Emilia Pattison to Eleanor Smith.

10 loc. cit. f. 63. 30 March 1881.

11 loc. cit. MS Pattison 140, ff.37–8. 23 November 1881. Emilia to Gertrude Tuckwell.

12 Quoted in Sheila R. Herstein, *A Mid-Victorian Feminist. Barbara Leigh Smith Bodichon* (1985) p. 189, from ed. Gordon S. Haight, *The George Eliot Letters* Vol VII, 1878–1880 (1955) p. 273. 8 May 1880.

13 Jalland, loc. cit. 'Victorian spinsters', p. 134.

14 Barbara Caine, *Destined To Be Wives. The Sisters of Beatrice Webb* (1986) pp. 90–1.

15 Ibid. p. 114.

16 Rosalind Mitchison, *British Population Change Since 1860*, (1977) pp. 25–7.

17 Martine Senegalen, *Historical Anthropology of the Family* (1986) p. 162.

18 The demographic information in this passage owes much to the help of Bruce Bellingham, to whom go my thanks.

19 Millicent Garrett Fawcett, *What I Remember* (1924) p. 40.

20 Fawcett Library, London. Lydia Becker Papers. LEB/1. Newspaper Cuttings. Mrs Alexander Ireland, 'Manchester men and women. I – Lydia Ernestine Becker', *Manchester Examiner and Times* 1 September 1891.

21 Ibid.

22 Banks, op. cit. p. 90.

23 Tricia Davis, Martin Durham, Catherine Hall, Mary Langan and David Sutton, '"The public face of feminism": early twentieth century writings on women's suffrage', in eds R. Johnson, G. McLennan, B. Schwarz and D. Sutton, *Making Histories. Studies in History-writing and Politics* (1982) p. 314. Other writers (see especially Martha Vicinus in *Independent Women. Work and Community for Single Women 1850–1920* (1985) would, of course, disagree and the point is a highly charged one.

24 W. D. Rubinstein, 'Education and the social origins of British elites, 1880–1970,' *Past and Present* 112 (1986) p. 179.

25 E. F. Richards, *Mazzini's Letters to an English Family* (1920) I. 23.

26 See Frances Widdowson, *Going Up Into The Next Class. Women and Elementary Teacher Training 1840–1914* (1980).

27 Jihang Park, 'Women of their time: the growing recognition of the second sex in Victorian and Edwardian England', *Journal of Social History* 21 (Fall 1987) 1, p. 51.

28 Rosemary van Arsdel, 'Mrs Florence Fenwick Miller and *The Woman's Signal*, 1895–99', *Victorian Periodicals Review* XV (1982) p. 107.

29 Nevinson, op. cit. p. 71.

30 Herstein, op. cit. p. 96.

31 Banks, op. cit. p. 12.
32 *The Autobiography of Mary Smith, Schoolmistress and Nonconformist* (1892) p. 179.
33 My thanks to David Rubinstein for pointing this out.
34 See Janet Howarth and Mark Curthoys, 'Gender, curriculum and career: a case study of women university students before 1914', unpublished paper, 1987, pp. 14–15.
35 Banks, op. cit. p. 13.
36 Janet Howarth and Mark Curthoys, 'The political economy of women's higher education in late nineteeth and early twentieth century Britain', *Historical Research* 60 (June 1987) 142, p. 217.
37 Janet E. Courtney, *Recollected in Tranquillity* (1926) p. 96.
38 Janet Howarth and Mark Curthoys, 'Gender, curriculum and career', p. 3.
39 M. Jeanne Peterson, 'No angel in the house: the Victorian myth and the Paget women', *American Historical Review* 89 (1984) 3, p. 693.
40 Jalland, op. cit, p. 195.
41 Banks, op. cit. p. 14; Peterson, loc. cit.
42 W. D. Rubinstein, loc. cit. pp. 188–9.
43 Ibid. p. 166.
44 Girton College, Cambridge. Emily Davies Papers. Family Chronicle, f. 241.
45 Barbara Stephen, *Emily Davies and Girton College* (1927) p. 110. Letter dated 1866.
46 Fawcett Library, London. Autograph Letter Collection. Women's Movement 1888–96. 24 April 1896.
47 Banks, op. cit. pp. 11–12.

CHAPTER 4: UNDERSTANDING THE EMPTY PLACES:
LOVE, FRIENDSHIP AND WOMEN'S NETWORKS

1 Girton College, Cambridge. Emily Davies Papers. Box I. Family Chronicle, f. 423.
2 Ibid. Family Chronicle, f. 95.
3 For a discussion of one specific feminist friendship, see Jane Rendall, 'Friendship and politics: Barbara Leigh Smith Bodichon (1827–91) and Bessie Rayner Parkes (1829–1925)', in eds Susan Mendus and Jane Rendall, *Sexuality and Subordination. Interdisciplinary Studies of Gender in the Nineteenth Century* (1989) pp. 136–70.
4 Patricia Jalland, *Women, Marriage and Politics 1860–1914* (1986) pp. 3–4.
5 Cobbe, *Life of Frances Power Cobbe By Herself.* 2 vols (1894) II. 204.
6 Mary L. Bruce, *Anna Swanwick. A Memoir and Recollections. 1813. 1899* (1903) p. 145.
7 Edwin A. Pratt, *A Woman's Work for Women, being the Aims, Efforts and Aspirations of 'L. M. H.' (Miss Louisa M. Hubbard)* (1898) p. 20.
8 ed. Margaret J. Shaen, *Memorials of Two Sisters. Susannah and Catherine Winkworth* (1908) p. 25.

9 Fawcett Library, London. Autograph Letter Collection. I. Women's Suffrage, 1851–94. Louise Creighton to Miss Fullagar, n.d.

10 Josephine Butler, *Personal Reminiscences of a Great Crusade* (1896) p. 405.

11 See, for instance, William R. Taylor and Christopher Lasch, 'Two "kindred spirits": sorority and family in New England, 1839–1846', *New England Quarterly* 36 (1963) 25–41, and Carroll Smith-Rosenberg, 'The female world of love and ritual: relations between women in nineteenth century America', *Signs* 1 (1975) pp. 1–29. For a critique of this school of thought, see Nancy A. Hewitt, 'Beyond the search for sisterhood: American women's history in the 1980s', *Social History* 10 (1985) 3, 299–321.

12 Margaret Bondfield, *A Life's Work* (1949) p. 44. Varley's revelatory experience of education was an echo, of course, of the determination of middle-class feminists a generation earlier to improve themselves through education. See chapter 7.

13 eds. Bertrand and Patricia Russell, *The Amberley Papers. The Letters and Diaries of Lord and Lady Amberley* (1937) II. 41.

14 See ed. Liz Stanley, *The Diaries of Hannah Cullwick. Victorian Maidservant* (1984).

15 Derek Hudson, *Munby. Man of Two Worlds. The Life and Diaries of Arthur J. Munby, 1828–1910* (1972).

16 See E. F. Richards, *Mazzini's Letters to an English Family* (1920) I.

17 Sheila Herstein's assessment of *NAPSS* constituents as 'a coalition between . . . the manufacturing middle class and . . . evolving professionalism' perhaps explains why its embracing of the women's movement remained qualified. *A Mid-Victorian Feminist, Barbara Leigh Smith Bodichon* (1985) p. 131.

18 Girton College, Cambridge. Emily Davies Papers. Family Chronicle, f. 259. (1862).

19 Brian Harrison, *Prudent Revolutionaries. Portraits of British Feminists between the Wars* (1987) p. 133.

20 Judith R. Walkowitz, 'Science, feminism and romance: the Men and Women's Club, 1885–89', *History Workshop Journal* 21 (1986) p. 53.

21 Estelle Freedman, 'Separatism as strategy: female institution building and American feminism, 1870–1930', *Feminist Studies* 5 (1979) 3, p. 517.

22 Eva Anstruther, 'Ladies' Clubs', *Contemporary Review* 45 (1899) p. 600.

23 Blanche Wiesen Cook, 'Female support networks and political activism. Lillian Wald, Crystal Eastman, Emma Goldman', in eds Nancy F. Cott and Elizabeth H. Pleck, *A Heritage of Her Own. Toward A New Social History of American Women* (1979) pp. 413; 437; Martha Vicinus, '"One life to stand beside me": emotional conflicts in first-generation college women in England', *Feminist Studies* 8 (1982) 3, p. 603.

24 Recent scholarship pursuing ideas of male friendship in this period also points to the dyadic consonance of close male friendship and romantic love. See Dorothy Hammond and Alta Jablow, 'Gilgamesh and the Sundance Kid: the myth of male friendship', in ed. Harry Brod, *The Making of Masculinities*, pp. 241–58.

25 Leila J. Rupp's '"Imagine my surprise": women's relationships in historical perspective', *Frontiers* 5 (1980) 3, pp. 61–70 offers a valuable discussion of the unfortunate polarization between the complete denial of physicality between women and the tendency to over-read commitment as a sure index of it.

26 See Blanche Wiesen Cook, loc. cit. for this and for the mythologies which have surrounded lesbianism historically. Adrienne Rich's work on the 'lesbian continuum' as a means of identifying strong female homosocial bonding is an important addition to the literature. See her 'Compulsory heterosexuality and lesbian existence', *Signs* 5 (1980) 4, pp. 631–660.

27 Freedman, loc. cit. p. 525.

28 Quoted in Martha Vicinus, loc. cit. p. 610 – Constance Maynard, unpublished autobiography, section 30, pp. 161–2.

29 Fawcett Library, London. Autograph Letter Collection. Women's Movement, 1865–71. 20 May 1865.

30 Smith-Rosenberg, loc. cit. p. 11.

31 Diana Mary Chase Worzala, 'The Langham Place Circle: the beginnings of the organized women's movement in England, 1854–70', unpublished PhD thesis, University of Wisconsin-Madison, 1982, p. 55.

32 The subject of Jane Rendall's article in *Sexuality and Subordination*, loc. cit.

33 British Library, London. Add. MS 47451, f. 20. Margaret H. Illingworth to Elizabeth Wolstenholme Elmy, 24 November 1896.

34 Martha Vicinus, loc. cit. p. 609.

35 For a fuller discussion of Maynard's views on marriage at this time, see Martha Vicinus, ibid.

36 Girton College, Cambridge. Bessie Rayner Parkes Collection. BRP I. MSS writings. Item 4. Diary for August–December 1849, 4/14; 4/10.

37 Bodleian Library, Oxford. MS Eng. misc. d. 494. Edith Jemima Simcox, 'Autobiography of a Shirtmaker' f.1. 1 October 1877.

38 A point made, too, by Jane Rendall in her article in *Sexuality and Subordination*, loc. cit. p. 142.

39 Tallahassee, Florida. Letters in private possession of Barbara S. McCrimmon. Parkes to Leigh Smith, 5 January 1848.

40 See my introduction to Amelia Edwards, *Untrodden Peaks and Unfrequented Valleys. A Midsummer Ramble in the Dolomites* (1986).

41 Shaen, op. cit. pp. 111–12. Catherine Winkworth to Emma Shaen, 8 May 1854.

42 Jalland, op. cit. p. 100.

43 Liz Stanley, 'Feminism and friendship: two essays on Olive Schreiner', *Studies in Sexual Politics* 8 (1985) p. 11.

44 Ibid. p. 2.

45 June Hannam, 'Usually neglected in standard histories: some issues in working on the life of Isabella Ford, 1855–1924', *Studies in Sexual Politics* 13 & 14 (double issue) *Writing Feminist Biography* (1986) p. 13.

46 Quoted in Lillian Faderman, *Surpassing the Love of Men. Romantic Friendship and Love between Women from the Renaissance to the Present* (1981) pp. 205–6.

47 Frances Power Cobbe, *Life.* II. 210.
48 Jane Ellen Harrison, *Reminiscences of A Student Life* (1925) p. 88.
49 Quoted in Worzala, op. cit. p. 164. 14 January 1863.
50 See Adrian Wilson, 'Participant or patient? Seventeenth century childbirth from the mother's point of view', in ed. Roy Porter *Patients and Practitioners* (1985) pp. 129–144, and – albeit somewhat different in its perspective – Edward Shorter's *A History of Women's Bodies* (1984).
51 Quoted in Margaret Todd, *Life of Sophia Jex-Blake* (1918) p. 65.
52 British Library, London. Add. MS 43946. Dilke Papers. Vol. LXXIII. Sir Charles Dilke's typescript memoirs of his wife, p. 101.
53 Russell, op. cit. II. 20.
54 This is a point noted, too, by Olive Banks in her *Becoming A Feminist*, p. 39.
55 Quoted in Joseph W. Reed Jr's edition of Barbara Leigh Smith Bodichon, *An American Diary 1857–8* (1976) p. 51.
56 Bodleian Library, Oxford. MS Eng. misc. d. 494. op. cit. f. 6.
57 Ibid. f. 1.
58 Janet E. Courtney, *Recollected in Tranquillity* (1926) p. 132.

CHAPTER 5 DISRUPTING THE DARK CONTINENT

1 See, as good examples, Jeffrey Weeks, *Sex, Politics and Society. The Regulation of Sexuality Since 1800* (1981) and Ben Barker-Benfield, 'The spermatic economy: a nineteenth century view of sexuality', *Feminist Studies* 1 (1972) 1, pp. 45–74.
2 Rachel Harrison and Frank Mort, 'Patriarchal aspects of nineteenth century state formation: property relations, marriage and divorce, and sexuality', in ed. Philip Corrigan, *Capital, State Formation and Marxist Theory. Historical Investigations* (1980) p. 105.
3 Nancy Chodorow, 'Mothering, male dominance and capitalism', in ed. Zillah R. Eisenstein, *Capitalist Patriarchy and the Case for Socialist Feminism* (1979) p. 92.
4 We should, however, note the revisionist historiography on eighteenth century sexuality now being authored by such scholars as G. S. Rousseau and Roy Porter whose work demonstrates with skill that a more subtle approach yields better results. See especially their *Sexual Underworlds of the Enlightenment* (1987). See also Paul-Gabriel Boucé, *Sexuality in Eighteenth Century Britain* (1982).
5 Elizabeth Janeway, 'Who is Sylvia? On the loss of sexual paradigms', in eds Catharine R. Stimpson and Ethel Spector Person, *Women: Sex and Sexuality* (1980) p. 5.
6 The most well-known of the many authors who deal with prostitution in this way – other than those reporting to governmental committees – are the historian William Lecky in his *History of European Morals from Augustus to Charlemagne* (1877) and William Acton, author of *Prostitution considered in its moral, social, and sanitary aspects, in London and other large*

Cities and Garrison Towns: with Proposals for the Control and Prevention of its Attendant Evils (1857).

7 Judith R. Walkowitz, 'Male vice and female virtue: feminism and the politics of prostitution in nineteenth century Britain', in eds Ann Snitow, Christine Stansell and Sharon Thompson, *Powers of Desire. The Politics of Sexuality* (1983) p. 422.

8 Carroll Smith-Rosenberg, 'A richer and gentler sex', *Social Research* 53 (1986) 2, p. 293.

9 *Women's Suffrage Journal* VI (1 January 1875) 59. Both Susan Kingsley Kent, *Sex and Suffrage in Britain 1860–1914* (1987) esp. p. 3, and Lucy Bland, 'Marriage laid bare: middle class women and marital sex, 1880s–1914', in ed. Jane Lewis, *Labour and Love. Women's Experience of Home and Family 1850–1940* (1986) pp. 122–46, esp. p. 135 discuss this in greater detail.

10 27 & 28 Vic. c. 85. 29 July 1864. An Act for the Prevention of Contagious Diseases at certain Naval and Military Stations.

11 *Parliamentary Papers*, House of Commons. 1871 C. 408. xix. *Report of the Royal Commission upon the Administration and Operation of the Contagious Diseases Acts*, p. 4.

12 Susan Sontag. 'AIDS and its metaphors' *New York Review of Books* XXXV (1988) 16, p. 89.

13 Andrew T. Scull, *Museums of Madness. The Social Organization of Insanity in Nineteenth Century England* (1982).

14 Derek Hudson, *Munby, Man of Two Worlds* p. 50. Monday 13 February 1860.

15 See Frank Mort, 'Purity, feminism and the state; sexuality and moral politics 1880–1914', in eds Mary Langan and Bill Schwarz, *Crises in the British State 1880–1930* (1985) pp. 209–25, and Jeffrey Weeks, *Sexuality and its Discontents. Meanings, Myths and Modern Sexualities* (1985) for more elaborate discussions of this issue.

16 We need to exercise some caution in yoking social purity and feminism unreservedly. Social purity organizations demonstrated considerable divergence of opinion, and only some were comfortable in identifying their perspective as a feminist one.

17 Carroll Smith-Rosenberg offers some comments on similar activities in the USA in her 'Writing history; language, class and gender', in ed. de Lauretis, *Feminist Studies/Critical Studies* (1986) pp. 31–54.

18 Interestingly, by 1902 habitual intoxication on the part of *either* spouse was made an explicit ground for marital separation under the Licensing Act of that year.

19 Susan Kingsley Kent, op. cit. p. 88.

20 Mary Lyndon Shanley, '"One must ride behind": married women's rights and the Divorce Act of 1857', *Victorian Studies* XXV (1982) 3, p. 369.

21 *Parliamentary Papers*, House of Commons, 1852–3 [1604] xl. *First report of the Commission appointed to enquire into The Laws of Divorce* p. 22.

22 Gail Savage, 'The operation of the 1857 Divorce Act, 1860–1910. A research note', *Journal of Social History* 16 (1983) p. 108.

23 The 1878 Matrimonial Causes Act which granted separation orders provided divorce only *a mensa et thoro* and not *a vinculo*, thus preventing its
recipients from re-marrying.

24 *Parliamentary Debates*. Second Reform Bill (1867). Quoted in Albie Sachs
and Joan Hoff Wilson, *Sexism and the Law. A Study of Male Beliefs and
Legal Bias in Britain and the United States* (1978) p. 54.

25 Patricia Jalland, *Women, Marriage and Politics 1860–1914* (1986) e.g.
p. 121.

26 See Judith R. Walkowitz, 'Jack the Ripper and the myth of male violence',
Feminist Studies 8 (1982) 3, pp. 534–74 for a feminist interpretation of the
significance of the Ripper murders.

27 Gail Savage, 'The wilful communication of a loathsome disease: marital
conflict and venereal disease in Victorian England', unpublished paper,
1988. With thanks to the author for permission to reproduce.

28 loc. cit.

29 *The Storm Bell* (1 January 1898) p. 2.

30 It should be noted, however, that in her medical practice, Elizabeth Garrett
Anderson did, on occasion, apparently counsel her women patients on
contraceptive methods. Mary Costelloe (née Smith) wrote of 'Dr Garrett
Anderson's "other ways"' in a letter to her mother, quoted in Maureen E.
Montgomery's *Gilded Prostitution. Status, Money and Transatlantic Marri-
ages 1870–1914* (1989) p. 196.

31 At no point in the century was significant mention of female homosexuality
made; laws dealing with homosexuality touched only upon male behaviour.

32 See Jeffrey Weeks, *Coming Out. Homosexual Politics in Britain from the
Nineteenth Century to the Present* (1977) for a complete discussion of these
Acts of Parliament.

33 It is an interesting side-note that the sponsor of the anti-homosexual
legislation of 1885 was radical MP Henry Labouchere. It was not only
women among England's political dissidents who took a conservative stance
on such issues.

34 See Weeks, *Coming Out*, p. 23.

35 Frances Power Cobbe, 'Wife-torture in England', *Contemporary Review* 32
(1878) p. 65.

36 Smith-Rosenberg, 'A richer and gentler sex', op. cit. p. 297.

37 Patricia Hollis, *Ladies Elect. Women in English Local Government
1850–1914* (1987) pp. 50; 234.

38 Information on Martindale, her mother and her sister will be found in
chapter 2.

39 Paul McHugh, *Prostitution and Victorian Social Reform* (1980) p. 25.

40 Martin Durham, 'Suffrage and after: feminism in the early twentieth
century', in eds Langan and Schwarz, *Crises in the British State,
1880–1930*, p. 179.

41 Jeffrey Weeks, *Sexuality and its Discontents*, p. 67.

42 Florence Fenwick Miller, *On the Programme of the Women's Franchise
League. An Address delivered at the National Liberal Club* (1890).

43 'Sixteen reasons for women's suffrage', *Women's Suffrage Journal* II (2 January 1871) I.

44 *'The Woman and the Age': a Letter Addressed to the Rt. Hon. W. E. Gladstone, MP* (London, 1881) p. 12.

45 For feminist attitudes to religion, see Nancy Boyd, *Josephine Butler, Octavia Hill, Florence Nightingale. Three Victorian Women who Changed their World* (1982).

46 Gayle Rubin, 'Thinking sex: notes for a radical theory of the politics of sexuality', in ed. Carole S. Vance, *Pleasure and Danger. Exploring Female Sexuality* (1984) p. 274.

47 Frank Mort, *Dangerous Sexualities. Medico-moral Politics in England since 1830* (1987); Michel Foucault, *The History of Sexuality* Vol I (1978); Jeffrey Weeks, *Sexuality and its Discontents*, op. cit.

48 Peter Gay, *Education of the Senses*. Vol I of *The Bourgeois Experience. Victoria to Freud* (1984) p. 420.

49 Harrison and Mort, loc. cit. p. 97.

50 Sheila Jeffreys, *The Spinster and her Enemies. Feminism and Sexuality 1880–1930* (1985) pp. 18–19.

51 *The Dawn* I (November 1888) 3. p. 19.

52 British Library, Add. MS 49611, f.142. 1 March 1895.

53 Ibid., f.144. n.d.

54 Manchester Reference Library Suffrage Collection. Letters of Millicent Garrett Fawcett M50/2/1/68, f.68. Letter, n.d.

55 Fawcett Library, London. Autograph Letter Collection. Women's Movement 1865–71. Millicent Garrett Fawcett to Elizabeth Wolstenholme Elmy, 10 December 1875.

56 British Library Add. MS 47451, f.99ᵛ. Elizabeth Wolstenholme Elmy to Harriet McIlquham. 20 May 1897.

57 Brian Harrison, 'Women's health and the Women's Movement in Britain: 1840–1940', in ed. Charles Webster, *Biology, Medicine and Society 1840–1940* (1981) p. 24.

58 Elizabeth Garrett, *An Enquiry into the Character of the Contagious Diseases Acts of 1866–69* (1870).

59 Mort, *Dangerous sexualities*, p. 70.

60 Kent, op. cit. p. 131.

CHAPTER 6   BREAKING THE MALE MONOPOLY: POLITICS, LAW AND FEMINISM

1 Florence Fenwick Miller, *On the Programme of the Women's Franchise League. An Address delivered at the National Liberal Club* (1890).

2 Frances Power Cobbe, Preface, *The Duties of Women. A Course of Lectures* (1881) p. v.

3 Norma Basch has pointed out in her *In the Eyes of the Law. Women , Marriage and Property in Nineteenth Century New York* (1982) that English coverture was far stronger than in countries such as France where marital property was deemed to be in communal possession (p. 18).

4 John Stuart Mill and Harriet Taylor, 'The Enfranchisement of Women', *Westminster and Foreign Quarterly Review* 55 (1851) p. 292.

5 Albie Sachs and Joan Hoff Wilson, *Sexism and the Law. A Study of Male Beliefs and Legal Bias in Britain and the United States* (1978) p. 41.

6 See Ibid. pp. 48–9 for a more involved discussion of this point. In her *The Female Body and the Law* (1988), Zillah Eisenstein states flatly that the law as well as specific laws are 'authorized discourses for the state'. (p. 20).

7 Sachs and Wilson, op. cit. p. 38.

8 T. O. Lloyd, *Empire to Welfare State. English History 1906–1985* (1986) p. 9.

9 Rachel Harrison and Frank Mort, 'Patriarchal aspects of nineteenth century state formation: property relations, marriage and divorce, and sexuality', in ed. Philip Corrigan, *Capitalism, State Formation and Marxist Theory: Historical Investigations* (1980).

10 For a compelling discussion advancing the ideological connections between these two concerns, see chapter 3 of Mary Poovey's *Uneven Developments. The Ideological Work of Gender in Mid-Victorian England* (1988).

11 J. Brophy and C. Smart, 'Locating law: a discussion of the place of law in feminist politics' in eds Brophy and Smart, *Women in Law. Explorations in Law, Family and Sexuality* (1985) p. 2.

12 Janet E. Courtney, *The Women of My Time* (1934) pp. 24–5.

13 Andrew Rosen, 'Emily Davies and the Women's Movement, 1862–1867', *Journal of British Studies* XIX (1979) 1, p. 121.

14 Olive Banks, *Becoming A Feminist. The Social Origins of 'First Wave' Feminism* (1986) p. 63.

15 See, for example, E. P. Thompson, *Whigs and Hunters: The Origin of the Black Act* (1975) and Steven Spitzer, 'The Dialectics of Formal and Informal Control', in ed. Richard L. Abel, *The Politics of Informal Justice*. Volume I *The American Experience* (1982) pp. 167–205.

16 See Sachs and Wilson, op. cit. pp. 14–22 for an analysis of the decision.

17 S. J. Tanner, *How The Women's Suffrage Movement Began in Bristol Fifty Years Ago* (1918) p. 9.

18 Manchester Central Reference Library. M/50/1/4. *First Annual Report of the Executive Committee of the Manchester National Society for Women's Suffrage, 1867 and 1868*, p. 4.

19 Frances Power Cobbe, Introduction, in ed. Theodore Stanton, *The Woman Question in Europe. A Series of Original Essays* (1884) p. xvi.

20 *Women's Emancipation Union. Its Origins and Its Work* (1892) p. 9.

21 Brophy and Smart, loc. cit. p. 2.

22 Spitzer, loc. cit. p. 168.

23 See my '"So few prizes and so many blanks": marriage and feminism in later nineteenth century England', *Journal of British Studies* 28 (1989) 2, pp. 150–74.

24 See Carole Pateman, 'The shame of the marriage contract', in ed. Judith Hicks Stiehm, *Women's Views of the Political World of Men* (1980) p. 78.

25 Mary L. Shanley, '"One must ride behind": married women's rights and the Divorce Act of 1857', *Victorian Studies* XXV (1982) 3, p. 369.

26 Norma Basch, op. cit. p. 38.
27 Millicent Garrett Fawcett, 'Why women require the franchise', in. eds H. and M. G. Fawcett, *Essays and Lectures on Social and Political Subjects* (1872) p. 276.
28 For a lengthy discussion of the fate of the property of wealthy women in this period, see Patricia Jalland, *Women, Marriage and Politics 1860–1914* (1986) pp. 58–72.
29 Frances Power Cobbe, *Criminals, Idiots, Women and Minors. Is the Classification Sound? A Discussion on the Laws concerning the Property of Married Women* (1869) p. 11.
30 Shanley, loc. cit. p. 373.
31 Ibid.
32 Mary Ashton Dilke, *Women's Suffrage* (1885) p. 73.
33 Frances Power Cobbe, 'Wife torture in England', *Contemporary Review* 32 (1878) pp. 55–87.
34 Tallahassee, Florida. Private Autograph Collection of Barbara S. McCrimmon. Letter from Helen Taylor to Barbara Bodichon, 7 June 1866.
35 Letter from Elizabeth Wolstenholme in the *Women's Suffrage Journal* II (March 1871) 12, p. 23.
36 Brophy and Smart, loc. cit. p. 9; Sachs and Wilson, op. cit. p. 137.
37 Susan Atkins and Brenda Hoggett, *Women and the Law* (1984) p. 106. Rachel Harrison and Frank Mort (q.v.), however, adopt a more favourable assessment in their belief that the 1882 Act lessened women's economic dependency on their husbands. (loc. cit. p. 90).
38 Mill and Taylor, loc. cit. p. 311.
39 Derek Hudson, *Munby: Man of Two Worlds* (1965) pp. 281–2.
40 See Sandra Holton, *Feminism and Democracy* (1987) and Patricia Hollis, *Ladies Elect* (1987) for a discussion of their role respectively in parliamentary and in municipal politics.
41 Hollis, op. cit. p. 33.
42 Margaret Wynne Nevinson, *Life's Fitful Fever. A Volume of Memories* (1926) p. 178.
43 Hollis, op. cit. pp. 189; 187.
44 Ibid. p. 284.
45 See Sachs and Wilson, op. cit. pp. 25–7; Hollis, op. cit. pp. 310–11; A. E. Metcalfe, *Woman's Effort. A Chronicle of British Women's Fifty Years' Struggle for Citizenship 1865–1914* (1917) pp. 12–13.
46 Caroline Ashurst Biggs, *A Letter from an Englishwoman to Englishwomen* (1889) unpaginated (p. 2).
47 Even today, the work of the locally elected councillor is a formidable task slotted into the working day and necessitating a great deal of late night work.
48 Rosemary van Arsdel, 'Victorian periodicals yield their secrets: Florence Fenwick Miller's three campaigns for the London School Board', *History of Education Society* 38 (1986) p. 35.
49 British Library, London. Add. MS 47450, f.120. Elizabeth Wolstenholme Elmy to Harriet McIlquham, 28 May 1894.

50 Tallahassee, Florida. Private Autograph Collection of Barbara S. McCrimmon. Letter dated 10 June 1866.
51 *Women's Suffrage Journal* 8 (October 1, 1870) p. 78.
52 Banks, op. cit. p. 66.
53 Brian Harrison, *Prudent Revolutionaries. Portraits of British Feminists Between the Wars* (1987) p. 3.
54 Hollis, op. cit. p. 6.
55 Andrea Nye, *Feminist Theory and the Philosophies of Man* (Beckenham, 1988) p. 5.
56 British Library, London. Add. MS 47451, f. 33. 11 December 1896.
57 Linda J. Nicholson, *Gender and History. The Limit of Social Theory in the Age of the Family* (1986) p. 56.
58 Lydia Becker, 'Female Suffrage', *Contemporary Review* (March 1867) p. 316.

CHAPTER 7 INVADING THE PUBLIC SPHERE: EMPLOYMENT, EDUCATION AND THE
MIDDLE-CLASS WOMAN

1 Frances Power Cobbe, 'The Final Cause of Women', in ed. Josephine Butler, *Woman's Work and Woman's Culture. A Series of Essays* (1869) pp. 1–26; 13–14. The reference to Starrs and Saurins relates to a celebrated legal case, *Starr v. Saurin*, between a Mother Superior and a young Roman Catholic nun. For details, see ch. XVIII of Anon. (Mary Frances Cusack), *Five Years in a Protestant Sisterhood and Ten Years in a Catholic Convent. An Autobiography* (1869).
2 Jane Lewis, *Women in England 1870–1950: Sexual Divisions and Social Change* (1984).
3 The one obvious exception to this lack of interest in elementary schooling is the Portman Hall School which Barbara Leigh Smith undertook with the aid of her friends.
4 A. J. Hammerton's work on female emigration in this period discusses one contemporary solution to this growing 'problem'. See his *Emigrant Gentlewomen. Genteel Poverty and Female Emigration 1830–1914* (1979).
5 See, for example, Carol Dyhouse, *Girls Growing Up in Late Victorian and Edwardian England* (1981).
6 Peter Gay, *The Bourgeois Experience. Victoria to Freud.* Vol. I: *The Education of the Senses* (1984) p. 179.
7 Girton College, Cambridge. Emily Davies Papers, Box I: Family Chronicle, f. 500.
8 Ibid. Family Chronicle f. 210.
9 Ibid. f. 506.
10 Bertrand and Patricia Russell, *The Amberley Papers. The Letters and Diaries of Lord and Lady Amberley*, 2 vols (1937) II. 268.
11 Josephine Butler, 'Introduction', in her *Woman's Work and Woman's Culture*, op. cit. xli.

12 Gordon S. Haight, ed., *The George Eliot Letters* 7 vols (1955) IV (1862–8) 399. November 1867.
13 Elizabeth Barrett Browning, *Aurora Leigh*, in ed. Cora Kaplan, *Aurora Leigh with other Poems* (1978) lst book, ll.832–44.
14 *Parliamentary Papers*, House of Commons. 1867–8. xxviii. *Report of Schools Inquiry Commission*. Part V. 16,006.
15 C. E. V. Leser, 'The supply of women for gainful work in Britain', *Population Studies* IX (1955–6) 2, p. 142.
16 Jessie Boucherett, 'The Industrial Movement', in ed. Theodore Stanton, *The Woman Question in Europe. A Series of Original Essays* (1884) p. 104.
17 Quoted in Hammerton, op. cit. p. 27.
18 The degrees to which women were admitted did not extend to medical qualifications in the first instance.
19 Joyce Senders Pedersen, 'The reform of women's secondary and higher education: institutional change and social values in mid and late Victorian England', *History of Education Quarterly* (Spring, 1979) p. 77.
20 'Our Daughters', *The Times*, 29 December 1894.
21 Barbara Caine, *Destined To Be Wives. The Sisters of Beatrice Webb* (1986) p. 144.
22 Rhoda Garrett, *The Electoral Disabilities of Women. A Lecture* (1872) p. 7.
23 Lady Stanley of Alderley, 'Personal recollections of women's education', *The Nineteenth Century* 6 (1879) p. 319.
24 Janet Howarth and Mark Curthoys, 'The political economy of women's higher education in late nineteenth and early twentieth century Britain', *Historical Research* 60 (June 1987) 142, pp. 213–4.
25 Joyce Senders Pedersen, 'Schoolmistresses and headmistresses: élites and education in nineteenth century England', *Journal of British Studies* XV (1975) 1, pp. 135–62.
26 Janet E. Courtney, *Recollected in Tranquillity* (1926) p. 112.
27 H. M. Swanwick, *I Have Been Young* (1935) p. 76.
28 Ibid. p. 81.
29 Millicent Garrett Fawcett, 'A short review of the portion of the Report of the Schools Inquiry Commission which refers to girls' education', in eds Henry and Millicent Fawcett, *Essays and Lectures on Social and Political Subjects* (1872) p. 188.
30 Frances Power Cobbe, *Life of Frances Power Cobbe by Herself* (1894) I. pp. 63; 64.
31 Mary L. Bruce, *Anna Swanwick. A Memoir and Recollections. 1813–1899* (1903) p. 19.
32 Mary Paley Marshall, *What I Remember* (1947) p. 7.
33 Constance Maynard, 'From early Victorian schoolroom to university: some personal experiences', *The Nineteenth Century and After* 76 (1914) p. 1063.
34 H. M. Swanwick, op. cit. p. 75.
35 Janet E. Courtney, *The Women of My Time* (1934) pp. 13–14.
36 Millicent Garrett Fawcett, 'A short review . . . of girls' education', loc. cit. p. 193.

37 Margaret Wynne Nevinson, *Life's Fitful Fever. A Volume of Memories* (1926) p. 8.
38 Ibid.
39 Fawcett Library, London. Autograph Letter Collection: Education 4A. 1850–64. Emily Davies to Dyke Acland, 30 January 1863.
40 Sheila Fletcher, *Feminists and Bureaucrats. A Study in the Development of Girls' Education in the Nineteenth Century* (1980) p. 171.
41 Margaret Bryant, *The Unexpected Revolution. A Study in the History of the Education of Women and Girls in the Nineteenth Century* (1979) pp. 94; 101.
42 See Sheila Fletcher, *Women First: the Female Tradition in English Physical Education 1880–1980* (1984) and Kathleen McCrone, *Sport and the Physical Emancipation of English Women 1870–1914* (1988).
43 Margaret Bondfield, *A Life's Work* (1949) p. 21.
44 *Journal of the Women's Education Union* I (January 1873) p. 15; H. M. Swanwick, op. cit. p. 75.
45 Janet E. Courtney, *The Women of My Time* p. 32.
46 James S. Stone, 'More light on Emily Faithfull and the Victoria Press', *The Library* XXXIII (1978) p. 63.
47 Girton College, Cambridge. Family Chronicle, op. cit. f. 472. Emily Davies to W. H. Hutton, 1866.
48 *Parliamentary Papers*, House of Commons, op. cit. 11,470.
49 Stone, loc. cit. p. 63.
50 Fawcett Library, London. MS LEB/1. Press cuttings.
51 *Parliamentary Papers*, House of Commons, op. cit. 15,461.
52 Family Chronicle, f. 392. Emily Davies to Dyke Acland, 28 December 1864.
53 Ibid. f. 201.
54 Barbara Stephen, *Emily Davies and Girton College* (1927) p. 221.
55 Family chronicle, f. 557. 27 November 1867.
56 Quoted from Maynard's diary for April 1891 in Janet Sondheimer, *Castle Adamant in Hampstead. A History of Westfield College 1882–1982* (1983) p. 48.
57 B. Stephen, op. cit. p. 89.
58 Marshall, op. cit. p. 10.
59 Pedersen, 'Schoolmistresses and headmistresses', *Journal of British Studies*, loc. cit.
60 *Parliamentary Papers*, House of Commons, 1895, xliii. *Royal Commission on Secondary Education*, p. 15.
61 Diana Mary Chase Worzala, 'The Langham Place Circle: The beginnings of the organized women's movement in England, 1854–70', unpublished PhD thesis, University of Wisconsin-Madison, 1982, pp. 249–50.
62 Family Chronicle, f. 432. Emily Davies to Anna Richardson, 25 October 1865.
63 Bedford College Archives, RF/103/6. Elizabeth Reid to Jane Martineau and Eliza Bostock, n.d. (?1860).
64 Ibid.

65 As Janet Howarth and Mark Curthoys point out in their 'Gender, curriculum and career: a case study of women university students before 1914', unpublished paper, 1987, 'it was these three universities [Oxford, Cambridge and London] that attracted the great majority of women who wished to follow a specialised course of study to degree level.' (p. 2).
66 Elizabeth Wordsworth, *Glimpses of the Past* (1913) pp. 159–60.
67 Marshall, op. cit. p. 15.
68 Wordsworth, op. cit. p. 169.
69 Nevinson, op. cit. p. 17.
70 Caine, op. cit. p. 141.
71 Maynard, loc. cit. p. 1066.
72 Janet E. Courtney, *Recollected in Tranquillity* pp. 100–101.
73 Mabel Tylecote, *The Education of Women at Manchester University 1883–1933* (1941) pp. 32–3.
74 Marshall, op. cit. p. 15.
75 Ibid. p. 15.
76 This raises the issue of what course of study women students followed and, in general, it appears that they followed much the same curriculum as men. The work of Janet Howarth and Mark Curthoys has established that a higher proportion of Cambridge women read for the Classics, Mathematics and Natural Sciences Tripos than men (loc. cit. 'Gender, curriculum, career', p. 11).
77 Blanche Athena Clough, *A Memoir of Anne Jemima Clough* (1897) pp. 155; 312.
78 Alice M. Gordon, 'The after-careers of university-educated women', *The Nineteenth Century. A Monthly Review* 37 (1895) pp. 956; 955.
79 Marshall. op. cit. p. 11.
80 Lilian M. Faithfull, *In the House of My Pilgrimage* (1924) p. 53.
81 Quoted in Janet E. Courtney, *The Women of My Time* p. 27.
82 Janet E. Courtney, *An Oxford Portrait Gallery* (1931) p. 243.
83 Lady Stanley of Alderley, 'Personal recollections', loc. cit. p. 314.
84 Janet Howarth's and Mark Curthoys' piece on 'Gender, curriculum, career', (loc. cit. pp. 7–8) offers an enlightening discussion of feminist attitudes to prevailing theories of education.
85 Elizabeth Wordsworth, op. cit. p. 160.
86 Janet E. Courtney, *Recollected in Tranquillity* p. 93.
87 Family Chronicle, f. 432. 25 October 1865.
88 Worzala, 'The Langham Place Circle', op. cit. p. 278.
89 Derek Hudson, *Munby. Man of Two Worlds. The Life and Diaries of Arthur J. Munby, 1828–1910* (1972) p. 216.
90 Ibid. p. 211.
91 Ibid. p. 236.
92 Frances Power Cobbe. *The Duties of Women. A Course of Lectures* (2nd edn, 1881) p. 113.
93 ed. L. M. H[ubbard], *The Year-Book of Women's Work* (1875) pp. 6–7.
94 A. Amy Bulley and Margaret Whitley, *Women's Work* (1894) p. 113.
95 Butler, op. cit. p. xxxv.

96 Gordon, loc. cit. p. 956.
97 Emily Faithfull, *On Some of the Drawbacks Connected with the Present Employment of Women* (1862) p. 3.
98 Hammerton, op. cit. p. 32.
99 Hester Burton, *Barbara Bodichon, 1827–91* (1949) p. 111.
100 Edwin A. Pratt, *Pioneer Women in Victoria's Reign. Being Short Histories of Great Movements* (1897) pp. 15–16.
101 The very use of the pseudonym by so many women offers an interesting comment on the whole question of knowing the author and, indeed, the author's intention. In deliberately masking their usual identity, women in fact fully acknowledged authorship. The *nom de plume* ironically becomes the most effective guarantee of authorship and of authorial intent.
102 Family Chronicle, f. 244.
103 Cobbe, *Life*, op. cit. I. 276.
104 British Library Add. MS 47451, f. 253. 18 September 1898.
105 David Rubinstein, *Before the Suffragettes. Women's Emancipation in the 1890s* (1986) p. 75.
106 Nevinson, op. cit. p. 62.
107 Quoted in Hammerton, op. cit. p. 125.
108 Angela John, *By The Sweat Of Their Brow. Women Workers at Victorian Coal Mines* (1984) p. 148.
109 Butler, op. cit. pp. xxviii–xxix.
110 Johann Handl, 'Educational chances and occupational opportunities of women: a sociohistorical analysis', *Journal of Social History* 17 (1984) 3, p. 480.
111 Anna Davin, 'Telegraphists and clerks', *Bulletin of the Society for the Study of Labour History* 26 (1973) p. 9.
112 Barbara L. Hutchins, *Statistics of Women's Life and Employment* (1909) pp. 8; 12.
113 Gordon, loc. cit. pp. 955–8.

CHAPTER 8   NURTURING THE SICKLY PLANTS: WOMEN, LABOUR AND UNIONISM

1 See my *Victorian Feminism 1850–1900* (1987) for a fuller discussion of these bodies as well as such monographs as the reprint of Barbara Drake's *Women in Trade Unions* (1984), Sarah Boston's *Women Workers and the Trade Union Movement* (1980) and Norbert Soldon's *Women in British Trade Unions 1874–1976* (1978) for concrete details on the various organizations.
2 See Jane Humphries, 'Protective legislation, the capitalist state and working class men: the case of the 1842 Mines Regulation Act', *Feminist Review* 7 (1981) p. 8, for some discussion of the importance of regionalism in determining female labour patterns.
3 British Library, London. Add. MS 43946. Dilke Papers Vol LXXIII. Typescript memoir by Sir Charles Dilke of Emilia Dilke, n.d. p. 156. Text of

a speech delivered by Emilia; neither date nor venue given. See also chapter 2 for details of Emilia's asceticism.

4 Rosemary Feurer has argued that this second period of interest in protective legislation is coincident with the rise of the women's movement in Britain. (See her 'The meaning of "sisterhood": the British Women's Movement and protective labour legislation 1870–1900', *Victorian Studies* 31 (1988) 2, p. 233.) Whilst there is certainly a considerable overlap between the two, women's activism in this phase of the movement had begun to have substantial impact as early as the 1850s, before this legislative interest saw fully-fledged revival.

5 James A. Schmiechen, *Sweated Industries and Sweated Labour. The London Clothing Trades 1860–1914* (1984) p. 139.

6 Jane Lewis, *Women in England 1870–1950: Sexual Divisions and Social Change* (1984) p. 189.

7 Olive Banks, *Becoming A Feminist. The Social Origins of 'First Wave' Feminism* (1986) p. 82.

8 Judith Baer, *The Chains of Protection. The Judicial Response to Women's Labor Legislation* (1978) p. 9.

9 Mrs Jane M. E. Brownlow, *Women and Factory Legislation* (1896) p. 6.

10 Ibid. p. 4.

11 Hal Draper and Ann G. Lipow, 'Marxist women versus bourgeois feminism', *Socialist Register* 13 (1976) p. 185; Enid Stacy, 'A century of women's rights', in ed. E. Carpenter, *Forecasts of the Coming Century by a decade of writers* (1897) pp. 94–95.

12 Anne Phillips, *Divided Loyalties. Dilemmas of Sex and Class* (1987) p. 87.

13 Rosemary Feurer, loc. cit. p. 247.

14 Jane Lewis, 'Dealing with dependency: state practices and social realities 1870–1945', in ed. Jane Lewis, *Women's Welfare. Women's Rights* (1983) p. 31.

15 In accusing women of assuming an effective alliance with employers (as Feurer does in her article in *Victorian Studies*, see footnote 13 above), such judgements make precisely the same error as contemporary claims that women arguing the case against freely available pornography are aligning themselves with organizations premised on censorship and a ban on free expression. The issue is not one of censorship but of exploitation; for nineteenth-century feminists, the issue centred more on the oppressive behaviour of the state than on how their opposition to its laws might serve the needs of manufacturers.

16 The *WUJ* changed its name to the *Women's Trade Union Review* in tandem with the organization's overall change of nomenclature.

17 Helen Jones, 'Women health workers: the case of the first women factory inspectors in Britain', *Journal of the Society for the Social History of Medicine* 1 (1988), p. 171.

18 Ibid.

19 It is interesting to note in passing that whilst the hiring of experienced

women was recommended, male inspectors continued to be hired from the educated classes without corresponding outcry or comment.

20 James D. Young, *Women and Popular Struggles. A History of British Working Class Women 1560–1984* (1985) p. 71.

21 Olive Banks, op. cit. p. 65.

22 James A. Schmiechen, op. cit. p. 187.

23 The category was a difficult one in which to be specific. The delineation of class boundaries, defined by occupation, is a tricky exercise requiring much caution. As an example of the pitfalls awaiting the unwary researcher, the case of cousins Agnes and Rhoda Garrett is instructive. Women from substantial middle-class backgrounds (one a merchant's daughter, the other a parson's daughter), they operated a highly successful house decorating partnership. Today their business would doubtless operate under the rubric of interior design, a grandiose title designed not simply to elicit considerably higher fees but to distinguish the practitioners from the lesser business of painting and decorating. Agnes and Rhoda called their work house decorating but it is clear that they none the less do not belong in the same category as women engaged in manual trades.

24 Banks, op. cit. p. 56.

25 Ibid. p. 3.

26 'How to help our own', *Women's Union Journal* January 1882, p. 2. See, too, Norbert Soldon, op. cit. p. 16 for a more comprehensive list of towns in which the WPPL was active.

27 Teresa Olcott, 'Dead centre: the women's trade union movement in London, 1874–1914', *London Journal* 2 (1976) 1, p. 33.

28 Ellen Mappen, *Helping Women At Work. The Women's Industrial Council 1889–1914* (1985) p. 13.

29 *Women Workers. The Official Report of the Conference held at Nottingham on October 22nd, 23rd, 24th and 25th, 1895* (1896).

30 Soldon, op. cit. p. 21.

31 See Jane Lewis, 'The debate on sex and class', *New Left Review* 149 (1985), p. 111; and Joanna Bornat, 'Home and work. A new context for trade union history', *Radical America* 12 (1978) pp. 52–69.

32 Judy Lown, 'Not so much a factory, more a form of patriarchy: gender and class during industrialisation', in eds. Eva Gamarnikow, David Morgan, June Purvis and Daphne Taylerson, *Gender, Class and Work* (1983) pp. 43–44.

33 Feurer, loc. cit. p. 255.

34 Carole Pateman, *The Sexual Contract* (1988) p. 14.

35 Feurer, loc. cit. p. 243.

36 Pateman, op. cit. p. 208.

37 Ibid. p. 6.

38 Brownlow, op. cit. p. 2.

39 Millicent Garrett Fawcett, 'Mr Sidney Webb's article on women's wages', *Economic Journal* 2 (1892) 1, quoted in Heidi Hartmann, 'Capitalism,

6

6

patriarchy and job segregation by sex', in eds Elizabeth and Emily K. Abel, *The Signs Reader. Women, Gender and Scholarship* (1983) p. 213.

40 Draper and Lipow, loc. cit. p. 180.

41 Dame Anne Godwin, 'Early years in the trade unions', in ed. Lucy Middleton, *Women in the Labour Movement. The British Experience* (1977) p. 95.

CHAPTER 9   ORGANIZING PRINCIPLES: RE-READING THE POLITICAL
GENEAOLOGY OF FEMINISM

1 Radical History Review Editorial Collective, 'Patrolling the borders: feminist historiography and the new historicism', comments of Judith R. Walkowitz, *Radical History Review* 43 (1989) pp. 23–43.

2 Joan Scott, 'On language, gender and working class history', *International Labour and Working Class History* 31 (1987) p. 8.

3 See, for example, the influential work of F. K. Prochaska, *Women and Philanthrophy in Nineteenth Century England* (1980).

4 R. W. Connell, *Gender and Power. Society, the Person and Sexual Politics* (1987) p. 131.

5 See the work of Michel Foucault, and most specifically his multi-volumed *History of Sexuality* (1978–86).

6 See Zillah Eisenstein, *The Female Body and the Law* (1988) p. 16.

Bibliography

MANUSCRIPT SOURCES

Bodleian Library, Oxford

Pattison Collection: MSS Pattison 118; 140.
Pearson Collection: MS Eng. lett. d. 187.
Primrose League: Ladies' Executive Committee Minute Book, 1885–6.
Rogers Collection: MS Eng. lett. c. 334; Eng. misc. c. 585.
Simcox, Edith Jemima, Autobiography of a Shirtmaker. MS Eng. misc. d. 494

British Library, London

Dilke Papers: Additional Manuscripts 43907; 43908; 43946; 49611.
Wolstenholme Elmy Papers: Additional Manuscripts 47449; 47450; 47451.

Fawcett Library, London

Autograph Letter Collection:
  Education 1850–64 4A
  Women's Movement 1865–71 2B
  Women's Movement 1872–86
  Women's Movement 1888–96
  Women's Movement 1897–1900
  Women's Suffrage 1851–94
  Women's Suffrage 1895–98 1B1
Becker Letters and Autograph Collection: LEB/1.
Central National Society for Women's Suffrage, Manuscript Minute Book for 1890.
Fawcett Collection: Box 89.
Hubbard Papers.

Girton College, Cambridge

Davies Papers: Family Chronicle; Schools Inquiry Commission.
Parkes Collection.

Manchester Central Reference Library

Fawcett Correspondence: M 50/2/1/6; M50/2/1/68
Manchester and North of England National Society for Women's Suffrage:
  Correspondence: M50/1/2, 1/9; Reports: M50/1/2/1–98; M50/1/4/27;
  M50/1/10/187.
National Union of Working Women: M50/4/10/1.
Society for Promoting the Employment of Women: membership and donations:
  M50/4/1/1.
Women's Franchise League papers: M50/2/32/1.

Royal Holloway and Bedford New College, London

Bedford College papers: GB 112/3/1; 112/4/1; 121/2; 122/1/1.
Reid papers: RF/103/1–3; RF/103/6.

Tallahassee, Florida

Barbara Leigh Smith Bodichon: autograph letters in the private collection of
Barbara S. McCrimmon.

BIOGRAPHICAL AND AUTOBIOGRAPHICAL SOURCES

Alcott, Louisa M.: *Shawl-Straps* (London, 1873).
Anon. [Mary Frances Cusack]: *Five Years in a Protestant Sisterhood and Ten
  Years in a Catholic Convent. An Autobiography* (London, 1869).
Balfour, Frances: *Ne Obliviscaris. Dinna Forget* 2 vols (London, 1930).
Banks, Olive: *Biographical Dictionary of British Feminists* (Brighton, 1985).
Bondfield, Margaret: *A Life's Work* (London, 1949).
Boyd, Nancy: *Josephine Butler, Octavia Hill, Florence Nightingale. Three
  Victorian Women who Changed their World* (London, 1982).
Bruce, Mary L.: *Anna Swanwick. A Memoir and Recollections. 1813–1899*
  (London, 1903).
Burton, Hester: *Barbara Bodichon 1827–91* (London, 1949).
Butler, Josephine E.: *Personal Reminiscences of a Great Crusade* (London,
  1896).
Caine, Barbara: 'Millicent Garrett Fawcett: a Victorian liberal feminist?', in eds
  Barbara Caine, E. A. Grosz and Marie de Lepervanche, *Crossing Boundaries.
  Feminisms and the Critique of Knowledges* (Sydney, 1988).
Clough, Blanche Athena: *A Memoir of Anne Jemima Clough* (London, 1897).

Cobbe, Frances Power: *Life of Frances Power Cobbe by Herself* 2 vols (London, 1894).

Courtney, Janet E.: *Recollected in Tranquillity* (London, 1926).

———: *An Oxford Portrait Gallery* (London, 1926).

———: *The Women of My Time* (London, 1934).

Cruikshank, M.: 'Mary Dendy', *Journal of Educational Administration and History* 8 (1976) pp. 26–9.

Ethelmer, Ellis [pseudonym of Benjamin Elmy]: 'A woman emancipator. A biographical sketch', *Westminster Review* 145 (April 1896) pp. 424–8.

Faithfull, Lilian M.: *In the House of My Pilgrimage* (London, 1924).

Fawcett, Millicent Garrett: *What I Remember* (London, 1924).

Gautrey, Thomas: *'Lux Mihi Laus': School Board Memories* (London, 1937).

Gurney, Ellen Mary: *Letters of Emelie Russell Gurney* (London, 1902).

Hannam, June: 'Usually neglected in standard histories: some issues in working on the life of Isabella Ford, 1855–1924', *Studies in Sexual Politics* 13 & 14 (double issue): *Writing Feminist Biography* (1986) pp. 4–27.

Harrison, Jane Ellen: *Reminiscences of A Student Life* (London, 1925).

Heath, Henry J. B.: *Margaret Bright Lucas. The Life Story of a 'British Woman'* (London, 1890).

Herstein, Sheila R.: *A Mid-Victorian Feminist, Barbara Leigh Smith Bodichon* (Yale, 1985).

Holmes, Marion: *Lydia Becker. A Cameo Life Sketch* (London, 1913).

Lerner, Gerda: *The Grimké Sisters from South Carolina: Pioneers for Women's Rights and Abolition* (New York, 1971).

Levine, Philippa: Introduction to Amelia Edwards, *Untrodden Peaks and Unfrequented Valleys. A Midsummer Ramble in the Dolomites* (London, 1986).

Lowndes, M. Belloc: *'I, Too, Have Lived in Arcadia'. A Record of Love and of Childhood* (London, 1941).

Manton, Jo: *Mary Carpenter and the Children of the Streets* (London, 1976).

Markham, Violet R.: *May Tennant. A Portrait* (London, 1949).

Marshall, Mary Paley: *What I Remember* (Cambridge, 1947).

Martindale, Hilda: *From One Generation to Another, 1839–1944. A Book of Memoirs* (London, 1944).

Matthews, Jacqui: 'Barbara Bodichon: integrity in diversity (1827–91)' in ed. Dale Spender, *Feminist Theorists. Three Centuries of Women's Intellectual Traditions* (London, 1983) pp. 90–123.

Maynard, Constance: 'From early Victorian schoolroom to university: some personal experiences', *The Nineteenth Century and After* 76 (1914) pp. 1060–73.

Metcalfe, Ethel E.: *Memoir of Rosamund Davenport-Hill* (London, 1904).

Mills, Isabel Petrie: *From Tinder-Box to the 'Larger' Light. Threads from the Life of John Mills, Banker (Author of 'Vox Humana'): Interwoven with some early century Recollections by his Wife* (Manchester, 1899).

Nevinson, Margaret Wynne: *Life's Fitful Fever. A Volume of Memories* (London, 1926).

Oakley, Ann: 'Millicent Garrett Fawcett: duty and determination (1847–1929)', in ed. Spender (1983) pp. 184–202.

Pratt, Edwin A.: *A Woman's Work for Women, being the Aims, Efforts and Aspirations of 'L. M. H.' (Miss Louisa M. Hubbard)* (London, 1898).

Raikes, Elizabeth: *Dorothea Beale of Cheltenham* (London, 1909).

Ridley, Annie E.: *Frances Mary Buss and her Work for Education* (London, 1895).

Shaen, Margaret J.: *Memorials of Two Sisters. Susannah and Catherine Winkworth* (London, 1908).

Sharp, Evelyn: *Hertha Ayrton, 1854–1923. A Memoir* (London, 1926).

Smith, Mary: *The Autobiography of Mary Smith, Schoolmistress and Nonconformist. A Fragment of Life* (London, 1892).

Somerville, Rose: *Brief Epitomes of the Lives of Women* (London, n.d.).

Soutter, Francis William: *Recollections of a Labour Pioneer* (London, 1923).

Stanley, Liz ed.: *The Diaries of Hannah Cullwick. Victorian Maidservant* (London, 1984).

Stephen, Barbara: *Emily Davies and Girton College* (London, 1927).

Strachey, Ray: *Millicent Garrett Fawcett* (London, 1931).

Sturge, Elizabeth: *Reminiscences of My Life* (London, 1928).

Swanwick, Helena M.: *I Have Been Young* (London, 1935).

Thomas, Clara: *Love and Work Enough. The Life of Anna Jameson* (Toronto and London, 1967).

Todd, Margaret: *The Life of Sophia Jex-Blake* (London, 1918).

Uglow, Jennifer: 'Josephine Butler: from sympathy to theory (1828–1906)', in ed. Spender (1983), pp. 146–64.

Wordsworth, Elizabeth: *Glimpses of the Past* (London, 1913).

FEMINIST PERIODICALS CONSULTED

Alexandra Magazine and Englishwoman's Journal (1864).

The Dawn. An Occasional Sketch of the Progress of the Work of the British, Continental and General Federation for the Abolition of State Regulation of Vice (1888).

English Woman's Journal (1858).

Englishwomen's Review (1866).

The Gatherer (1883).

Journal of the Women's Education Union (1873).

Kettledrum (1869).

The Pioneer. Being the Organ of the Social Purity Alliance and the Moral Reform Union (1887).

The Shield. The Anti-Contagious Diseases Acts Association's Weekly Circular (1870).

Shafts. A Monthly Magazine of Progressive Thought (1892).

The Storm Bell for the Ladies' National Association for the Abolition of State Regulation of Vice (1898).

Victoria Magazine (1863).

Woman. A Weekly Journal Embodying Female Interests from an Educational, Social and Domestic Point of View (1872).

Woman's Herald (1891).
Woman's Opinion (1874).
Woman's Signal (1894).
Woman's World (1868).
Women's Industrial News (1895).
Women's Penny Paper (1888).
Women's Suffrage Journal (1870).
Women's Trade Union Review (1891).
Women's Union Journal (1876).
Women and Work. A Weekly Industrial Educational and Household Register for Women (1874).
Work and Leisure (1880).

PARLIAMENTARY PAPERS

House of Commons:

1847–8 [973] xxviii. *First Report of the Commissioners appointed to inquire into the state and operation of the Law of Marriage.*
1852–3 [1604] xl. *First Report of the Commissioners appointed to enquire into the Laws of Divorce.*
1859 Sess. 2. (131) xix. *Returns Relative to Divorce and Matrimonial Causes.*
1867–8 [4059] xxxii. *Report of the Royal Commission on the Laws of Marriage.*
1867–8 [4031] xxxvii. *First Report of the Committee Appointed to enquire into the Pathology and Treatment of the Venereal Diseases.*
1867–8 [441] vii. *Special Report from the Select Committee on the Married Women's Property Bill.*
1867–8 xxviii. *Report of Schools Inquiry Commission.*
1868–9 (210) vii. *Report from the Select Committee on the Married Women's Property Bill.*
1871 C. 408. xix. *Report of the Royal Commission upon the Administration and Operation of the Contagious Diseases Acts.*
1894 lxxx. Part 2. 845. *Report by Miss Collett on the Statistics of Employment of Women and Girls.*
1895 xliii. *Royal Commission on Secondary Education.*

OTHER PRIMARY PRINTED SOURCES

Acton, William: *The Functions and Disorders of the Reproductive Organs in Youth, in Adult Age and in Advanced Life, considered in their Physiological, Social and Psychological Relations* (London, 1857).
——: *Prostitution considered in its Moral, Social and Sanitary Aspects, in London and other Large Cities and Garrison Towns: with Proposals for the Control and Prevention of its Attendant Evils* (London, 1857).
Anderson, Adelaide Mary: *Women in the Factory. An Administrative Adventure, 1893–1921* (London, 1922).

Anstruther, Eva: 'Ladies' Clubs', *Contemporary Review* 45 (1899) pp. 598–611.
B. T. [Bertha Thomas]: 'Latest intelligence from the planet Venus', *Fraser's Magazine* 90 o.s., 10 n.s., (December 1874) pp. 763–66.
Becker, Lydia: 'Female suffrage', *Contemporary Review* (March 1867) pp. 307–16.
Biggs, Caroline Ashurst: *Women as Poor Law Guardians* (London, 1887).
——:A Letter from an Englishwoman to Englishwomen (London, 1889).
Black, Clementina: *An Agitator* (London, 1894).
Blackburn, Helen: *A Handbook for Women engaged in Social and Political Work* (1st edn, Bristol, 1881; 2nd edn, Bristol, 1895).
Bodichon, Barbara: *Reasons for the Enfranchisement of Women* (London, 1866).
——: 'Authorities and precedents for giving the suffrage to qualified women', *Englishwomen's Review* II (January 1867) pp. 63–75.
——: *An American Diary 1857–8*, ed. Joseph W. Reed Jr, (London, 1972).
Boucherett, Jessie: 'The employment of women', *Nowadays* (July 1869) pp. 52–9.
——: 'The industrial movement', in ed. Theodore Stanton, *The Woman Question in Europe. A Series of Original Essays* (London, 1884) pp. 90–107.
——: with Helen Blackburn and some others: *The Condition of Working Women and the Factory Acts* (London, 1896).
Brownlow, Jane M. E.: *Women and Factory Legislation* (London, 1896).
Browning, Elizabeth Barrett: 'Aurora Leigh', in ed. Cora Kaplan, *Aurora Leigh with other Poems* (London, 1978).
Bulley, A. Amy and Margaret Whitley: *Women's Work* (London, 1894).
Butler, Josephine E.: *Woman's Work and Woman's Culture. A Series of Essays* (London, 1869).
Caird, Mona: 'Marriage', *Westminster Review* 130 (1888) 2, pp. 186–201.
——: *The Morality of Marriage and other Essays on the Status and Destiny of Woman* (London, 1897).
Chapman, Rachel: 'Marriage rejection and marriage reform', *Westminster Review* 130 (1888) 3, pp. 358–77.
Cobbe, Frances Power: *Essays on the Pursuits of Women* (London, 1863).
——: *Criminals, Idiots, Women and Minors. Is the Classification Sound? A Discussion on the Laws Concerning the Property of Married Women* (Manchester, 1869).
——: *The Duties of Women. A Course of Lectures* (London, 1881).
——: 'The final cause of women', in ed. Josephine Butler, *Woman's Work and Woman's Culture. A Series of Essays* (London, 1869).
——: 'Introduction' to ed. Theodore Stanton (1884).
——: 'Wife torture in England', *Contemporary Review* 32 (1878) , pp. 55–87.
Collett, Clara E.: *Women in Industry* (London, n.d.).
——: *Educated Working Women* (London, 1902).
Cornwallis, Caroline Frances: 'The property of married women', *Westminster Review* 66 (October 1856) pp. 331–360.
Cusack, M. F.: *Women's Work in Modern Society* (Kenmare, 1874).
Davies, Emily: *The Higher Education of Women* (1866) ed. Janet Howarth

(London and Ronceverte, 1988).

Dilke, Mary Ashton: *Women's Suffrage* (London, 1885).

Dilke, Emilia, F. S.: *Benefit Societies and Trades Unions for Women* (London, 1889).

Faithfull, Emily: *On Some of the Drawbacks connected with the Present Employment of Women* (2nd edn, London, 1862).

Fawcett, Henry and Millicent Garrett: *Essays and Lectures on Social and Political Subjects* (London, 1872).

Fawcett, Millicent Garrett: *On Women's Suffrage* (Birmingham, 1872).

——: 'Why women require the franchise', in eds H. and M. G. Fawcett, *Essays and Lectures on Social and Political Subjects* (London, 1872).

——: 'A short review of the portion of the Report of the Schools Enquiry Commission which refers to Girls' Education' in eds H. and M. G. Fawcett, *Essays and Lectures on Social and Political Subjects* (London, 1872).

——: 'The Women's Suffrage Movement' in ed. Theodore Stanton (1884) pp. 1–29.

——: *Home and Politics* (London, n.d. 1894?).

Ford, Isabella O.: *On the Threshold* (London, 1895).

Garrett, Elizabeth: *An Enquiry into the Character of the Contagious Diseases Acts of 1866–69* (London, 1870).

Garrett, Rhoda: *The Electoral Disabilities of Women. A Lecture* (Cheltenham, 1872).

Garton, R. L.: 'A modern socialist. An interview with Miss Enid Stacy, B.A.', *The Woman's Signal* IV (1895) 89, pp. 161–2.

Girton College Register 1869–1946 (Cambridge, 1948).

Glennie, J. S. Stuart: 'The proposed subjection of men', *Fortnightly Review* XLV (1889) pp. 568–78.

Gordon, Alice M.: 'The after-careers of university-educated women', *The Nineteenth Century. A Monthly Review* 37 (1985) pp. 955–60.

Grey, Maria: *The National Union for Improving the Education of Women. A Letter to the Editor of The Times* (London, 1872).

——: *Idols of Society; or Gentility and Femininity* (London, 1874).

——: *Old Maids. A Lecture* (London, 1875).

—— and Emily Shirreff: *Thoughts on Self-Culture Addressed to Women* (London, 1872).

Grote, Harriet: *Collected Papers In Prose and Verse, 1842–62* (London, 1862).

Gurney, Mary: *Are We To Have Education for our Middle Class Girls? or The History of Camden Collegiate Schools* (London, 1872).

H. B. [Helen Blackburn]: *A Women's Suffrage Calendar for 1886* (Bristol and London, 1885).

Haight, Gordon S. ed.: *The George Eliot Letters: IV and VIII, 1862–8* (Yale, 1955).

Hoggan, Frances Elizabeth: 'Women in medicine', in ed. Theodore Stanton (1884) pp. 63–89.

Holdsworth, Annie E.: *A Garden of Spinsters* (London and Newcastle-upon-Tyne, 1904).

Hubbard, Louisa M. ed.: *The Year-Book of Women's Work* (London, 1875).

Hutchins, Barbara L.: *Statistics of Women's Life and Employment* (privately printed, 1909).

——: *Conflicting Ideals. Two Sides of the Woman's Question* (London, 1913).

——: *Women in Modern Industry* (London, 1915).

Justina: *Letters in reply to Miss Garrett's Defence of the Contagious Diseases Acts* (London, 1870).

Lecky, William H.: *A History of European Morals from Augustus to Charlemagne* (London, 1877).

M. A. [Mabel Atkinson]: *The Economic Foundations of the Women's Movement* (London, 1914).

McLaren, Eva: *History of the Women's Suffrage Movement in the Women's Liberal Federation* (London, 1903).

Married Women's Property Committee Tracts, 1869–82.

Manchester National Society for Women's Suffrage: *Annual Report of the Executive Committee, 1867 and 1868.*

Mill, John Stuart and Harriet Taylor: 'The enfranchisement of women', *Westminster and Foreign Quarterly Review* 55 (July 1851) pp. 289–311.

Miller, Florence Fenwick: *On the Programme of the Women's Franchise League. An Address delivered at the National Liberal Club* (London, 1890).

——: *In Ladies' Company. Six Interesting Women* (London, 1892).

National Society for Women's Suffrage: *Declaration in favour of Women's Suffrage* (London, 1889).

——: *The Work of the Central Committee. A Sketch* (London, 1893).

Newnham College Register Volume I: 1871–1923 (n.d.).

Page, Hamilton [pseudonym of Frances Martin]: *The Lady Resident* 3 vols (London, 1880).

Parkes, Bessie: *Essays on Woman's Work* (London, 1865).

Philipps, Mrs: *A Dictionary of Employments open to Women – with details of Wages, Hours of Work and other Information* (London, 1898).

Richards, E. F.: *Mazzini's Letters to An English Family* 3 vols (London, 1920–22).

Russell, Bertrand and Patricia, eds: *The Amberley Papers. The Letters and Diairies of Lord and Lady Amberley* 2 vols (London, 1937).

Sewall, May Wright, ed.: *The World's Congress of Representative Women* (Chicago and New York, 1894).

Snowden, Ethel: *The Feminist Movement* (London, 1911).

Society for Promoting the Return of Women as Poor Law Guardians: *Annual Report* (1883).

Squire, Rose E.: *Thirty Years in the Public Service. An Industrial Retrospect* (London, 1927).

Stacy, Enid: 'A century of women's rights', in ed. Edward Carpenter, *Forecasts of the Coming Century* pp. 86–101.

Stanley, Lady: 'Personal recollections of women's education', *The Nineteenth Century* 6 (1879) pp. 308–21.

Sturge, E. M.: *On Women's Suffrage* (Birmingham, 1872).

'The Woman' and The Age: A Letter from the International Association for the Total Suppression of Vivisection (London, 1881).

Women's Emancipation Union. Its Origin and Its Work (Manchester, 1892).
Women's Franchise League: *Report of Proceedings at the Inaugural Meeting, London, July 25 1889* (London, 1889).
Women's Industrial Council pamphlets (Fawcett Library, London).
Women Workers. The Official Report of the Conference held at Manchester 1896 (1896).

OTHER SECONDARY SOURCES

Abel, Elizabeth and Emily K. Abel, eds: *The Signs Reader. Women, Gender and Scholarship* (Chicago and London, 1983).
Abel, Richard L., ed.: *The Politics of Informal Justice*. Vol. I, *The American Experience* (New York, 1982).
Alexander, Sally: 'Women's work in nineteenth century London; a study of the years 1820–50', in eds Juliet Mitchell and Ann Oakley, *The Rights and Wrongs of Women* (Harmondsworth, 1976) pp. 59–111.
——: 'Women, class and sexual difference in the 1830s and 1840s: some reflections on the writing of a feminist history', *History Workshop Journal* 17 (Spring 1984) pp. 125–149.
Altick, Richard D.: 'The social origins, education and occupations of 1100 British writers, 1800–1935, *Bulletin of the New York Public Library* 66 (June 1962) 6, pp. 389–404.
Amsden, Alice, ed.: *The Economics of Women's Work* (London, 1980).
Anderson, Michael: *Approaches to the History of the Western Family, 1500–1914* (London, 1980).
——: 'The social position of spinsters in mid-Victorian Britain', *Journal of Family History* 9 (1984) 4, pp. 377–93.
Anderson, Olive: 'Women preachers in mid-Victorian Britain: some reflections on feminism, popular religion and social change', *Historical Journal* XII (1969) 3, pp. 467–84.
Annan, Noel: 'The intellectual aristocracy', in ed. J. H. Plumb, *Studies in Social History. A Tribute to G. M. Trevelyan* (London, 1955) pp. 243–87.
Armstrong, Nancy and Leonard Tennenhouse: *The Ideology of Conduct. Essays on Literature and the History of Sexuality* (New York and London, 1987).
Atkins, Susan and Brenda Hoggett: *Women and the Law* (Oxford, 1984).
Babcock, B. A., A. E. Freedman, E. H. Norton and S. C. Ross: *Sex Discrimination and the Law. Causes and Remedies* (Boston and Toronto, 1975).
Baer, Judith A.: *The Chains of Protection. The Judicial Response to Women's Labor Legislation* (Westport, Connecticut, 1978).
Ball, T.: 'Utilitarianism, feminism and the franchise: James Mill and his critics', *History of Political Thought* 1 (1980) 1, pp. 91–115.
Banks, J. A.: *Victorian Values. Secularism and the Size of Families* (London, 1981).
Banks, J. A. and Olive: 'The Bradlaugh-Besant trial and the English newspapers', *Population Studies* VIII (1954–5) pp. 22–34.
——: 'Feminism and social change – a case study of a social movement', in eds

G. K. Zollschan and W. Hirsch, *Explorations in Social Change* (London, 1964) pp. 547–69.

Banks, Olive: *Faces of Feminism. A Study of Feminism as a Social Movement* (Oxford, 1981).

——: *Becoming a Feminist. The Social Origins of 'First Wave' Feminism* (Brighton, 1986).

Barker, Diana Leonard: 'The regulation of marriage: repressive benevolence', in eds. Gary Littlejohn, Barry Smart, John Wakeford and Nira Yuval-Davis, *Power and the State* (London, 1978) pp. 238–66.

—— and S. Allen eds: *Dependence and Exploitation in Work and Marriage*, (London, 1976)

Barker-Benfield, Ben: 'The spermatic economy: a nineteenth century view of sexuality', *Feminist Studies* 1 (1972) 1, pp. 45–74.

Barrett, Michèle and Mary McIntosh: 'The "family wage": some problems for socialists and feminists', *Capital and Class* 11 (1980) pp. 51–72.

——: 'The "Family Wage"' in ed. N. Whitehead, *The Changing Experience of Women* (Milton Keynes, 1982) pp. 71–87.

Basch, Françoise: 'Women's rights and the wrongs of marriage in mid-nineteenth century America', *History Workshop Journal* 22 (1986) pp. 18–40.

Basch, Norma: *In the Eyes of the Law: Women, Marriage and Property in Nineteenth Century New York* (Ithaca, 1982).

Bauer, C. and L. Ritt: '"A husband is a beating animal": Frances Power Cobbe confronts the wife-abuse problem in Victorian England', *International Journal of Women's Studies* 6 (1983) 2, pp. 99–118.

——: 'Wife abuse, late-Victorian English feminism and the legacy of Frances Power Cobbe', *International Journal of Women's Studies* 6 (1983) 3, pp. 195–207.

Bayley, David H., ed.: *Police and Society* (California, 1977).

Becher, Harvey W.: 'The social origins and post-graduate careers of a Cambridge intellectual élite 1830–1860', *Victorian Studies* 28 (1984) 1, pp. 97–127.

Behrman, Cynthia Fansler: 'The annual blister', *Victorian Studies* 11 (1968) 4, pp. 483–502.

Bell, Moberly E.: *Storming the Citadel. The Rise of the Woman Doctor* (London, 1953).

Bennett, Tony, Colin Mercer and Janet Wollacott, eds: *Popular Culture and Social Relations* (Milton Keynes and Philadelphia, 1986).

Bentley, Michael and John Stevenson, eds: *High and Low Politics in Modern Britain. Ten Studies* (Oxford, 1986).

Billington, Rosamund: 'Ideology and feminism: why the suffragettes were "wild women"', in ed. Elizabeth Sarah, *Reassessments of 'First Wave' Feminism* (Oxford, 1982) pp. 663–74.

Bland, Lucy: 'In the name of protection: the policing of women in the First World War', in eds Julia Brophy and Carol Smart, *Women in Law: Explorations in Law, Family and Sexuality* (London, 1985) pp. 23–49.

——: 'Marriage laid bare: middle class women and marital sex, 1880s–1914', in ed. Jane Lewis, *Labour and Love. Women's Experience of Home and Family,*

1850–1940 (Oxford, 1986) pp. 122–46.

Bolt, Christine and Seymour Drescher, eds: *Anti-Slavery, Religion and Reform: Essays in Memory of Roger Anstey* (Connecticut, 1980).

Boone, Gladys: *The Women's Trade Union Leagues in Great Britain and the United States of America* (New York, 1942).

Bordin, Ruth: *Woman and Temperance. The Quest for Power and Liberty, 1873–1900* (Philadelphia, 1981).

Bornat, Joanna: 'Home and work. A new context for trade union history', *Radical America* 12 (1978) pp. 52–69.

Bose, Christine: 'Dual spheres', in eds Beth B. Hess and Myra Marx Ferree, *Analyzing Gender. A Handbook of Social Science Research* (Newbury Park, California, 1987) pp. 267–85.

Bostick, Theodora P.: 'Women's suffrage, the Press and the Reform Bill of 1867', *International Journal of Women's Studies* 3 (1980) 4, pp. 373–90.

Boston, Sarah: *Women Workers and the Trade Union Movement* (London, 1980).

Boucé, Paul-Gabriel: *Sexuality in Eighteenth Century Britain* (Manchester, 1982).

Boxer, Marilyn J.: '"First Wave" feminism in nineteenth century France: class, family and religion', in ed. Elizabeth Sarah (1982) pp. 551–9.

—— and Jean H. Quataert: *Socialist Women. European Socialist Feminism in the Nineteenth and Early Twentieth Centuries* (New York, 1978).

Bradbrook, Muriel C.: *'That Infidel Place': A Short History of Girton College 1869–1969* (London, 1969).

——: 'Barbara Bodichon, George Eliot and the limits of feminism', in her *Women and Literature 1779–1982: The Collected Papers of Muriel Bradbrook* Vol. 2 (Brighton, 1982).

Branca, Patricia: 'A new perspective on women's work: a comparative typology', *Journal of Social History* 9 (1975) pp. 129–53.

Brennan, Teresa and Carole Pateman: '"Mere auxiliaries to the Commonwealth": women and the origins of Liberalism', *Political Studies* XXVII (1979) pp. 183–200.

Brittain, Vera: *The Women At Oxford. A Fragment of History* (London, 1960).

Brod, Harry, ed.: *The Making of Masculinities. The New Men's Studies* (Boston, 1987).

Brophy, Julia and Carol Smart: *Women in Law. Explorations in Law, Family and Sexuality* (London, 1985).

Bryant, Margaret: *The Unexpected Revolution. A Study in the History of the Education of Women and Girls in the Nineteenth Century* (London, 1979).

Burman, Sandra, ed.: *Fit Work for Women* (London, 1979).

Burstyn, Joan N.: *Victorian Education and the Ideal of Womanhood* (London, 1980).

——: 'Religious arguments against higher education for women in England, 1840–90', *Women's Studies* 1 (1972) 1, pp. 111–31.

Caine, Barbara: 'Woman's "natural state": marriage and the nineteenth century feminists' *Hecate* 3 (1977) pp. 84–102.

——: 'John Stuart Mill and the English Women's Movement', *Historical Studies* 18 (1978) 70, pp. 52–67.

——: 'Feminism, suffrage and the nineteenth century English Women's Movement', *Women's Studies International Forum* 5 (1982) 6, pp. 537–50.

——: *Destined to be Wives. The Sisters of Beatrice Webb* (Oxford, 1986).

——, E. A. Grosz and Marie de Lepervanche, eds: *Crossing Boundaries. Feminisms and the Critique of Knowledges* (Sydney, 1988).

Callen, Anthea: *Women in the Arts and Crafts Movement 1870–1914* (London, 1979).

Carpenter, Edward, ed.: *Forecasts of the Coming Century* (Manchester, 1897).

Charvet, John: *Feminism* (London, 1982).

Chodorow, Nancy: 'Family structure and feminine personality', in eds Michelle Zimbalist Rosaldo and Louise Lamphere, *Woman, Culture and Society* (Stanford, California, 1974) pp. 43–6.

——: 'Mothering, male dominance and capitalism', in ed. Zillah R. Eisenstein, *Capitalist Patriarchy and the Case for Socialist Feminism* (New York, 1979) pp. 83–106.

Coll, Robert and Philip Dodd, eds: *Englishness, Politics and Culture 1880–1920* (Beckenham, 1986).

Cominos, Peter T.: 'Late Victorian sexual respectability and the social system', *International Review of Social History* 8 (1963) pp. 18–48 and 216–50.

Connell, R. W.: *Gender and Power. Society, the Person and Sexual Politics* (Oxford, 1987).

Cook, Blanche Wiesen: 'Female support networks and political activism. Lillian Wald, Crystal Eastman, Emma Goldman', in eds Nancy F. Cott and Elizabeth H. Pleck, *A Heritage of Her Own. Toward A New Social History of American Women* (New York, 1979) pp. 412–46.

Corrigan, Philip, ed.: *Capitalism, State Formation and Marxist Theory. Historical Investigations* (London, 1980).

Cott, Nancy F.: *The Bonds of Womanhood. 'Woman's Sphere' in New England, 1780–1835* (New Haven and London, 1977).

—— and Elizabeth H. Pleck, eds: *A Heritage of Her Own. Toward a New Social History of American Women* (New York, 1979).

——: *The Grounding of Modern Feminism* (New Haven and London, 1987).

Crawford, Patricia, ed.: *Exploring Women's Past* (Sydney, 1983).

Davidoff, Leonore: 'The rationalization of housework', in eds D. L. Barker and S. Allen (London, 1976) pp. 121–51.

——: 'Class and gender in Victorian England', in eds Judith Newton, Mary Ryan and Judith Walkowitz, *Sex and Class in Women's History* (London, 1983) pp. 17–71.

—— and Catherine Hall: 'The architecture of public and private life. English middle class society in a provincial town 1780–1850', in eds Derek Fraser and Anthony Sutcliffe, *The Pursuit of Urban History* (London, 1983) pp. 327–45.

——: *Family Fortunes. Men and Women of the English Middle Class 1780–1850* (London, 1987).

Davies, Celia: 'Making sense of the census in Britain and the U.S.A.: the changing occupational classification and the position of nurses', *Sociological Review* n.s.

28 (1980) 3, pp. 581–609.

Davin, Anna: 'Telegraphists and clerks', *Bulletin of the Society for the Study of Labour History* 26 (1973) pp. 7–9.

Davis, Tricia, Martin Durham, Catherine Hall, Mary Langan and David Sutton: '"The public face of feminism": early twentieth century writings on women's suffrage', in eds R. Johnson, G. McLennan, B. Schwarz and D. Sutton, *Making Histories. Studies in History-writing and Politics* (London and Birmingham, 1982) pp. 302–72.

de Lauretis, Teresa: 'Feminist studies/critical studies: issues, terms and contexts', in ed. de Lauretis, *Feminist Studies/Critical Studies* (Bloomington, Indiana, 1986) pp. 1–19.

——, ed.: *Feminist Studies/Critical Studies* (Bloomington, 1986).

Deckard, Barbara Sinclair: *The Women's Movement: Political, Socioeconomic and Psychological Issues* (New York, 1978).

Delphy, Christine: *Close To Home. A Materialist Analysis of Women's Oppression* (London, 1984).

Dex, Shirley: 'Issues of gender and employment', *Social History* 13 (1988), pp. 141–50.

Donnison, Jean: 'Medical women and lady midwives. A case study in medical and feminist politics', *Women's Studies* 3 (1976) 3, pp. 229–50.

Doughan, David and Denise Sanchez: *Feminist Periodicals 1855–1984. An Annotated Critical Bibliography of British, Irish, Commonwealth and International Titles* (Sussex, 1987).

Drake, Barbara: *Women in Trade Unions* (reprinted, London, 1984).

Draper, Hal and Anne G. Lipow: 'Marxist women versus bourgeois feminism', *Socialist Register* 13 (1976) pp. 178–226.

Drescher, Seymour: 'Two variants of anti-slavery: religious organization and social mobilization in Britain and France, 1780–1870', in eds Christine Bolt and Seymour Drescher, *Anti-Slavery, Religion and Reform: Essays in Memory of Roger Anstey* (Connecticut, 1980) pp. 43–63.

Dubois, Ellen: 'The nineteenth century woman suffrage movement and the analysis of women's oppression', in ed. Zillah Eisenstein (1979) pp. 137–50.

Durham, Martin: 'Suffrage and after: feminism in the early twentieth century', in eds Mary Langan and Bill Schwarz, *Crises in the British State 1880–1930* (London, 1985) pp. 179–91.

Dyhouse, Carol: *Girls Growing Up in Late Victorian and Edwardian England* (London, 1981).

——: 'Miss Buss and Miss Beale: Gender and authority in the history of education', in ed. Felicity Hunt, *Lessons for Life. The Schooling of Girls and Women 1850–1950* (Oxford, 1987) pp. 22–38.

Edwards, Amelia: *Untrodden Peaks and Unfrequented Valleys. A Midsummer Ramble in the Dolomites* (London, 1986).

Eisenstein, Zillah R., ed.: *Capitalist Patriarchy and the Case for Socialist Feminism* (New York, 1979).

——: *The Radical Future of Liberal Feminism* (New York and London, 1981).

——: *The Female Body and the Law* (Berkeley, California and London, 1988).

Ellsworth, Edward W.: *Liberators of the Female Mind. The Shirreff Sisters,*

Educational Reform and the Women's Movement (Westport, Connecticut, 1979).

Elshtain, Jean Bethke: *Public Man, Private Woman* (Princeton, New Jersey, 1981).

Evans, Richard J.: *The Feminists. Women's Emancipation Movements in Europe, America and Australasia 1840–1920* (Beckenham, 1979).

——: 'The history of European women: a critical survey of recent research', *Journal of Modern History* 52 (1980) 4, pp. 656–75.

Faderman, Lillian: *Surpassing the Love of Men. Romantic Friendship and Love between Women from the Renaissance to the Present* (New York, 1981).

Farnham, Christie, ed.: *The Impact of Feminist Research in the Academy* (Bloomington, 1987).

Feurer, Rosemary: 'The meaning of "sisterhood": the British women's movement and protective labor legislation 1870–1900', *Victorian Studies* 31 (1988) 2, pp. 233–60.

Fletcher, Sheila: *Feminists and Bureaucrats. A Study in the Development of Girls' Education in the Nineteenth Century* (Cambridge, 1980).

——: *Women First: the Female Tradition in English Physical Education 1880–1980* (London, 1984).

Foucault, Michel: *The History of Sexuality* 3 vols (New York, 1978–86).

Fraser, Derek and Anthony Sutcliffe, eds: *The Pursuit of Urban History* (London, 1983).

Fredeman, William E.: 'Emily Faithfull and the Victoria Press: an experiment in sociological bibliography', *The Library* 5th series XXIX (June 1974) 2, pp. 139–64.

Freedman, Estelle: 'Separatism as strategy: female institution building and American feminism 1870–1930' *Feminist Studies* 5 (1979) 3, pp. 512–29.

Freeman, Ruth and Patricia Klaus: 'Blessed or not? The new spinster in England and the United States in the late nineteenth and early twentieth century', *Journal of Family History* 9 (1984) 4, pp. 394–414.

Gamarnikow, Eva: 'Sexual division of labour: the case of nursing', in eds Annette Kuhn and Anne Marie Wolpe, *Feminism and Materialism. Women and Modes of Production* (London, 1978) pp. 98–123.

——, David Morgan, June Purvis and Daphne Taylerson, eds: *Gender, Class and Work* (London, 1983).

Gay, Peter: *The Bourgeois Experience. Victoria to Freud* Vol. I: *Education of the Senses* (New York and Oxford, 1984).

Geiger, Susan N. G.: 'Women's life histories: method and content', *Signs* 11 (1986) 2, pp. 334–51.

Gillis, John R.: *For Better, For Worse: British Marriages 1600 to the Present* (Oxford, 1985).

Gladstone, Florence M.: *Aubrey House, Kensington 1698–1920* (London, 1922).

Glenday, Nonita and Mary Price: *Reluctant Revolutionaries. A Century of Head Mistresses 1874–1974* (London, 1974).

Gordon, Linda: 'The struggle for reproductive freedom: three stages of feminism', in ed. Eisenstein (1979) pp. 107–132.

——: 'What's new in women's history', in ed. de Lauretis (1986) pp. 20–30.

—— and Ellen DuBois: 'Seeking ecstasy on the battlefield: danger and pleasure in nineteenth century feminist sexual thought', *Feminist Review* 13 (1983) pp. 42–54.

Gordon, Shirley C.: 'Studies at Queen's College, Harley Street, 1848–1868', *British Journal of Educational Studies* 3 (1954–5) pp. 144–54.

Gorham, Deborah: 'Victorian reform as family business: the Hill family', in ed. Anthony S. Wohl, *The Victorian Family. Structure and Stresses* (London, 1978) pp. 119–47.

Hakim, Catherine: 'Census reports as documentary evidence: the Census Commentaries 1801–51', *Sociological Review* 28 (1980) 3, pp. 551–80.

Halevy, Elie: *A History of the English People in the Nineteenth Century* Vol. III, 2nd edn (London, 1952).

Hall, Catherine: 'The early formation of Victorian domestic ideology' in ed. Sandra Burman, *Fit Work for Women* (London, 1979) pp. 15–32.

——: 'The historical separation of home and workplace', in ed. Whitehead (1982) pp. 2–29.

——: 'The tale of Samuel and Jemima: gender and working class culture in early nineteenth century England', in eds Tony Bennett, Colin Mercer and Janet Wollacott, *Popular Culture and Social Relations* (Milton Keynes and Philadelphia, 1986) pp. 73–92.

Hammerton, A. James: *Emigrant Gentlewomen. Genteel Poverty and Female Emigration 1830–1914* (Canberra, 1979).

Hammond, Dorothy and Alta Jablow: 'Gilgamesh and the Sundance Kid: the myth of male friendship', in ed. Harry Brod, *The Making of Masculinities. The New Men's Studies* (Boston, 1987) pp. 241–58.

Handl, Johann: 'Educational chances and occupational opportunities of women: a sociohistorical analysis', *Journal of Social History* 17 (1984) 3, pp. 463–85.

Harrison, Brian: 'The British prohibitionists 1853–72. A biographical analysis', *International Review of Social History* XV (1970) 3, pp. 375–467.

——: *Drink and the Victorians. The Temperance Question in England 1815–72* (London, 1971).

——: 'Dictionary of British temperance biography', *Society for the Study of Labour History Bulletin, Supplement I* (1973).

——: 'State intervention and moral reform in nineteenth century England', in ed. Patricia Hollis, *Pressure from Without in early Victorian England* (London, 1974) pp. 289–322.

——: *Separate Spheres. The Opposition to Women's Suffrage in Britain* (London, 1978).

——: 'A genealogy of reform in modern Britain', in eds. Christine Bolt and Seymour Drescher (1980) pp. 119–48.

——: 'Women's health and the Women's Movement in Britain: 1840–1940', in ed. Charles Webster, *Biology, Medicine and Society 1840–1940* (Cambridge, 1981) pp. 15–71.

——: 'The act of militancy: violence and the suffragettes, 1904–14' in Harrison, *Peaceable Kingdom. Stability and Change in Modern Britain* (Oxford, 1982) pp. 26–81.

——: 'Women's suffrage at Westminster, 1866–1928', in eds. Michael Bentley and John Stevenson, *High and Low Politics in Modern Britain. Ten Studies* (Oxford, 1986) pp. 80–122.

——: *Prudent Revolutionaries. Portraits of British Feminists between the Wars* (Oxford, 1987).

Harrison, Rachel and Frank Mort: 'Patriarchal aspects of nineteenth century state formation: property relations, marriage and divorce, and sexuality', in ed. Philip Corrigan, *Capitalism, State Formation and Marxist Theory. Historical Investigations* (London, 1980) pp. 79–109.

Hartmann, Heidi: 'Capitalism, patriarchy and job segregation by sex', in eds Elizabeth and Emily K. Abel, *The Signs Reader. Women, Gender and Scholarship* (Chicago and London, 1983) pp. 193–225.

Hersh, Blanche Glassman: *The Slavery of Sex. Feminist-Abolitionists in America* (Urbana, 1978).

Hess, Beth B. and Myra M. Ferree, eds: *Analyzing Gender. A Handbook of Social Science Research* (Newbury Park, California, 1987).

Hewitt, Nancy A.: 'Beyond the search for sisterhood: American women's history in the 1980s', *Social History* 10 (1985) 3, pp. 299–321.

——: 'Feminist friends: agrarian Quakers and the emergence of woman's rights in America', *Feminist Studies* 12 (1986) 1, pp. 27–49.

Hiley, Michael: *Victorian Working Women. Portraits from Life* (London, 1979).

Hinton, R. J.: *English Radical Leaders* (New York, 1875).

Holcombe, Lee: *Victorian Ladies At Work. Middle Class Working Women in England and Wales 1850–1914* (Newton Abbot, 1973).

——: 'Victorian wives and property', in ed. Martha Vicinus, *A Widening Sphere. Changing Roles of Victorian Women* (London, 1977) pp. 3–28.

Hollis, Patricia: *Ladies Elect. Women in English Local Government 1865–1914* (Oxford, 1987).

——, ed.: *Pressure from Without in Early Victorian England* (London, 1974).

Holt, Raymond V.: *The Unitarian Contribution to Social Progress in England* (London, 1938).

Holton, Sandra Stanley: *Feminism and Democracy* (Cambridge, 1987).

Howarth, Janet: 'Public schools, safety-nets and educational ladders: the classification of girls' secondary schools, 1880–1914', *Oxford Review of Education* 11 (1985) 1, pp. 59–71.

—— and Mark Curthoys: 'The political economy of women's higher education in late nineteenth and early twentieth century Britain', *Historical Research* 60 (June 1987) 142, pp. 208–31.

——: 'Gender, curriculum and career: a case study of women university students before 1914', unpublished paper, 1987.

Hudson, Derek: *Munby. Man of Two Worlds. The Life and Diaries of Arthur J. Munby, 1828–1910* (London, 1972).

Hume, Lesley Parker: *The National Union of Women's Suffrage Societies* (London, 1982).

Humphries, Jane: 'The working class family, women's liberation and class struggle: the case of nineteenth century British history', *Review of Radical*

Political Economics 9 (1977) 3, pp. 25–41.

——: 'Protective legislation, the capitalist state and working class men: the case of the 1842 Mines Regulation Act', *Feminist Review* 7 (1981) pp. 1–33.

——: '"The most free from objection . . . "': the sexual division of labor and women's work in nineteenth century England', *Journal of Economic History* XLVII (1987) 4, pp. 929–49.

Hunt, Felicity: 'The London trade in the printing and binding of books: an experience in exclusion, dilution and de-skilling for women workers', *Women's Studies International Forum*, 6 (1983) 5, pp. 517–24.

——: 'Divided aims: the educational implications of opposing ideologies in girls' secondary schooling', in ed. Hunt (1987), pp. 3–21.

——, ed.: *Lessons for Life. The Schooling of Girls and Women, 1850–1950* (Oxford, 1987).

Isichei, Elizabeth: *Victorian Quakers* (Oxford, 1970).

Jalland, Patricia: 'Victorian spinsters: dutiful daughters, desperate rebels and the transition to the New Women', in ed. Patricia Crawford, *Exploring Women's Past* (Sydney, 1983) pp. 129–170.

——: *Women, Marriage and Politics 1860–1914* (Oxford, 1986).

Janeway, Elizabeth: 'Who is Sylvia? On the loss of sexual paradigms' in Catharine R. Stimpson and Ethel Spector Person, *Women: Sex and Sexuality* (Chicago and London, 1980), pp. 4–20.

Jardine, Alice: *Gynesis. Configurations of Woman and Modernity* (Ithaca and London, 1985).

Jeffreys, Sheila: '"Free from all uninvited touch of man": women's campaigns around sexuality 1880–1914', *Women's Studies International Forum* 5 (1982) 6, pp. 629–45.

——: *The Spinster and her Enemies. Feminism and Sexuality 1880–1930* (London, 1985).

John, Angela: *By The Sweat of Their Brow. Women Workers at Victorian Coal Mines* (2nd edn, London, 1984).

Johnson, R., G. McLennan, B. Schwarz and D. Sutton, eds: *Making Histories. Studies in History-writing and Politics* (London and Birmingham, 1982).

Jones, Helen: 'Women health workers: the case of the first women factory inspectors in Britain', *Journal of the Society for the Social History of Medicine* 1 (1988) pp. 165–181.

Kamm, Josephine: *Hope Deferred. Girls' Education in English History* (London, 1965).

——: *Rapiers and Battleaxes. The Women's Movement and its Aftermath* (London, 1966).

Kaplan, Cora, ed.: *Aurora Leigh with other Poems* (London, 1978).

Kent, Susan Kingsley: *Sex and Suffrage in Britain 1860–1914* (Princeton, New Jersey, 1987).

Kuhn, Annette and Anne Marie Wolpe, eds: *Feminism and Materialism. Women and Modes of Production* (London, 1978).

Lake, Marilyn: 'The politics of respectability: identifying the masculinist context', *Historical Studies* 22 (April 1986) 86, pp. 116–31.

Langan, Mary and Bill Schwarz, eds: *Crises in the British State 1880–1930*

(London, 1985).

Leser, C. V.: 'The supply of women for gainful work in Britain', *Population Studies* IX (1955–6), 2, pp. 142–7.

Levine, Philippa: *Victorian Feminism 1850–1900* (London, 1987).

——: '"So few prizes and so many blanks"': marriage and feminism in later nineteenth century England', *Journal of British Studies* 28 (1989) pp. 150–74.

Lewenhak, Sheila: *Women and Work* (London, 1980).

Lewis, Jane, ed.: *Women's Welfare. Women's Rights* (London, 1983).

——: *Women in England 1870–1950: Sexual Divisions and Social Change* (Brighton and Bloomington, Indiana, 1984).

——: 'The debate on sex and class', *New Left Review* 149 (1985) pp. 108–120.

——, ed.: *Labour and Love. Women's Experience of Home and Family, 1850–1940* (Oxford, 1986).

Littlejohn, Gary, Barry Smart, John Wakeford and Nira Yuval-Davis, eds: *Power and the State* (London, 1978).

Lloyd, T. O.: *Empire to Welfare State. English History 1906–85* (3rd edn, Oxford, 1986).

Lown, Judy: 'Not so much a factory, more a form of patriarchy: gender and class during industrialisation', in eds. Eva Gamarnikow, David Morgan, June Purvis and Daphne Taylerson, *Gender, Class and Work* (London, 1983).

Lush, Montague: *A Century of Law Reform. Twelve Lectures on the Changes in the Law of England during the Nineteenth Century* (London, 1901).

McCrone, K. E.: 'The assertion of women's rights in mid-Victorian England', *Canadian Historical Association Historical Papers* (1972), pp. 39–53.

——: 'Feminism and philanthropy in Victorian England: the case of Louisa Twining', *Canadian Historical Association Historical Papers* (1976), pp. 123–39.

——: 'The National Association for the Promotion of Social Science and the advancement of Victorian women', *Atlantis* 8 (1982) 1, pp. 44–66.

——: *Sport and the Physical Emancipation of English Women 1870–1914* (London, 1988).

McGregor, O. R.: *Divorce in England. A Centenary Study* (London, 1957).

McHugh, Paul: *Prostitution and Victorian Social Reform* (London, 1980).

Mackay, Jane and Pat Thane: 'The Englishwoman' in eds Robert Coll and Philip Dodd, *Englishness. Politics and Culture 1880–1920* (Beckenham, 1986) pp. 191–229.

McWilliams-Tulberg, Rita: *Women at Cambridge. A Men's University – Though of a Mixed Type* (London, 1975).

Malmgreen, Gail, ed.: *Religion in the Lives of English Women 1760–1930* (London and Sydney, 1986).

Mangan, J. A. and James Walvin, eds: *Manliness and Morality. Middle Class Masculinity in Britain and America 1800–1940* (Manchester, 1987).

Mappen, Ellen: *Helping Women At Work. The Women's Industrial Council 1889–1914* (London, 1985).

Marcus, Jane: 'Transatlantic sisterhood: labor and suffrage links in the letters of Elizabeth Robins and Emmeline Pankhurst', *Signs* 3 (1978) pp. 744–55.

Mark-Lawson, Jane and Anne Witz: 'From "family labour" to "family wage"? The case of women's labour in nineteenth century coalmining', *Social History* 13 (1988) 2, pp. 151–74.

Marks, Pauline: 'Femininity in the classroom. An account of changing attitudes' in eds Mitchell and Oakley (1976) pp. 176–98.

Martin, D. E. and David Rubinstein, eds: *Ideology and the Labour Movement. Essays presented to John Saville* (London, 1979).

Mason, Bertha: *The Story of the Women's Suffrage Movement* (London, 1912).

Maynard, Constance: *We Women. A Golden Hope* (London, 1924).

Maynard, Mary: 'Privilege and patriarchy: feminist thought in the nineteenth century', in eds Susan Mendus and Jane Rendall, *Sexuality and Subordination. Interdisciplinary Studies of Gender in the Nineteenth Century* (London and New York, 1989) pp. 221–47.

Mendus, Susan and Jane Rendall, eds: *Sexuality and Subordination. Interdisciplinary Studies of Gender in the Nineteenth Century* (London and New York, 1989).

Metcalfe, A. E.: *Woman's Effort. A Chronicle of British Women's Fifty Years' Struggle for Citizenship 1865–1914* (Oxford, 1917).

Middleton, Lucy, ed.: *Women in the Labour Movement. The British Experience* (London, 1977).

Minor, Iris: 'Working class women and matrimonial law reform', in eds D. E. Martin and David Rubenstein, *Ideology and the Labour Movement. Essays presented to John Saville* (London, 1979) pp. 103–24.

Mintz, Steven: *A Prison Of Expectations. The Family in Victorian Culture* (New York and London, 1983).

Mitchell, Juliet and Ann Oakley, eds: *The Rights and Wrongs of Women* (Harmondsworth, 1976).

Mitchison, Rosalind: *British Population Change Since 1860* (London, 1977).

Montgomery, Maureen E.: *Gilded Prostitution. Status, Money and Transatlantic Marriages 1870–1914* (London, 1989).

Moore, T. and D. C. Sturge: *Works and Days. From the Journal of Michael Field* (London, 1933).

Morgan, David: *Suffragists and Liberals. The Politics of Women's Suffrage in Britain* (Oxford, 1975).

Mort, Frank: 'Purity, feminism and the state: sexuality and moral politics 1880–1914' in eds Langan and Schwarz (1985) pp. 209–25.

——: *Dangerous Sexualities. Medico-moral Politics in England since 1830* (London and New York, 1987).

Newton, Judith, Mary Ryan and Judith Walkowitz, eds: *Sex and Class in Women's History* (London, 1983).

Nicholson, Linda J.: *Gender and History. The Limits of Social Theory in the Age of the Family* (New York, 1986).

Nye, Andrea: *Feminist Theory and the Philosophies of Man* (Beckenham, 1988).

O'Donovan, K.: 'The male appendage – legal definitions of women', in ed. Burman (1979) pp. 134–52.

Offen, Karen: 'Defining feminism: a comparative historical approach', *Signs* 14

(1988) 1.

Olcott, Teresa: 'Dead centre: the women's trade union movement in London, 1874–1914', *London Journal* 2 (1976) 1, pp. 33–50.

Olsen, Frances E.: 'The family and the market: a study of ideology and legal reform', *Harvard Law Review* 96 (1983) 7, pp. 1497–1578.

Padgug, Robert A.: 'Sexual matters: on conceptualizing sexuality in history', *Radical History Review* 20 (1979) pp. 3–23.

Palmegiano, Eugenia: 'Feminist propaganda in the 1850s and 1860s', *Victorian Periodicals Newsletter* 11 (1971) pp. 5–9.

Pankhurst, Sylvia: *The Suffragette Movement. An Intimate Account of Persons and Ideals* (London, 1931).

Park, Jihang: 'Women of their time: the growing recognition of the second sex in Victorian and Edwardian England', *Journal of Social History* 21 (1987) 1, pp. 49–67.

Pateman, Carole: *The Sexual Contract* (Stanford, California, 1988).

——: 'The shame of the marriage contract', in ed. Judith Hicks Stiehm, *Women's Views of the Political World of Men* (New York, 1980) pp. 69–97.

Paulson, Ross Evans: *Women's Suffrage and Prohibition. A Comparative Study of Equality and Social Control* (Illinois, 1973).

Pedersen, J. S.: 'Schoolmistresses and headmistresses: élites and education in nineteenth century England', *Journal of British Studies* XV (1975) 1, pp. 135–62.

——: 'The reform of women's secondary and higher education: institutional change and social values in mid and late Victorian England', *History of Education Quarterly* (1979) pp. 61–91.

Peterson, M. Jeanne: 'No angel in the house: the Victorian myth and the Paget women', *American Historical Review* 89 (1984) 3, pp. 677–708.

——: 'Dr Acton's enemy: medicine, sex and society in Victorian England', *Victorian Studies* 29 (1986) 4, pp. 569–90.

Phillips, Anne: *Divided Loyalties. Dilemmas of Sex and Class* (London, 1987).

Pinchbeck, Ivy: *Women Workers and the Industrial Revolution 1750–1850* (London, 1930).

Plumb, J. H., ed: *Studies in Social History. A Tribute to G. M. Trevelyan* (London, 1955).

Poovey, Mary: *Uneven Developments. The Ideological Work of Gender in Mid-Victorian England* (Chicago, 1988).

——: 'Feminism and deconstruction', *Feminist Studies* 14 (1988) 1, pp. 51–65.

Porter, Roy, ed.: *Patients and Practitioners* (Cambridge, 1985).

Pratt, Edwin A.: *Pioneer Women in Victoria's Reign. Being Short Histories of Great Movements* (London, 1897).

Prochaska, F. K.: *Woman and Philanthropy in Nineteenth Century England* (Oxford, 1980).

Pugh, Evelyn L.: 'Florence Nightingale and J. S. Mill debate women's rights', *Journal of British Studies* 21 (1982) pp. 118–38.

Pugh, Martin: *Women's Suffrage in Britain, 1867–1928* (London, 1980).

——: *The Tories and the People, 1880–1935* (Oxford, 1985).

Rabkin, Peggy: *Fathers to Daughters. The Legal Foundations of Female Emancipation* (Westport, Connecticut, 1980).

Radical History Review Editorial Collective: 'Patrolling the borders: feminist historiography and the new historicism', *Radical History Review* 43 (1989) pp. 23–43.

Reed, Joseph W., Jnr, ed.: *An American Diary 1857–8* (London, 1972).

Rendall, Jane: *The Origins of Modern Feminism: Women in Britain, France and the United States 1780–1860* (Basingstoke, 1985).

——, ed.: *Equal or Different. Women's Politics, 1800–1914* (Oxford, 1987).

——: 'Friendship and politics: Barbara Leigh Smith Bodichon (1827–91) and Bessie Rayner Parkes (1829–1925)', in eds. Susan Mendus and Jane Rendall (1989) pp. 136–70.

Rich, Adrienne: 'Compulsory heterosexuality and lesbian existence', in eds Ann Snitow, Christine Stansell and Sharon Thompson, *Powers of Desire. The Politics of Sexuality* (New York, 1983) pp. 177–205, and in *Signs* 5 (1980) 4, pp. 631–60.

Richards, Eric: 'Women in the British economy since about 1700: an interpretation', *History* lix (1974) pp. 337–357.

Richards, Jeffrey: '"Passing the love of women": manly love and Victorian society', in eds J. A. Mangan and James Walvin, *Manliness and Morality. Middle Class Masculinity in Britain and America 1800–1940* (Manchester, 1987) pp. 92–122.

Robson, A. P. W.: 'The Founding of the National Society for Women's Suffrage, 1867–67', *Canadian Journal of History* VIII (1973) 1, pp. 1–22.

Rogers, Annie M. A. H.: *Degrees by Degrees. The Story of the Admission of Oxford Women Students to Membership of the University* (Oxford, 1938).

Rosaldo, Michelle Z. and Louise Lamphere, eds: *Woman, Culture and Society* (Stanford, California, 1974).

Rose, Sonya O.: 'Gender at work', *History Workshop Journal* 21 (1986) pp. 113–31.

Rosen, Andrew: 'Emily Davies and the Women's Movement 1862–7', *Journal of British Studies* XIX (1979) 1, pp. 101–21.

Ross, Ellen and Rayna Rapp: 'Sex and society: a research note from social history and anthropology', in eds Snitow et al. (1983) pp. 51–73.

Rossi, Alice S.: *The Feminist Papers: From Adams to de Beauvoir* (New York, 1973).

Rousseau, G. S. and Porter, Roy: *Sexual Underworlds of the Enlightenment* (Manchester, 1987).

Rowbotham, Sheila, ed.: *The Daughters of Karl Marx. Family Correspondence 1866–98* (London, 1982).

Rubin, Gayle: 'Thinking sex: notes for a radical theory of the politics of sexuality', in ed. Carole S. Vance *Pleasure and Danger: Exploring Female Sexuality* (Boston, 1987), pp. 267–319.

Rubinstein, David: *Before the Suffragettes. Women's Emancipation in the 1890s* (Brighton, 1986).

Rubinstein, W. D.: 'Education and the social origins of British elites 1880–1970',

Past and Present 112 (1986) pp. 163–207.

Rupp, Leila J.: 'Imagine my surprise: women's relationships in historical perspective', *Frontiers* 5 (1980) 3, pp. 61–70.

Sachs, Albie and Joan Hoff Wilson: *Sexism and the Law. A Study of Male Beliefs and Legal Bias in Britain and the United States* (New York, 1978).

Sarah, Elizabeth, ed.: *Reassessments of 'First Wave' Feminism* (Oxford, 1982).

Savage, Gail: 'The operation of the 1857 Divorce Act, 1860–1910. A research note', *Journal of Social History* 16 (1983) 4, pp. 103–110.

——: 'The wilful communication of a loathsome disease: marital conflict and venereal disease in Victorian England', unpublished paper presented to the North East Victorian Studies Association, U.S.A., 1988.

Schmiechen, James A.: *Sweated Industries and Sweated Labour. The London Clothing Trades 1860–1914* (London, 1984).

Scott, Joan 'Gender: a useful category of historical analysis', *American Historical Review* 91 (1986) 5, pp. 1053–75.

——: 'Women's history and the rewriting of history', in ed. Christie Farnham, *The Impact of Feminist Research in the Academy* (Indiana, 1987) pp. 34–50.

——: 'On language, gender and working class history', *International Labor and Working Class History* 31 (1987) pp. 1–13.

——: 'Deconstructing equality-versus-difference: or, The uses of poststructuralist theory for feminism', *Feminist Studies* 14 (1988) 1, 33–50.

Scull, Andrew T.: *Museums of Madness. The Social Organization of Insanity in Nineteenth Century England* (Harmondsworth, 1982).

Seccombe, Wally: 'Patriarchy stabilized: the construction of the male bread-winner wage norm in nineteenth century Britain', *Social History* XI (1986) 1, pp. 53–76.

Sen, Gita: 'The sexual division of labour and the working-class family: towards a conceptual synthesis of class relations and the subordination of women', *Review of Radical Political Economics* 12 (1980) 2, pp. 76–85.

Senegalen, Martine: *Historical Anthropology of the Family* (Cambridge, 1986).

Shanley, M.: '"One must ride behind": married women's rights and the Divorce Act of 1857', *Victorian Studies* XXV (1982) 3, 355–76.

——: 'Suffrage, protective legislation and married women's property laws in England', *Signs* 12 (1986) 1, pp. 62–77.

Sheppard, M. G.: 'The effects of the franchise provisions on the social and sex compositions of the municipal electorate 1881–1914', *Bulletin of the Society for the Study of Labour History* (1982), pp. 19–25.

Shiman, Lillian Lewis: '"Changes are dangerous": women and temperance in Victorian England', in ed. Malmgreen (1986) pp. 193–215.

Shorter, Edward: *A History of Women's Bodies* (Harmondsworth, 1983).

Silverstone, Rosalie: 'Office work for women: an historical review', *Business History* XVIII (January 1976) 1, pp. 98–110.

Smart, Carol: *The Ties That Bind. Law, Marriage and the Reproduction of Patriarchal Relations* (London, 1984).

—— with Julia Brophy: 'Locating law: a discussion of the place of law in feminist politics', in eds Brophy and Smart (1985) pp. 1–20.

Smith-Rosenberg, Carroll: 'The female world of love and ritual: relations between women in nineteenth century America', *Signs* 1 (1975) pp. 1–29.

——: 'A richer and gentler sex', *Social Research* 53 (1986) 2, pp. 288–309.

——: 'Writing history: language, class and gender', in ed. Teresa de Lauretis (1986) pp. 31–54.

Snitow, Ann, C. Stansell and S. Thompson, eds: *Powers of Desire. The Politics of Sexuality* (New York, 1983).

Soldon, Norbert C.: *Women in British Trade Unions 1874–1976* (Dublin, 1978).

Sondheimer, Janet: *Castle Adamant in Hampstead. A History of Westfield College 1882–1982* (London, 1983).

Sontag, Susan: 'AIDS and its metaphors', *New York Review of Books* XXXV (27 October 1988) 16, pp. 89–99.

Spender, Dale, ed.: *Feminist Theorists. Three Centuries of Women's Intellectual Traditions* (London, 1983).

Spitzer, Steven: 'The dialectics of formal and informal control', in ed. Richard L. Abel, *The Politics of Informal Justice.* Vol. I *The American Experience* (New York, 1982) pp. 167–205.

Stange, Douglas Charles: *British Unitarians against American Slavery 1835–65* (London, Ontario and New Jersey, 1984).

Stanley, Liz: 'Whales and minnows: some sexual theorists and their followers and how they contribute to making feminism invisible', *Women's Studies International Forum* 7 (1984) 1, pp. 53–62.

——: 'Feminism and friendship: two essays on Olive Schreiner', *Studies in Sexual Politics* 8 (1985).

Stanton, Theodore, ed.: *The Woman Question in Europe. A Series of Original Essays* (London, 1984).

Stearns, Carol and Peter: 'Victorian sexuality: can historians do it better?', *Journal of Social History* 18 (1985) pp. 625–34.

Stetson, Dorothy: *A Woman's Issue. The Politics of Family Law Reform in England* (Connecticut and London, 1982).

Stiehm, Judith H., ed.: *Women's Views of the Political World of Men* (New York, 1980).

Stimpson, Catharine R. and Ethel S. Person, eds: *Women: Sex and Sexuality* (Chicago and London, 1980).

Stone, S. James: 'More light on Emily Faithfull and the Victoria Press', *The Library* XXXIII (1978) pp. 63–7.

Storch, Robert D.: 'Police control of street prostitution in Victorian London: a study in the context of police action', in ed. David H. Bayley, *Police and Society* (California, 1977) pp. 49–72.

Strachey, Ray: *The Cause* (London, 1928).

Summers, Anne: 'Pride and prejudice: ladies and nurses in the Crimean War', *History Workshop Journal* 18 (1983) pp. 32–56.

——: *Angels and Citizens. British Women as Military Nurses 1854–1914* (London, 1988).

Tanner, S. J.: *How the Women's Suffrage Movement Began in Bristol Fifty Years Ago* (Bristol, 1918).

Taylor, William R. and Christopher Lasch: 'Two "kindred spirits": sorority and family in New England, 1839–1846', *New England Quarterly* 36 (1963) pp.

23–41.

Thomas, Keith: 'The double standard', *Journal of the History of Ideas* XX (1959) 2 pp. 195–216.

Thompson, Dorothy: 'Women, work and politics in nineteenth century England: the problem of authority', in ed. Jane Rendall, *Equal or Different. Women's Politics, 1800–1914* (Oxford, 1987) pp. 57–81.

Thompson, E. P.: *Whigs and Hunters: the Origin of the Black Act* (New York, 1975).

Todd, Janet: *Feminist Literary History* (New York, 1988).

Tylecote, Mabel: *The Education of Women at Manchester University 1883–1933* (Manchester, 1941).

Tyrrell, Alex: '"Woman's mission" and pressure group politics in Britain (1825–60)', *Bulletin of the John Rylands University Library of Manchester* 63 (1980) 1, pp. 194–230.

Valenze, Deborah: *Prophetic Sons and Daughters. Female Preaching and Popular Religion in Industrial England* (Princeton, New Jersey, 1985).

Van Arsdel, Rosemary: 'Mrs Florence Fenwick Miller and *The Woman's Signal*', *Victorian Periodicals Review* XV (1982) pp. 107–18.

——: 'Victorian periodicals yield their secrets: Florence Fenwick Miller's three campaigns for the London School Board', *History of Education Society* 38 (1986) pp. 26–42.

Vance, Carole S., ed.: *Pleasure and Danger: Exploring Female Sexuality* (Boston, 1987).

Vicinus, Martha: 'Sexuality and power: a review of current work in the history of sexuality', *Feminist Studies* 8 (1982) 1, pp. 133–56.

——: '"One life to stand beside me": emotional conflicts in first-generation college women in England', *Feminist Studies* 8 (1982) 3, pp. 603–28.

——: *Independent Women. Work and Community for Single Women 1850–1920* (London, 1985).

——, ed.: *A Widening Sphere. Changing Roles of Victorian Women* (London, 1977).

Walkowitz, Judith R.: 'The politics of prostitution' in Stimpson and Person (1980), pp. 145–57.

——: *Prostitution and Victorian Society. Women, Class and the State* (Cambridge, 1980).

——: 'Jack the Ripper and the myth of male violence', *Feminist Studies* 8 (1982) 3, pp. 543–74.

——: 'Male vice and female virtue: feminism and the politics of prostitution in nineteenth century Britain', in eds Snitow et al. (1983) pp. 419–38.

——: 'Science, feminism and romance: the Men and Women's Club, 1885–89', *History Workshop Journal* 21 (1986) pp. 36–59.

Walvin, James: *Slavery and British Society 1776–1846* (London, 1982).

Webb, Catherine: *The Woman with the Basket. The History of the Women's Co-operative Guild 1883–1927* (Manchester, 1927).

Webster, Charles, ed.: *Biology, Medicine and Society 1840–1940* (Cambridge, 1981).

Weeks, Jeffrey: *Coming Out. Homosexual Politics in Britain from the Nineteenth Century to the Present* (London, 1977).

——: *Sex, Politics and Society. The Regulation of Sexuality Since 1800* (London, 1981).

——: 'Discourse, desire and sexual deviance: some problems in a history of homosexuality', in ed. Kenneth Plummer, *The Making of the Modern Homosexual* (Totowa, New Jersey, 1981) pp. 76–111.

——: *Sexuality and its Discontents. Meanings, Myths and Modern Sexualities* (London, 1985).

——: *Sexuality* (Chichester, 1986).

Whitehead, N., ed.: *The Changing Experience of Women* (Milton Keynes, 1982).

Widdowson, Frances: *Going Up into the Next Class. Women and Elementary Teacher Training 1840–1914* (London, 1980).

Williams, Perry: 'Pioneer women students at Cambridge, 1869–81', in ed. Hunt (1987) pp. 171–91.

Wills, Stella: 'The Anglo-Jewish contribution to the education movement for women in the nineteenth century', *Transactions of the Jewish Historical Society of England* XVII (1951–2) pp. 269–81.

Wilson, Adrian: 'Participant or patient? Seventeenth century childbirth from the mother's point of view', in ed. Roy Porter, *Patients and Practitioners* (Cambridge, 1985) pp. 129–44.

Wohl, Anthony S., ed.: *The Victorian Family. Structure and Stresses* (London, 1978).

Women in the Trade Union Movement (London, 1955).

Worzala, Diana Mary Chase: 'The Langham Place Circle: The beginnings of the organized women's movement in England 1854–70', unpublished PhD thesis, University of Wisconsin–Madison, 1982.

Young, James D.: *Women and Popular Struggles. A History of British Working Class Women 1560–1984* (Edinburgh, 1985).

Zollschan, G. K. and W. Hirsch, eds: *Explorations in Social Change* (London, 1964).

Index